Indian Saints and Sages

INDIAN SAINTS AND SAGES

From before Shankarâchârya to Vivekânand

Prof. Shrikant Prasoon

Published by

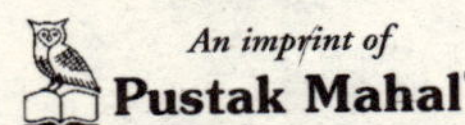

J-3/16 , Daryaganj, New Delhi-110002
☎ 23276539, 23272783, 23272784 • *Fax:* 011-23260518
E-mail: info@pustakmahal.com • *Website:* www.pustakmahal.com

Sales Centre

• 10-B, Netaji Subhash Marg, Daryaganj, New Delhi-110002
☎ 23268292, 23268293, 23279900 • *Fax:* 011-23280567
E-mail: rapidexdelhi@indiatimes.com

• Hind Pustak Bhawan

6686, Khari Baoli, Delhi-110006, ☎ 23944314, 23911979

Branches

Bengaluru: ☎ 080-22234025 • *Telefax:* 080-22240209
E-mail: pustak@airtelmail.in • pustak@sancharnet.in
Mumbai: ☎ 022-22010941 • 022-22053387
E-mail: rapidex@bom5.vsnl.net.in
Patna: ☎ 0612-3294193 • *Telefax:* 0612-2302719
E-mail: rapidexptn@rediffmail.com
Hyderabad: *Telefax:* 040-24737290
E-mail: pustakmahalhyd@yahoo.co.in

ISBN 978-81-223-1062-7

Edition 2011

Printed at : Glorious Printers, Delhi

Dedication

'Indian Saints and Sages'
Is dedicated to
All saintly figures
And to those
Who wish and try to follow the Sants
And to live like them;
And to
Shri Râmâgyâ Chaturvedi and
Smt. Âshâ Chaturvedi,
An excellent couple that stand by
And assist each other.

Contents

□□□

PREFACE

According to the need and nature of pronunciation, two spellings have been used in this book for a Saint (Saint and Sant); and two different spellings have been used to indicate the plural form Sant as Sants and Santas; besides the common word Saints. It is a necessity. Indian Sants are different to western Saints: in essence, appearance, nature, characteristics, deeds and accomplishments. The word Saints neither bears nor carries the meaning, weight, denotation and connotation of Indian Sants. So, they have been mostly called Sants through out the book.

In this book **Indian Saints and Sages,** I have not made use of Scriptural Transliteration, instead, only **â** has been taken from it for long 'a' sound which is otherwise impossible to write in Roman script. It is for enabling the general people to read it easily. Rest of everything is as written in government papers, magazines, newspapers and general books. It will help the readers to read the lines quoted in it and also the names of numerous persons and places.

I had the option and there is a tradition to divide the Santas, as from Northern India; Southern India and so on. There are many books that deal only with the Sants from Northern India or Western India and so on. It was the most successful policy of British Rulers, known to all, to divide India into fragments; and of course, it's a very subtle act. It's a wonder that the already known destructive policy is still very popular and is being vehemently used.

The fact is that the Sants are for all and for all times. They do not belong to a particular place, caste, religion, state, or age. They are above these petty and selfish considerations. They are Sants for all the Indians. They are Indians. They made us human and taught the ways to be divine. They united us for our survival. So, even when the place of their birth is given, South or North, is deliberately not mentioned. 'Indian Sants' have not been arranged place-wise or in chronological order. Most of such things are debatable and in many cases, they changed places and lived at so many places that they did not belong to a place even when they were alive. All the controversies should be absorbed and their teachings should be given preference.

The names of many Sants have been given but all of them have not been discussed in different chapters. How many of Sants are there? It is a futile effort to count the Indian Sants or to collect their names. They are numerous both in literal and spiritual sense. One Sant has a host of Sant-disciples and the disciples have a host of other disciples. There is not one but 'numerous' chains. There is no such effort here to count them or to collect their names. In giving the names, feelings have superimposed on the reason.

India is still full of Sants: both Grihsthas and Grihatyâgis. Countless will not be the correct word, only 'numerous' can satisfy.

Only â has been taken from scriptural transliteration for longer a sound. Rest is as given in government papers, magazines, newspapers and general books. It will help the reader in reading names and quotations.

Hari Aum Tatsat!

Prof. Shrikant Prasoon
M. 09868082133
Web: www.shrikantprasoon.com

1

Prayer

न धनं न जनं न सुन्दरीं कवितां वा जगदीश कामये।
मम जन्मनि जन्मनीश्वरे भक्ताद् भक्तिः हैतुकी त्वयि॥
महाप्रभु श्री चैतन्यदेव

Na dhanam na janam na sunderim
kavitâm wâ jagadisha kâmaye;
Mama janmani jananishware
bhaktâd bhaktih haituki tvayi.
Mahâprabhu Sri Chaitanyadeva

(O Jagannâth! I don't wish to get wealth, men, women or poetry. I wish to remain devoted to you without expectation for many more lives.)

नान्या स्पृहा रघुपते हृदयेऽस्मदीये
सत्यं वदामि च भवान अखिल अन्तरात्मा।
भक्ति प्रयच्छ रघु पुंगव निर्भरां मे
काम आदि दोष रहितं कुरू मानसं च॥
गोस्वामि तुलसीदास

Nânyâ sprihâ raghupate hridaye asmadiye
satyam vadâmi cha bhawân akhil antarâtmâ;
Bhaktim prayachchha raghu pungava nirbharâm mey
kâma âdi dosha rahitam kuru mânasam cha.

Goswâmi Tulasidâs

(O Raghunâth! I have no other desire at heart; I'm telling you the truth; you are the soul of all hence you know it well. O Raghu Shreshtha! Give me perfect devotion and free my mind from sensuousness and other vices.)

काहू सों न रोश तोष, काहू सों न राग द्वेश,
काहू सों न बैर भाव, काहू सों न घात है ।
काहू सों न बकबाद, काहू सों नहीं विशाद,
काहू सों न संग, न तौ काहू पच्छपात है ॥
काहू सों न दुष्ट बैन, काहू सों न लेन देन,
ब्रह्म को बिचार कछु, और न सुहात है ।

संत सुन्दरदास

Kâhu soen na rosha tosha, kâhu soen na râga dwesha;
kâhu soen na bair bhâwa, kâhu soen na ghâta hai.
Kâhu soen na bakavâda, kâhu soen nahin vishâd;
kâhu soen na sanga, na tau kâhu pachchhapâta hai.
Kâhu soen na dushta bain, kâhu soen na lena dena;
Brahman ko vichâr kachhu, aur na suhâta hai.

Sant Sunderdâs

(I'm neither angry nor friendly to anyone; neither attached nor jealous; neither I've enmity towards nor ready to attack on anyone; neither I start debates nor am aggrieved at someone; there is neither companionship nor inclination towards a person; I speak neither ill nor have any dealings with anyone. I like only to think of Brahman and nothing else.)

□□□

2

SAINTS IN SPIRITUAL QUADRUPLETS

(1)

The saints are absolutely pious, the emblem of goodness;
Sympathy, compassion, affection, piety, help and kindness;
Gracious in benevolence, philanthropy, charity and mercy:
They are lenient, humble, amiable: a living idol of kindliness.

(2)

The saints are blessed, blissful and they shower blessings.
They depend on intuitions, and are men of profound feelings.
Their presence relieves, gives sense of security, confidence:
They are incarnations, figures divine and natural paintings.

(3)

The saints are completely detached, candid and true devotee.
They clear for others the paths: muddy, thorny and dusty.
Their exemplary indifferent and unconcerned nature makes
Them God's responsible, dependable, and reliable trustee.

(4)

The saints possess peace, coolness and pacify others easily.
They also get relief that come to them only occasionally.
They have poise, serenity, equanimity, and perfect tranquility.
They never speak or act or announce conclusions hastily.

(5)

All are equal in the eyes of saints, neither high nor low.
In perception they are fast but in expression very slow.
They shower exuberant blessings on one and all.
They are bright, spread brightness and inwardly glow.

(6)

The saints have no pride, no dilemma and no lust.
Saluting God is their daily ritual, prayer to Him must.
Purity is their power, truthfulness strength, love energy:
In their declarations and verdicts they are always just.

(7)

The saints are real human and accept the hard realities.
They know one Absolute God, digest all sorts of dualities.
All is One and One is All is their philosophy, psychology.
They are not sants that lack any of the sublime qualities.

From *'Spiritual Quadruplets'*

□□□

3

INTRODUCTION

The History of Indian Sants and Sages

The history of Indians Sants can be divided into four parts: Pre-ancient; Ancient; Medieval and Modern. It is such a long period, that it is impossible to know the history, the men, life and the rare achievements of even the selected and famous people. Naturally, it is next to impossible to provide a list of the saints or of only the famous saints. There is another and very subtle difficulty that at one time and one place, a person is called a saint and another place a rishi; and there is a lot of difference in work and nature of a rishi and a saint. The other difficulty is that during the Middle Ages about 80% of the rare books were burnt to ashes.

But from time to time, many wise and diligent persons have tried to compile up names and life of saints. They are not exhaustive and never complete. A complete list can't be prepared. A lot of work was done after independence. Even though, the books are available yet it is difficult to know all the books, collect, read and prepare a complete list, at least on the basis of those research works.

The saints were so similar and so unlike each other that neither their lives nor words can be theorized, defined and expressed at a place.

Something concrete can be done only when some dedicated people from every region work hand in glove, forming groups and sharing their findings as it was done during the Pre-ancient and ancient periods, to come to a definite conclusion; or if some Veda Vyâsa appears to edit them after getting them collected. Yet, there is doubt that all the Sants will come to life.

The History of Sants can be summed up in few words that, numerous persons who followed the Vedas and the Eternal Human Religion, taught through thousands of Books of the Vedas, led a pure life, got revelation of God, and taught the people to live with piety, perform pious deeds, worship God and be happy. That way Salvation can be achieved. It was a balancing of reason and emotion; and of gyân and bhakti or knowledge and devotion.

It seems to be pertinent to mention here, that our saints taught the opposite of the following truth about the 21st Century, that I got from Internet. The saints never thought of making what we have become. We have changed because we have discarded the saints and relegated them into oblivion. The Truth will change. What will it become in the next fifty years or so? Within the last sixty years, the scientists have announced and brought the earth to annihilation for more than sixty times; the latest being the 'Big-Bang-Test'. Sri Aurobindo has claimed that some day some scientist will push on the wrong button and it will be extinction of the world, before the God can shout to save it. Will ever the scientists and leaders stop creating and storing powerful destructive 'Bombs'? There is a doubt. It is a matter of conjecture and hypothesis. What have we become today is being given below:

TRUTH: 21st Century

Our communication: Wireless

Our telephone: Cordless

Our cooking: Fireless

Our youth: Jobless

Our food: Fatless

Our labour: Effortless

Our conduct: Worthless

Our relation: Loveless

Our attitude: Careless

Our feelings: Heartless

Our follies: Countless

Our arguments: Baseless

Our Boss: Brainless

Our job: Thankless

Our salary: Very less

Our existence: Meaningless

Our movement: Heedless

Our action: Merciless

From *Internet*

The Definition of Sants

The broader definition of a saint is such that numerous pious souls may be claimed to be saints. Even people often say about a pious soul; that, *wey to sant âdami hain*, he is a saint. But the subtle difference is in the fact that a saint must have Brahman Gyâna, the knowledge of Cosmos and Cosmic power; the revelation of Brahman and the union with Him. It is an inner happening and can't be physically proven; and those that have the revelation would hardly reveal it. In any case, it is the most wonerful achievement. It happens to one out of millions; and after centuries apart. It is one thing that can't be guaranteed.

Brahman-gyâna is the reason, that many accepted saints can be omitted from the list as their Brahman-gyân has not established beyond doubt. But because they were closer to revelation, the people started calling them saints.

Charisma is not a criterion for sainthood or a quality of a saint. It is natural and hence, the plants feel first that a person has the revelation of Brahman; the animals are the second to feel it; man is the last one to feel the Brahman Gyâna of a person.

It must be mentioned here, that the best creation of the Absolute God is not man but plants. Man depends on plants. Plants depend on none. Plants depend only on Nature and they are the only creation that, follow Nature in its entirety. They are totally independent. They live and grow, bloom and bear fruits at one place. They collect their food well and survive on the things available at the place.

Plants are great. They have all the qualities of great saints. That is the reason that Indians treat plants as gods, and worship them. The plants collect, cook and eat their food without running from place to place or without killing other living beings. They have self-procreating ability. They have their own ways and means of scattering, improving and sowing seeds. They are the best creation and great saints, because each of their part is used and utilised in many ways. They serve all without reservations or prejudices. They have no lust and don't need companion to share the pleasure and pain. Man can never compete with plants.

Sant Tulasidâs gave a definition and noted two very important characteristics of the Sants: *sant saral chit jagat hit*: that the Sants are simple and gentle at heart; and they work for the welfare of all.

A Sant is a practical-form and a physical presentation of the spiritual knowledge. The Sants have personal experiences of what the spiritual philosophers and theorists have propounded in their philosophy. A Sant may not have his knowledge through those books but they have perceived it; he may not be able to explain and elucidate it but he has it in his inner self. A Sant is also a visionary. The outer curtains can't stop the inner sight of a Sant from looking at the eternal and cosmic truth. For him only that truth is immortal and unchangeable. That infinite glow is the essence in his eyes. He prays in the words of Upanishadas when he first, experiences it:

Pushanne karshe yam suryam prâjâpatya vyuha rashmin samuh.

Tejo yatte rupam kalyântamam tatte pashyâmi.

(O That Fosters! O Sun! That created the Universe! Collect and absorb your rays! Enabling me to see your Glowing Benevolent Form.)

And that way he feels: *yo âsâwasau purushah soahamasmi*: I'm that what That Purush is. He becomes one like him. There is no duality. Oneness is established and felt. To pronounce *soahamasmi* is easier but to reach to that state of being, perceiving and revelation is very difficult. Those who accomplish that, they enjoy that bliss and beatitude, here and in this life: *atra Brahman samashnute*: as his body remains on the earth but his soul resides in heaven: *prithvi par dehi rahe, paramesur mein prân.*

The desires of the Sant are purged and pacified. Then, he is no longer under the threat by the six enemies: *kâma,* sex; *krodha,* anger; *lobha*, lust; *mada*, pride; *moha* affection; and *matsar*, jealousy. He feels no pain, no disgrace, no defeat and no victory. He is completely detached, and hence, he can sacrifice anything and everything: *mana hâth bhaye jinkae, tinake bana hi ghar hai, ghar hi ban hai*: (He who has control over his mind, the home is like a forest and the forest is like a home.)

The Sant feels elated in humility, compassion, kindness, sympathy, love and benevolence. He has to show it for he has that feeling of Oneness with all living creatures, and when he is all, he is in everyone, then how can he ignore any, or to whom can he show pride. The other one is not defeated, it is he who is defeated; other one has not won, he himself is victorious; for he is the essence: *tatwamasi*. It is the real nectar, the amrit: *ya yetadwiduh amritâste bhawanti*.

No definition can be perfect to show all the qualities of Sants. Sants are intuitively known and accepted as Sants. It is all the more difficult because the qualities and characteristics of the Sants are inner, and not visible. It can only be felt and accepted or rejected. A Sant is a Sant because of his inner experiences and revelation, and never because of the outer garments. It is always mentioned that one meets a real Sant only with the grace of god, the luckiest one. It is again always mentioned that each part of a real Sant emits the inner revelation. Dariyâ Saheb claims that it must be expressed from each part of the body, if it is not so, then it is a lie:

Pâras parasâ jâniye jo palate ang-ang;

Ang-ang palate nahin, to hai jhoothâ sang.

To conclude, one can use a negative way: Sants are not Rishis; they are not Munies; they are not Yogis; they are neither Swâmis nor Mahâtmâs; neither Bhakts nor Pandits nor Poojâries. They possess some characteristics from them all, and become a combined 'whole'; and hence, Sants are only Sants.

The Meaning of Sant

The meaning of the word *sat* in Samskrit is 'to be' because the original *dhâtu* is *asti*, that which exists. Its correct meaning is' existence'. But it is usually used as a synonym to good and goodness. The plural of sat is *Santah*; that who possesses goodness in enormity. In Hindi it is popular as *Sant*. The *visarga* from *Santah* vanished in the common language of the people.

Sant, Satjana, Sajjana, Sâdhu are used as synonyms. The word *sant* denotes God, the Brahman, Almighty as he exists so others exist: *sadeva somyedamagra âsit*. (Chhândogya 6). So, in reality, *the meaning of Sant is that person who has the revelation of and knows the Brahman*:

असन्नेव स भवति असद् ब्रह्मेति वेद चेत् ।
असति ब्रह्मेति चेद् वेद सन्तमेनं ततो विदुः ॥

Asanneva sa bhawati asad brahmeti veda chet;
Asti brahmeti ched veda santam yenam tato viduh.

Taittiriya 2nd Valli

(That is untrue and not existing that does not possess the realisation of Brahman at his heart. The Rishis say them to be *sants* that have realised that Brahman.)

In that sense, a person may have thousands of good deeds against his name but if he had not the realisation of God at his heart then he is not a sant. Brahman is true and Brahman exists so, the person that knows the Brahman is also existing: *brahmavid brahmaiva bhawati*; the knower of Brahman becomes like Brahman. The Sants follow any of the three ways: Karma (Action); Gyâna (Knowledge) and Bhakti (Devotion) but it has been seen that most of the Sants have followed all the three paths.

There is yet another analysis. It says that the word *sant* may have originated in two ways. It could have been the plural form of *sat*, and it has been used in Hindi in its singular form. *Sant* is always singular in Hindi, and *santon* is the plural form. It means that who is the essence or that who had experienced the essence. Or it could have originated as an *upabhransh* (deformed or broken or both) of *shânt*. It means, he whose desires have been pacified or who has no desires. Both the meanings are correct with reference to a Sant.

In the Gitâ, Sant word has been repeated five times in the 17th Chapter- Shlokas 23; 26 twice and once 27, and every time the meaning has changed. In the first, it claims that Sat is the Name of the Brahman: *Aum tatsaditi nirdesho brahman strividhah smritah.* In the second, **sadbhâva** (sympathy, kindness, mercy, compassion; and **sâdhubhâva**, pity and helping others; and *sarvabhutahite ratâh*, doing good to every living creature without discrimination and with full freedom from lust and jealousy is also called sat: *sadbhâwe sâdhubhâwe cha sadítye tâtprya uchyate.* In the third, **Prashashta karm**a, greater deeds for the liberation of soul are also called sat: *prashaste karmani tathâ sa cha shabdah pârtha yujyate.* In the fourth, it says that **tadartha karma**, selfless work, work for others, particularly for God or Godly or Divine work is called sat: *karma chaiva tadarthâyam sadityewâ abhidhiyate.* In the fifth, all the good deeds like performing yagya, offering charity and doing penance are called sat: *yagya tapasi dâne cha sthitah saditi cha uchyate.*

Characteristics of Sants

In short and nutshell, the characteristics of God are the characteristics of a Saint. He is all; All is in Him; He is different to all; He lacks all; He possesses all; He is God; Divine Power; Cosmic Energy; a Saint; a Sage; a Pious Soul. All these epithets are the same. They denote similar qualities and characteristics. A Saint is a worldly symbol and representative of God. As God is seen and perceived in idols, God is seen and perceived in Sants too. An individual's perception may not be the proof of Saint or Sainthood but the words and deeds of the Saints are ample proofs. There is a rare balance of Sat Chit and Ânand in a Saint that is his individuality and working for the welfare of all is his idiosyncratic identity. He is neither a friend nor a foe; he has neither a friend nor a foe ***complete detachment; Devotion and surrender to God; Peace and ease; Equality and belief in***

***All as One; Devoid of attachment and enchantment; without Ego and without pride; no doubt and no duality or dilemma; Clarity in vision and philosophy; a lonely life without wealth;* etc.** are the qualities and characteristics of the Saints:

सन्तोऽनपेक्षा मन्चित्ताः प्रषान्ताः समदर्षिन ।
निर्ममा निरंहकारा निर्द्वन्द्वा निश्परिग्रहा ॥

Santo anapekshâ manchitâh prashântâh samdarshinah;
Nirmamâ nirahankârâ nirdwandâ nishparigrahâh.

If someone lacks one or some of these qualities then he is not a Saint. Only the person that possesses these qualities, knows and feels the possession; others can't test him and know whether he possesses them or not. All of us should try one's best to possess all or some of these characteristics. Even some of them will give peace and happiness in life and liberate the soul from the bondage of birth, life and death.

What Krishna taught Arjun to be in the Gita (2:45) is the real characteristics of Sants:

त्रैगुण्य विशया वेदा निश्त्रैगुण्यो भव अर्जुन।
निर्द्वन्द्वो नित्य सत्त्वस्थो निर्योगक्षेम आत्मवान्॥

Traigunya vishayâ vedâ nistraigunyo bhaw arjuna;
Nirdwandwo nitya satwastho niryogakshema âtmawân.

Be free from all the three worldly qualities, **Nistraigunya**, (Tamo, Rajo and Sato); Be **Nirdwando**, Be free from duality, don't think in terms of this or that, here or there; Keep doing all the good deeds everyday, do **Nityasatwastho**; Be free from the desire of that which you don't possess; and the thought of saving that which you possess, be **Niryogakshema**, free from possessions and non-possessions; be **Âtmanishtha**, enter the self, feel God and be one with the Absolute in you. These five qualities are treated as Five Nectars given by the Gita.

In plain words: *Saints are the persons that are free from the three qualities; from the feelings of friend and foe, love and hatred, respect and disrespect; free from anger, laziness, sex, desires, lust; and possess simplicity, truthfulness, compassion, kindness, mercy, charity, helping attitude, contentment, peace and forgiveness.*

It is interesting to see what the Sants said about the Sants and the characteristics of Sants. Guru Gorakhnâth begins with physical postures and movements. He tells that one should not stand up suddenly, and beat the feet while moving; instead, one should put his foot slowly and patiently. He prefers an introvert and forbids from revealing the secrets. Sweet tongue be preferred and anger should be controlled; see all, hear all but don't express them. Have patience and control over the self, don't invite debate; the world is made up of thorns, see before you put your foot forward; and do everything carefully:

Habaki na bolibâ, thabaki na chalibâ, dheerai dharibâ pâwn;
Garab na karibâ, sahaje rahibâ, bhanat gorava râwn.
Mana mein rahinâ, bheda na kahinâ, bolibâ amrit vâni;
Âgilâ agani hoibâ awadhu, taun âpana hoibâ pâni.
Gorakh kahai sunahu re awadhu jaga mein yaise rahanâ;
Âkhai dekhibâ, kânai sunibâ, mukha te kachhu na kahanâ.
Nâth kahai tuma âpâ râkho, hatha kari vâda na karanâ;
Yehu jaga hai kânte ki bâri, dekhi dekhi paga dharanâ.

Sant Ekanâth says that the Sants see the world with the feeling of Oneness, as a result of it, the God overwhelms the heart, mind and sight. Duality disappears. Then the sense of I or You, Mine or Yours also vanishes. Then only God resides in meditation, in inner self and the outer world.

Samartha Guru Râmadâs says the same thing in a different way and a different imagery. To him the life of a Sant is a box of jewels. It is full of bright and shining jewels of bhajans. The

Sants have no worldly wealth but they are rich in the wealth of Brahman, and have incomparable pleasure. For him the pain of the world is a sort of bliss.

On a similar pattern, Sant Tukârâm says that the Sants are empty of desire and lust. They are free from ego. He has advised the Sants to remain away from the places of debates.

Sant Dâdu Dayâla declares that only he is a Sant who has offered body and heart with head to Shri Râm:

Kâyar kâma na âwai, yehu sure kâ khet;
Tana mana saupe râm koon, dâdu seesa sahet.

It is a very interesting declaration by Sant Sunderdâs who follows the same suit, and says that the Sants have nothing to do with others. They are all the time engrossed in Brahman:

Kâhu soen na rosha tosha, kâhu soen na râga dwesha;
Kâhu soen na bair bhava, kâhu soen na ghât hai.
Kâhu soen na bakabâd, kâhu soen nahi bishâd;
Kâhu soen na sang, na tau kâhu pachhapât hai.
Kâhu soen na dushta bain, kâhu soen na lena dena;
Brahman ko vichâr kachhu aur na suhât hai.

Such are the Sants.

Goodness: The Quality of Sants

Goodness is not just a quality; it is the state of being good, being a saint, divine and sublime. The forcible or artificial goodness, neither can last nor can have strength but the goodness and the positive quality that emerges out of the inner self is everlasting. Who are the Saints? The Saints are the emblems of goodness; of positive qualities; and not in abstraction but in deeds.

Goodness or the positive qualities emerge from the self, only when one dedicates oneself to God or to some divine act or some Godly cause. They are inherent, present from before, mostly in the form of seeds; one has to cultivate or culture them to bring them to the fore. Penance, Satsang, words of Saints and Sages, Positive Thinking and good deeds are the ways to cultivate one's inner land to make the seed of goodness sprout and grow into a sapling first and then into a tree. That goodness will last forever, otherwise, it will vanish easily at one heavy blow of negative force or terror. When it has grown into a sapling, only then it can stand against the heat, flood, and wind of different secret or apparent devilish forces. Saintliness and Sainthood comes from within and grows wide outside to give shade to numerous souls hovering in transition.

One must read the book that is lying inside, the Cosmic Book of Eternal System that gives the ability to distinguish between the Good and the Bad and forces one to do only good. It is the knowledge that frees one from all sorts of negative attitude and deeds: *sâ vidyâ yâ vimukataye*. Saints are the person that have deep knowledge taken from that Inner and Eternal Book and hence are free from desire, lust, fear, and bondage.

The meaning of the words *sâdhu* and *sant* is the same but the conditions are very difficult to observe, absorb and to follow: They must be content with what they get; maintain equanimity, be the same both in pleasure and pain; must have control over the sense organs, maintain balance everywhere; devotion to and shelter of the Brahman only; free from slander and censure; no enmity; kindness, mercy, peace, without ego or pride, no prejudice, asceticism, penance and absolute goodness. These are the real characteristics of the *sants*:

यथालब्धोऽपि संतुष्ठः समचित्तो जितेन्द्रियः ।
हरिपाद आश्रयो लोके विप्रः साधुः निन्दकः ॥

निर्बैरः सदयः शान्तो दम्भ अहंकार वर्जित ।
निरपेक्षो मुनिः वीतरागः साधुः उच्यते ॥

Yathâ labadhe api santusthah sama chitto jitendriyah;
Haripâda âshrayo loke viprah sâdhuh anindakah.
Nirvairah sadayah shânto dambha ahankâr varjitah;
Nirpeksho munih vitarâgah sâdhurih uchyate.

Some people like to and prefer to prostrate and salute the dust sticking to the feet of such sants, whose feelings have been purged; he is of pure mind and pure deeds, he is the sant, they are able to know and feel the Brahman; they are beyond Time and Place: millions of salutations in their adorable feet:

यत्पूजाया हरेः पूजा दृश्टया न यमदर्शनम् ।
पापक्षयः स्पर्षनाच्च्च किं परं सत्समागमात् ॥
नमः सद्‌भयः सदा मेऽस्तु येशां चरणधूलिभिः ।
धान्या वसुन्धारा नित्यं सन्तः साक्षाद् हरेः तनुः ॥

Yatpujâyâ hareh pujâ dristyâ na yamadarshanam;
Pâpakshayah sparshanâncha kim param satsamâgamât.
Namah sadbhayah sadâ mey astu yeshâm charan dhulibhih;
Dhanyâ vasundharâ nityam santah sâkshâd hareh tanuh.

Nature of Sants

The characteristics of Sants are given in detail in Shrimadbhâgawat. Lord Krishna says to Uddhava: (11:11:29 – 31)

"Sants are kind to all; they won't wrong anybody or have no grudge against anyone; they have endurance, patience, fortitude; are free from scandals; they take pleasure and pain in the same vein; help others; are not enchanted by worldly things; they have tender heart but full command over their sense organs; pure; benevolent; detached; they eat least only for survival and never for taste; totally and always at ease; unperturbed; devoted to me; thoughtful; alert and conscious; serious; patient in dangers; they have won all the six weaknesses: hunger, thirst, pain, lust, old age and death; they give due honour to others; skilled and dexterous; friendly to all; merciful and wise:

कृपालुरकतद्रोहस्तितिक्षुः सर्वदेहिनाम्।
सत्यसारोऽनवद्यात्मा समः सर्वोपकारकः ॥
कामैरहतधीर्दान्तो मृदुः शुचिः अकिंचनः ।
अनीहो मितभुक्शान्तः स्थिरो मच्छरणो मुनिः ॥
अप्रमत्तो गंभीरात्मा धृष्टतिमांजित षड्गुणः ।
अमानी मानदः कल्पो मैत्रः कारूणिकः कविः ॥

kripâluh akrit adrohah titikshuh sarvadehinâm;
satya asâro anwadyâtmâ samah sarva upakârakah;
kâmairahatdheerdânto mriduh shuchih akinchanah;
aniho mitbhuk shântah sthiro machchharano munih;
apramatto gambhir âtmâ dhrishtatim ânjita shadgunah;
amâni mânadah kalpo maitrah kârunikah kavih.

At another place in the same book, Bhagawân Kapildeo has said to his mother Dewâhuti: (3:25:21–24):

तितिक्षवः कारूणिकाः सुहृदः सर्वदेहिनाम् ।
अजातशत्रवः शान्ताः साधवः साधुभूषणाः ॥
मय्यनन्येन भावेन भक्तिं कुर्वन्ति ये दृढाम् ।
मत्कृते त्यक्त कर्माणः त्यक्त स्वजन बान्धवाः ॥
मदाश्रयाः कथा मृष्ताः श्रृण्वन्ति कथयन्ति च।
तपन्ति विविधाः तापा नैतान् मद्गतचेतसः ॥
त एते साधवः साध्वि सर्व संग विवर्जिताः ।
संगस्तेप्वथ ते प्रार्थ्यः संगदोषहरा हि ते ॥

Titikshawah kârunikâh suhridah sarvadehinâma;
Ajâtshatrawah shântâh sâdhawah sâdhubhushanâh;
Mayyannena bhâwena bhaktim kurvantim ye dridhâm;
Matkrite tyakt karmânah tyakt swajan bândhwâh;
Madâshrayâh kathâ mrishtâh shrinwanti kathayanti cha;
Tapanti vividhâh tâpâ naitân madagatchetasah;
Ta yaite sâdhawah sâdhwi sarva sang vivarjitâh;
Sangah te pwatha te prârthyah sang dosha harâ hi te.

(Those who endure and are kind; friend to all; without enemy; serene and tranquil; simplicity is their ornament; are the saintly people, the Sants. They have unlimited and boundless devotion for God; they detach themselves from all actions and all relatives only for God; they listen to and tell only the tales of God; because they have taken shelter in God, so they never get worldly pains and live with pleasure. O Mother! Sincere to husband! They have no inclination for anyone or anything. You should be only in the company of Sants endowed with the above-mentioned qualities, because they are the only figures that take off all ailments arising from attachment.)

Other than these, the characteristics of Sants have also been given in the Gitâ (12:13–20 and 14: 22–25) and Shrimadbhâgawat (11:45–55). According to Bhartrihari, the Sants keep themselves busy in helping others: *santah swayam parhite vihitâ abhiyogâh.*

Bhartrihari exclaimed, "How many such Sants are here that have filled the body, mind and speech with the nectar of virtues; that feel pleased, elevated and gratified in doing only good to the three worlds; that treat atom like quality of others, to be like mountains and are always pleased at heart":

मनसि वचसि काये पुण्य पीयूष पूर्णाः
त्रिभुवनम् उपकार श्रेणिभिः प्रीणयन्तः ।

परगुण परमाणून् पर्वती कश्त्य नित्यं
निजहृदि विकसन्तः सन्ति सन्तः कियन्तः ।

Manasi vachasi kâye punya piyush purnâh;
Tribhuwanam upakâr shrenibhih preenayantah;
Par guna parmânun parvati kritya nityam
Nija hridi vikasantah santi santah kiyantah.

A Sant must possess all the qualities described at these places. So, it is not easy to be a Sant. And, it is all the more difficult to describe the characteristics and qualities of a Sant. Kâlidâs openly accepted it:

महिमानं यदुः कीर्त्यं तव संह्रियते वचः ।
श्रमेण तदशक्तया वा न गुणानामियत्तया ॥

Mahimânam yaduh kirtyam tava sangrihyate wachah;
Shramena tad ashaktyâ wâ na gunâ nâmiyattayâ.

(My speech stops here in describing your qualities not because your qualities have come to an end but because it has got tired after describing it so far.)

Sants are Rare

Sants are rare. It's not easy to be a Sant. It's not easy to get a Sant. Sants know the Essence, the Essential, the First, the Infinite, that who creates all; and pervades all; His existence is the cause of the existence of all; He is pure consciousness, all consciousness and the consciousness in all; He is all life and life in all; He is all energy; energy in all; and energy in all parts of one's self. It is a description of only a part of Him; He is indescribable; beyond any and all description. The person that knows Him, lives in Him is the Truth, and that Truth is the essence and that essence is a Sant. So, Sants are rare.

There is a lot of difference between a man called Sant and an actual Sant. A real Sant is Brahman; he is in the Brahman; he knows Brahman; he adores Brahman and is thoroughly deluded in Him. Sants take shelter in God, God stays in Sants; Sants are replicas of God, His emblem; they love God and they are loving to God; they are sons of God; disciples of God and in direct shelter of God. Sants have seen the acts and plays of God; they enact the acts and plays of God; they are parts of His daily ritual; they assist Him; they have access to Him and they are His accessories. They know God and hence they know all; they have access to inner world; that caused the universe; and the wonder is that *they are aloof from the world, completely detached.* One must try to search out such a Sant for himself; at least he must remember such Sants from time to time. The very memory of the Sant is enough to purge the inner self of a man. He would grow and prosper. And, the most important of all; *try to be such a Sant.*

That is the reason that it is usually said: ***santam sushântam satatam namâmi***: I regularly bow and salute the Sants that are perfectly poised and patient.

Inseparable Music and Devotion

Rasa and rang, Aesthetics and Colour, individuality and variations play a significant role in Indian Music, and Music is the spiritual life force of Indian culture, religion and devotion. Not a single ritual is devoid of music, not a single ceremony is completed without music. Often, music starts a month, a fortnight or a week earlier and usually continues even when the main function is over. Sometimes the form and content is changed as in the case of *Holi*. The songs begin a month earlier and from the next day after *Holi* the music continues but it becomes *Chaitâvar*. The same is true to the birth of a child or the marriage of a girl. It is also a way to collect people. At the very first *thâp of dholak*, the beat of drum, people (both performers and audience) start moving towards the designated place. That is one reason that from gods to sâdhus, and from Brahmins to Shudra, all move with a musical instrument. The gents as well as the ladies play musical instruments freely and with ease, often without being taught by a guru or without rigorous practice. The last few decades had reduced the number of persons moving with the musical instruments.

There are numerous examples that, in the groups of religious preachers and Sants, there were musicians; and all the Sants of India were good singers: some general, others extraordinary. It was natural (and it continues) that all the temples were and are the centres of music, and devotional songs and dances are presented before the gods and deities.

It is because sound and life are born out of *swayambhu nâd* or *anhad nâd* or *anâhat nâd* AUM, the sound that is ceaselessly flowing in the universe and any one can listen this AUM sound by only closing both the ears with palm any time. It is un-struck, infinite and ceaseless music. It is the form and presence of the Brahman. It carries the *Prân Vâyu* rather it is the *Prân*, the living element. So music is the easiest way to concentrate, meditate and get united with the Absolute. So, music is also the *Prân* of spirituality and devotion in India.

It is not only with Kabir, Raidâs, Meerâ or Nânak; it was also with the Rishis and Munies, Gandharvas and Apasarâs or from the beginning in the *Damaru* and *Tândava* of Shiva; in the *Veenâ* of Saraswati for Brahmâ and in the *Ektâra* (single stringed instrument, also played by Meerâ) of *Nârad* for Nârâyan; flute for Krishna and *Kartâla* for Hanumân, etc. The list is really long.

AUM, the anhad nâd, is a divine melody, celestial music, which transcends all and which is perceived by senses and intellect and is also beyond senses and intellect, for it is universal, cosmic, everywhere and for everyone and everything. It can be easily heard, felt, sung, possessed and reproduced. It's a simple eternal phenomenon. One needs only the willingness and time to listen to it or to possess it because it is in the self, in the whole of body as the heart beat and it can be felt at every part of the universe at large, and every part of a body at hand.

AUM, Anhad nâd, soul, God and Brahman are in essence, the same. Brahman pervades all in that, those or similar forms. They are the same poles of the electromagnetic field of body and cosmos; naturally, there is natural repulsion. One has to detach oneself from the physical magnetic field to be the opposite in the self or soul to get attracted towards the Brahman, God or the Cosmic magnetic field as there is attraction only in the opposite. The opposition is to be created for attraction. The poles must be different.

The Creator rules and if the soul is the ruler and has the ego, there can't be attraction. So, the Sants taught to surrender the self and the ego. They declared themselves to be the servant, and got the revelation: *kaun dambha kar kâru vâdya ke sammukh âwe*; who can play the eternal instrument with ego? *Main hi to teri godi baithâ moda bharâ bâlak hun*; I'm a happy child sitting in your lap. There is complete surrender in it, and then the eternal music will flow easily and everywhere and for everyone. That is the crux, the pivotal point. Those that feel it and follow it, get blessed; those that remain at the bank and fail to submerge the self in the Bountiful All, *rahâ kinâre baith*; waited and waited for no avail.

The other way, the Sants taught, is to turn inside, to cut off completely from the outer electromagnetic field. It is another way, and simpler way, to become the opposite pole to get attracted and merged in the *Nirâkâr* Brahman, the Un-manifest Supreme God. As music, He takes âkâr, and felt and heard. If we think of Musical Instruments and Music, we can easily realise both *âkâr* and *nirâkâr*; manifest and un-manifest. Though, the difference is subtle yet can easily be felt.

It is one reason that **age** has made no difference. Shri Chângdeva waited for 1500 years and Sant Gyâneshwar got it at only 5. There are numerous Sants in between them.

That has made the music imperative in the field of devotion. *Bhakti-bhâva is expressed and shown easily through music*. It helps in concentration also. Haridâs used to sing only when he felt inner compulsion. Not only he, but Tulasi and others also refused to turn professionals. Despite the global professionalism, and despite the fact that they are trying very hard, yet even in 21st Millennium, Indian Sportsmen, Artists, Actors, Musicians, Writers, Poets, Philosophers, Spiritual Preceptors have badly failed to show the inner professional spirit.

It is because deep at their inner self, in their spiritual life force, they are so thrilled by so many other aspects, that in each field and at each time, they feel the union, the rhythmic vibration, the deep resonance, the conscious sensations in conscience; and deep within they listen to the *anahad nâd*. It is not strange in Indian context.

It is one reason that **wealth** has made no difference. It is true to the richest king Râjâ Janak and the Pauper Sant Raidâs and in between those, that left their kingdoms like Buddha or Meerâ, and those that remained householders like Kabir and Nânak.

The listeners are also impressed, enchanted and influenced by the same process and on the same grounds. They also go deep down in trance and forget the outer world; and their life is changed.

Ironically enough, in music, the beat is as important as the un-beat; the *tâli* is as musical as *khâli*; the un-beat string of *sitâr* helps the beat-string in definite and positive manner that creates the vibration and resonance or the music itself. It's really a wonderful world of Brahman and Music. They are the blessed ones that submerge their identity or succeed in total identification of their personality. It's not only diving deep, but also losing the self in the Absolute; lost in music. They have fine-tuning with the Cosmic Entity or the Cosmic Electro-magnetic Power, with the Incessant Flow of Music and Life: the *Akhand*, the *Anant*. They live. They get bliss. They get Beatitude. To repeat, they are the blessed ones.

The language of Sants

Language is the only proper means available to express the spiritual experiences, provided, that one has the experience and the language. When there is the spiritual experience, then there is no physical existence or entity. It is amalgamated in that One *Virât*. Words melt and, sound ceases to exist. There is only the feeling. So, it has been always a problem for the Sants to express the rare feelings or the scenario that they sighted.

When Râmakrishna Paramahans failed to convey and convince Vivekânand that, he could see the God or Mâ Shakti as clearly as he sees the other things of the world, then he touched the forehead of his great disciple to show him and experience it himself. Vivekânad, at once, came to know what the Mother is, and what the Shakti means. A similar thing happened in the battlefield of Kurukshetra when Arjuna failed to grasp the Cosmic reality and had numerous questions left, Lord Krishna showed him His *Virât Swaroopa* and blessed him with the realisation. It can be learnt by experience alone. It is stressed in the Kenopanishad: '*One, who declares to know Him, does not know Him; one who feels that he does not know Him, he alone knows. For the claimers, it is unknown; it is known to those that stress their ignorance.*'

It is about realisation of spiritual truth, not about the expression of it. Experience is a different matter and the expression of the experience is quite different. Experience carries the whole, while the descriptions begin from a part, and end at a part. The whole is not expressed at a time; and when one tries to combine together the piecemeal expressions, then he fails badly because he has no experience, and no knowledge of which piece to join first or next and which piece to join where. And, those that have the experience, don't need the expression, they know the whole. What is that whole that the Sants possess? It is far better and illuminating to see it in the words of Shri Râma Krishna Paramahans:

"This earth is the largest thing that we see around us. But larger than the earth is the ocean, and larger than the ocean is the sky. But Vishnu as Vâman covered earth, sky and the netherworld with one of His feet. And that foot of Vishnu is enshrined in the heart of a Sant. Therefore, the heart of a holy man is greatest of all": it possesses all; *yat brahmânde tat pinde*. How can a Sant express the whole in words that are parts of language or in language that are parts of human sound or in sound which are parts of a human's breath.

There is one hurdle in the realisation also. God manifests. One can't see Him without His will. He chooses the person, place, way, etc., and appears, rather manifests. Shri Shankarâchârya has put it in the following way in his *Vivekachudâmani*:

"Gods make themselves manifest. Both Âtman and Brahman make themselves manifest, provided, that they wish and the person fulfills certain criterion (that differs or varies from person to person as some has achieved something and lacks something). Âtman is an ever present reality and manifests itself as the right means of knowledge that are present; and does not depend on place, person or ceremonial purity."

Modern scholars are trying to express the mystic and spiritual experiences in scientific way and language. They possess neither the mystic and spiritual language, nor they have that experience or revelation. Naturally, they are unable to convey the experience. Then they blame the language, while they themselves are mixing some of the scientific terms, with some of the spiritual words or words from the world of spirituality. They have read some books of science and some spiritual books. The whole is always missing. There is no completeness as there is no fullness in their life. When they fail to express themselves and to register their ideas into the inquisitive and conscious mind of the alert readers; then they conclude, that language can't convey the spiritual and mystic experiences.

Our Sants did not express it. They felt no need of expressing their idiosyncratic experiences. They were interested only in showing the path to others. Actually, only that path is important. Others should know and follow that path to attain that devotion and exaltation and purity of thought and deeds to force the Almighty to manifest; to get the needed experience for Salvation and Freedom from the cyclical chain of birth-death and rebirth.

At certain places, some Sants have tried to give a glimpse of their spiritual and mystic experiences. Invariably, and at all such places, they have used the language of signs and symbols. Of, course, these signs and symbols have been expressed through words but the words are so rich in meaning and implications that each reader can analyse, explain and understand it in his own way. His meaning or grasp of the experiences will be limited to the extent of his achievement or accomplishment. He can't go beyond that. It is true about all the Sants in general but particularly about Kabir and Sri Aurobindo, to cite two examples: one from the medieval period and another from Modern period. It is needless to state that very few readers have been able to understand 'Sâvitri' of Sri Aurobindo.

All the Sants have taught Bhakti, devotion to God; and use poetic diction, the language of poetry to express it. As the Sants had command over music, *ragas* and *raginis*, in the same way, the Sants had command over different kinds of poetry: epics, pastoral epics, lyrics, hymns, songs, shepherd's songs, *dohâ, sorathâ, chhappaya,* and *chaupâi* etc; and also on metres and figures of speech: *rasa, chhanda* and *alankâr*. Ironically enough, they were most learned yet totally illiterate. From where did they get the command? Was it intuitive or traditional or divine?

The Sants taught everything through poetry, with a clear intention that, like poems and songs, the people will be able to memorise them easily and keep them in mind; and transfer them orally to the next generation. Most of the poems and songs and hymns of the Sants have been saved, only by the oral tradition. The devotional songs and hymns have been widely acclaimed as 'the most satisfying and elevating reading' 'the solace of life as well as death'.

The poetic creation of all the Sants, are known as *Sant-Kâvya*. They are an integral part of religious literature and a living document of social philosophy and social thinking. They represent the time and describe both the grandeur and weaknesses of the society. They have retained their entertaining values also because of the flow, rhyme and rhythm. Moreover, they are all inspiring as they are rich in religiosity and positive values.

The Sants must have thought that poetry touches deeply. The idea must have cropped up from their own experiences as they listened to numerous such poems and songs, before they ventured to compose some of their own, and when they got the needed control over the subject matter, poetic diction, rhyme and rhythm, there was nothing else to stop them. Some of them composed more than one thousand couplets or verses or both. There are dozens of such Sants that have given 'a lot'; some have given dozens of books. Their revelation and intuitive knowledge must have played a greater role or deeper part in shaping their mind and in helping them to create poetry. They must be regarded as creative genius.

Most of the Sants had the divine grace and quality to compose them, as they were endowed with inner insight to see the outer world and know its inner meaning. They had the power of imagination. In most of the cases, the verses are genuinely spontaneous overflow of religious and spiritual feelings.

The other reason was that they had a definite purpose behind their composition. The directness and the definite quality of the purpose, made them bold and presented a big platform to present them.

There were two more reasons behind the creation of so much of poetic works: one was the regular congregations and the other the combined encouragement of and by the disciples and audience. At least, in the case of Kabir and Dâdu Dayâl it is said that people gathered everyday and they had to sing something new to them. They did with pleasure and dexterity. Two things happened because of it: one that at least one new song was composed everyday, and the other, that they had to repeat the same theme many times. Naturally, there are many such things in their poetic creation that can be easily and readily accepted as repetition

The *Sant-Kâvya* includes: the verses that they composed, mostly hymns, devotional songs, mystic description of their experiences and teachings for the people. It is no wonder that there are many books against the names of many Sants or at least there is one collection of their 'Vâni'. Guru Arjun Deva went far ahead and got the works of the Sants collected. The collection became 'Shri Guru Grantha Sahib' better known as SGGS. Guru Govind Singh surpassed him when he declared the collection SGGS as the eleventh and the last Guru. The logic behind it is very simple that the teachings of the Sants are as good as Guru.

The Accomplishment of Sants

People may think it to be superficial, because modern life has become completely materialistic but the fact is that the greatest achievement and accomplishment of the Sants is that they felt, followed and declared 'devotion', 'the worship of the God' and complete surrender to God, as the aim of human life. What they rejected as rubbish: the physical pleasure and luxury, fulfillment of lust and desires, has unfortunately become the aim of modern human beings. It is not. The Sants concluded that these six are the enemies: *kâma*, sex; *krodha*, anger; *lobha*, lust; *mada*, pride; *moha* affection; and *matsar*, jealousy.

They work as enemies in two different ways: if they are a part of our own 'self' they spoil us; if they are in others, they attack us with vehemence and destroy us. These are the intrinsic qualities that the world, the countries, the society and the families are all divided into tiny fragments. The fragmentation, pain, suffering, ill health, anxiety and depression are all caused by them.

In modern times, they are counted as friends and all the good qualities and wholesome deeds are treated as enemies. As a result, neither anyone is satisfied nor happy; neither any one has compassion nor healthy. They indulge in different (rather all sorts of) unethical, immoral and illegal things to earn to pay the huge bills of the clinics, hospitals and medicine shops; but health and happiness has gone far away from modern life. Man discarded saintly life and behaviour and Nature took away everything valuable from their life. They have substituted those eternal precious things with costly living style; costly cars, luxurious hotels and accumulation and show of wealth.

The Sants made us realise that we can't take away a single needle from the world when we die; Alexander requested to put his empty palm out of the coffin to make people realise that Victor is doing his last journey empty handed. What we take away are the abstract effects of our good deeds and misdeeds.

It is a great accomplishment that great Rishis like Veda Vyâsa declared: *âchâr lakshano dharmah santashcha âchâr lakshanâ*. In nutshell; religion shows how to behave well; the Sants behave well.

The Sants acquired Truth and preached Truth. The acquisition of truth is their achievement, we don't believe in them and we don't follow the truth is our weakness. As a result of their spiritual, pious and divine accomplishments the Sants live happily, teach happiness, give happiness and are the causes of bliss and salvation: *alam prasannâ hi sukhâya santah*; and the Scriptures asked to go to the Sants: *sangah satasu vidhiyatâm*; because the company of Sants is rare, illuminates; and always shows good results: *mahat sangastu durlabho agamyo amoghashcha*.

The Sants accomplished three most needed human and divine qualities: **no jealousy or anger against anyone; charity and truthfulness.** Veda Vyâsa declared that for these three achievements the Sants hold a very high position:

Triga yeva tu satâmâhuh santah padam uttamam;

Na chaiva druhyâdyât satyam chaiva sadâ vadet.

The Sants have absorbed many virtues including kindness, mercy, and merciful ways of teaching, imparting and giving those qualities. The Sants spread these qualities, and there lies their greatness, and that is the reason that they are needed most.

Once Guru Nânak wished cruel and uncivilised persons to remain united and live at that place; but he wished kind and civilised persons to get scattered. The disciples raised questions and the Guru explained that it is good for others that the cruel remain confined to one place; while it is good for others that the civilised scatter everywhere to make others good and civilised. Sants are the most essential needs; for they help others without thinking of any return. They have ample of the wealth of satisfaction and contentment. That is the only important reason that Lord Ram said to Sabari in *Adhyâtma Râmâyana* that the company of the Sants is the best way to bliss and salvation: *satâm sangatih yewâtra sâdhanam prathamam smritam*. What is the need to accomplish anything else if such qualities are there in us.

The Gifts of Sants

The greatest gift of the Sants is that they kept us close to God. They declared fear God you don't need to fear anything else. If you are not afraid of the God, you will have to be afraid of everything. We have gone far away from God, and doubt the very existence of God, as a result we are afraid of everything: of climate and atmosphere; of cold and heat; of rains and famines; of religion and atheism, of our rulers and the rulers of other countries; of our country men and the citizens of other countries; of our sect and other sects; of terrorists and criminals, of Sants and older people; of cunning people and younger generation; of food and dress; of doctors and medicines, of our family and other families; of father and brother, of wife and sister, of mother and mother in law, of sons and cousins, of teachers and workers; and the climax is that we are afraid of ourselves, our shadow, our deeds and misdeeds. There is no wonder that worries, anxieties; depression, ill health, diseases and many other enemies have overpowered our life. We are working and earning but we are not living. *The Sants gave us the ways and means of happy, healthy, prosperous and peaceful life.*

The gifts of Sants can't be listed. They made man human. It is equal to the greatest gift. Life will survive if we can keep it; life will perish if we lose it. Only humanity can ensure the survival of life on the earth or the earth itself, animal qualities in man is sure to bring extinction. In between the survival and extinction are the Sants and Humanity. Oneness or *âtmavat sarvabhuteshu*; or all human beings are related or *vashundhavai kutumbakam* will help man to live using the least natural resources and saving a lot for the future and for the unborn for their survival and continuation of life. If the saintly teachings are disregarded then, man will use all machine: light and heavy; all resources: physical and spiritual; all techniques: traditional and modern and all knowledge: scientific and intuitive to mine out, and eat out all that the earth possesses within a hundred years or so. Life will then easily perish in absence of trees; crops; water; air and fertile soil. We are fast moving towards our extinction. Hence, the Gifts of Sants have become valuable.

Another Gift of the Sants, that needs special mention, is that in every general crisis and danger on life they kept the people united; and in their own way and style forced one to help others. The compassion, cooperation and charity helped people in surviving during the crisis. It is true to the Sants of all over the world. If we cite the example of India then one can proudly claimed that India and Indians; Indian life, knowledge, culture and civilization was saved by the numerous Sants that sacrificed their all during the one thousand years of slavery. It's a great achievement by any standard.

□□□

4

ALL KNOWN SANTS

The names of the Sants have been taken from various books but the names are not complete. There are many more Sants. Many scholars are working on the Sants of different areas. More and more Sants and their works are coming to the fore. There is an effort to divide them according to the sect they belonged to or the age they lived in but that is also not possible because of their number and the mystery that surrounds them. It is only an effort to put them separately. It should never be taken as true and final. So far the Indian Sants and Sages are concerned there can never be a correct and final list. Moreover, a simple detail of **only a few hundred** is being given. Even the details have been taken from various books. Honestly speaking, it is an effort to make others know what the Sants were and simply by going away from them what a great wealth we are losing!

In the Indian Scriptures the 12 Forms of Brahman, that came into being in the Beginning are accepted as the Sadaguru, the greatest Sants and in the 8th Skandha and 24th Adhyâya of Shrimad Bhâgawat it has been forcibly pleaded that only one of them should be accepted as the Guru. Human Gurus are themselves enchanted to the world, have attachments and desires. They can't be accepted as the real Guru. Once that Subtle Omnipresent is accepted as the Guru, then there is no need of any other Guru. The following are those twelve Original Forms; Original Powers, Original Gurus and Original Sants:

Ādināth: Pure, Without Ego, Desire, One, Peerless, Without Dimensions, Infinite, Immense, initial form of Sat Chit Ānand, Almighty, Absolute God, the Brahman.	**Ādishakti**: An integral part of the Absolute Brahman, the Original Power, Energy, Strength, Creative Force, the initial form of all Powers and Energy.	**Sadāshiva**: When the Existence is accepted with 'Ahamasmi' 'I am', then idiosyncratic and peculiar Sadāshiva, different from the Brahman is created. He is the one that gave life to all innate matters and made the Universe MOVE.
Sadāshivashakti: The original Prakriti, a part of the Eternal Purush, created by the wish of Sadāshiva, 'I don't indulge alone'; the knowledge existing from before the creation.	**Iswar**: As a replica of the Pride of Sadāshiva Iswar came into sight: with quality yet without quality; He is described by 'apānipādau', without hand and feet etc.	**Iswariyashakti**: The wish to be two is the Inshwariyashakti: '*tato dwitiyam yaikshat*'; Greater Elements are incorporated in this Energy. The Inner and Working Power of Ishwar is the Ishwarshakti.
Rudra: With the wish to be two, Brahman took form and shape and Rudra came into being: *yā te rudra shivā tanuh;* the Universe exists in Him during the great deluge. He is famous as the seventh Sant Guru.	**Rudrashakti**: *Ekoaham bahushyām*, I'm one and multiply. This wish of Brahman brought Rudrashaki. He separates the action, profession and Great Elements.	**Vishnu**: *Ekoaham bahushyām*, I'm one and wish to multiply. In order to multiply He gave His brightness to Great Elements (Gross Elements) to feed and sustain the world. He protects and sustains.

Vishnushakti:	Brahmā:	Brāhmnishakti:
With my power I sustain the world' gave form to energy and power. The power of Vishnu, in the form of elements, is the 10th Sadguru and Sant.	Totally engrossed in the self, He visualized the Universe while looking at the Elements and appeared as Brahmā and created everything diverse as their Life-element, is the Form of All and Life in All.	He wished that my creation should act, perform all actions through yagyas; and the *Kriyārupa*, Power appeared to be the twelfth Sadguru, and resides in Veda, the knowledge. He is the Power of Knowledge and Power in Knowledge.

The following is the List of the First Sants. Surprisingly enough it includes Munies and Rishies also:

Sanakâdi (Sanaka etc Sanaka, Sanandan, Sanâtana, Sanatkumâr and Sanatsujât	**Saptarishies:** Marichi, Atri, Angirâ, Pulastya, Pulah, Kratu, Vashishtha,	Nârad
Bhrigu	Ribhu	Kashyap
Brihaspati	Shukrâchârya	Nara - Narâyana
Bhardwâja	Dattâtreya	Chyavan
Shândilya	Vaishampâyan	Yâgyavalkya
Vishwâmitra	Jamadagni	Markandeya
Upamanyu	Âruni	Uddâlaka
Ashtâvakra	Agashtya	Jadabharat
Kapildeva	Dadhichi	Raivataka
Saubhari	Bâsudeva	Vâlmiki
Sutikshna	Mankanaka	Gautam
Akrtitavrana	Patanjali	Kanâda
Sharbhanga	Pundarika	Jaratkâru

Vyâsa	Shukadeva	Maitreya
Shaunaka	Uttanka	Animândavya
Mudgal	Upamanyu	Sudâmâ
Gokarna	Swâyambhuva Manu	Priyavrat
Dhruva	Utakala	Rishabhadeva
Bharat	Prithu	Prachetâ etc
Aswapati	Nala	Rantideva
Shivi	Chandrahâsa	Nimi
Ikshawâku	Mândhâtâ	Muchukunda
Khatwâng	Bhagiratha	Ambarisha
Rukmângad	Harishchandra	Dilip
Raghu	Janak	Dasaratha
Bharat	Lakshaman	Shatrughna
Keshidhwaja	Khândikya	Bhishma
Marich	Nandabâbâ	Akrura
Uddhava	Yudhistir	Bhima
Arjuna	Sudhanvâ	Mayurdhwaja
Pradyuman	Aniruddha	Parikshit

Other Sants of Unspecified Period

Sant Veer	Sankarpana	Vainateya
Kâkabhushundi	Gajendra	Sugriva
Hanumân	Angad	Jambawâna
Jatâyu	Vidur	Romaharshana
Samâdhi Vaishya	Tulâdhâra	Tulâdhâra Shudra
Chakrika Bhila	Gudâkesha	Vritrâsura
Vrishparvâ	Prahlâd	Bali
Vânâsura	Vibhishana	

List of Woman Sants (Primeval Period)

Shatarupâ	Sandhyâ	Arundhati
Devahuti	Madâlasâ	Sulabhâ
Maitreyi	Gârgi	Sâvitri

Anusuyâ	Shândili	Damayanti
Kausalyâ	Sumitrâ	Kaikeyi
Mandodari	Shabari	Târâ
Devaki	Yashodâ	Kunti
Draupadi	Gopikâs	Sukhiyâ Mâlina
Yagyapatni	Shaivyâ	Prâtitheyi
Sukalâ´	Sumanâ	Andâla Rangnâyaki
Meerâbâi	Muktâ Bâi	Janâbâi
Sâdhwi Sakhubâi	Rukmini Bâi	Sahajo Bâi

The Sants of Transition Period

Nrisingh Muni	Mahesh Muni	Bhâskar Yogi
Mahendra Muni	Mâdhavânand	Jishnudeva
Gaudpâda	Govindbhagawatpâda	Vishnuswâmi
Bhartrihari	Shridhar Swâmi	Vidyâranya Mahâmuni
Jagadhar Bhatta	Laxmidhar	Vilvamangal
Appayya Dikshit		

The Sants from Medieval Period

Jagadguru Shankarâchârya	Yâmunâchârya	Ramânujâchârya
Nimbârkâchârya Râmânandâchârya	Madhwâchârya Chaitanya Mahâprabhu	Ballabhâchârya Râmânand Râi
Nârâyana	Basudeva	Prabodhânand
Bhattâchârya	Bhattâchârya	
Sanâtana Goswâmi	Roopa Goswâmi	Jiva Goswâmi
Raghunâthdâs	Mahâkavi	Madhusudan
Goswâmi	Karnapur	
Vitthalnâthji	Viswanâth Chakravarti	Harirâiji
Goswâmi	Srikrishna Mishra	Vishnuchitta
Raghunâthji	Yati	

Pandit Jagannâth	Kulashekhar Âlwâra	Poygai Âlwâra
Vipra Nârâyana Âlwâra	Muniwâhana Âlwâra	Peya Âlwâra
Bhutattâ Âlwâra	Tirumdisai Âlwâra	Nilana Âlwâra
Madhura Kavi Âlwâra	Nammâ Âlwâra	Appâra
Mânik Wâchaka	Sambandha	Sunder Murti
Vashweswar	Tirvalluvar	Vemanâ
Kundkunda	Râma Singh	Devasena
Ânandghana	Gyâna Sâgar	Chidânand
Jinadâs	Bhikhanji	Sarahapâda
Tillopâda	Macchendranâth	Gorakhanâth
Nibritinâth	Jâlandharnâth	Nâmadeva
Sant Gyâneswar	Sâwatâ Mâli	Senâ Nâi
Narahari Sunâr	Jagamitra Nâgâ	Chokhâ Melâ
Sant Trilochana	Sant Eknâth	Sant Tukârâma
Samartha Guru	Vinâyakânand	Sant Mahipati
Râmadâsa	Swâmi	
Sant Amritrâi	Sant Tikârâmanâth	Sant Mânapuri
Keshava Kashmiriji	Shri Bhatta	Harivyâsadeva
Bhatta		
Parashurâma	Hari Nâth	Raghunâth
Devâchârya		
Mukunda Râja		

The Sants of Mughal Period

Sant Kabir	Sant Kamâlji	Sant Raidâs
Sant Dhani Dharamdâs	Sant Nipataniranjan	Govinda Prabhu
Nâgadevâchârya	Vitthal Pant	Sopâna Deva
Chângadeva Mahârâja	Gorâ Kumbhâr	Visobhâ Khechar
Kânhu Pâtrâ	Kurma Dâs	Jogâ Parmânand
Gangânâth	Shankarânand	Sant Pipâji

Dhannâ Jâta	Bâbâ Lâl Dayâlu	Râmâlingam
Shrivallabha	Sarvânand Thâkur	Nrisingh Saraswati
Narasi Mehtâ	Goswâmi Tulasidâs	Madhusudan Saraswati
Hitâchârya	Gadâdhar Bhatta	Jagannâth Dâs
Gangâdhardâs	Sant Tyâgarâja	Dâmâji Pant
Bhânudâs	Janârdan Swâmi	Sant Gopinâth
Jani Janârdana	Sant Arun Giri Nâth	Tâyumânawar
Ramlinga Swâmi	Meyakand	Chadamber Swâmi
Kumargurupar Swâmi	Guru Nânak	Guru Angad
Guru Râmadâs	Shrichandraji Mahâraj	Sant Veerbhân
Sant Surdâs	Sant Nandadâs	Sant Krishnadâs
Sant Kumbhandâs	Sant Cahturbhuja Dâs	Chhetaswâmi
Govind Swâmi	Sant Vyasa Dâs	Sant Singâji
Mâreyâ Gosâwi	Parameshthi Darji	Kubâ Kumbhâr
Raghu Kevat	Sant Mâdhava Dâs	Sant Dâdu Dayâl
Sant Rajjab	Sant Sunderdâs	Trayambaka Râj
Ramâ Ballabha Dâs		
Sant Tukârâm	Vâman Pandit	Nijânandâchârya
Prânanâth	Sant Bhikhâ	Dariyâ Sâheb
Tailang Swâmi	Sahirobâ Mahârâj	Sant Prahlâd Mahârâj
Bhashkar Râi	Krishnadâsji	Bâbâ Âmanâthji
Sant Mâdhava Dâs	Swâmi Nârâyana	Sant Hansdâsji
Râmkrishna Paramhans	Sant Somaji	Bandâ Bairâgi
Sant Vijaya Krishna	Sant Gomatidâs	

The Sikh Gurus

Guru Nânak Devaji	Guru Angad Devaji	Guru Amardâsji
Guru Râmdâsji	Guru Arjundevaji	Guru Hargovindji
Guru Harirâiji	Guru Harikrishnaji	Guru Tegbahâdurji
Guru Govindsinghji		

The Sants of Nâth Sampradâya (Sect)

	Ādināth (Shiva)		
Umā	Matsyendra Nāth	Jālandhar Nāth	
Gorakh Nāth	Chaurangi Nāth	Kāniph Nāth	Maināwati
Gaini Nāth	Charpati Nāth		
Nibriti Nāth			
Gyāneshwar	Sopān Deva	Muktābai	

The Sants of Modern Age I

Munnâdâs	Govinddâs	Gajâdhar Dâs
Siddhadâs	Haridâs	Pahalwândâs
Âula Chând	Mahârâja Gosain	Sudhishta Gosai
Karan Gosain	Bâbâ Kapildeva Gosain	Albeli Ali
Shri Dhruva Dâs	Harerâm Brahmachâri	Gunâteetânand Swâmi
Gopâlânand Swâmi	Nityânand Swâmi	Shatânand Swâmi
Nishkulânand Swâmi	Muktânand Swâmi	Brahmânand Swâmi
Shiva Nârâyan	Dedharâja	Siddha Hansdâs
Sant Somaji	Pitâmbar Puri	Bhakta Purâji
Gumân Singhji	Mahârâja Chatursingh	Nathuni Bâbâ
Yukteshwar Giri	Subbarâidâs Swâmi	Shri Ânandâ Bâbâ
Shri Lalit Kishori	Shri Lalit Mâdhuri	Swâmi Nigamânand

Shri Gambhir Nâthji	Dayâl Dâs Swâmi	Swâmi Krishnânand
Swâmi Keshavânand	Shri Nâgâ Bâbâ	Sant Nâga Mahâshaya
Swâmi Vivekânand	Prabhu Jagat Bandhu	Sant Vijaya Krishna
Harnâth Thâkur	Shri Mâdhava Dâsji	Bâbâ Premânand Bhârti
Swâmi	Vishuddhânand	Swâmi
Bhâshkarânand	Saraswati	Shivarâmkinkar Yogatrayânandji
Shri Awinâshiji	Shri Shankar Swâmi	Shri Yugalânand Sharanji
Jânakivar Sharanji	Râmballabh Sharanji	Sitâsharanji
Shri Hanskalâji	Sant Rupa Kalâji	Sant Gomatidâsji
Shri Râmâji	Shri Râmdâsji	Shri Shyâmadâsji
Siyârâmsharanji	Shri Siyâsakhiji	Bâbâ Bharatdâsji
Bâbâ Sâwaldâsji	Swâmi Mângilâlji	Swâmi Râmânuja Dâsji

The Sants of Modern Age II

Shri Râdhikâ Dâsji	Shri Saryuji Dâs	Shri Bâlkrishnaji
Yogi Vanrâja	Swâmi Phool Râmji	Shri Vishnudâsji
Dolurâmji Sâchihar	Shri Râmji Mahârâj	Ajaneshwarji
Devidânji Amyâsi	Mangalnâthji	Pt. Ganeshji
Brahmchârini Gorânji	Shri Kushalânandji	Bâbâ Râmnâthji
Shri Permânandji	Shri Amritnâthji	Shri Sitârâmdâsji
Râmcharan Râmsanehi	Shri Uttamnâthji	Shri Agradâsji
Shri Vriti Nârâyanji	Bhâratiji Siddha	Maujânandji
Shri Heerâdâsji	Bâbâ Mehârdâsji	Sant Siyârâmji
Swâmi Shrutânandji	Bâbâ Hajârâ	Anant Mahâprabhu

Bâbâ Houriakhân	Somawâri Bâbâ	Shankar Râmkrishna Teerthaji
Hariharji Mahârâja	Sant Shri Râmchandraji	Sant Sri Kachchâ Bâbâ
Lakhanji Paramhans	Laxmipati Paramhans	Mâdhava Lâlji
Pt Shri Gattulâlji	Shri Dayârâm Bhâi	Anantâchâryaji
Laxamanâchâryaji	Swâmi Mathurâdâsji	Siddhâpâ Swâmi
Shri Mânik Prabhu	Sant Balabhimaji	Shri Krishna Bhatta
Shri Vishnu Kavi	Âtmânandji	Shri Gulâb Râo
Shri Sâinâthji Mahârâja	Sri Padmanâbh Teertha	Rishirâja Mahârâja
Upendrâchâryaji	Laghurâja Swâmi	Shri Mohan Giriji
Shri Nârâyan Dâsji	Maluka Dâsji	Rupa Bhawâni
Purnânand Giri	Nârâyan Teertha Swâmi	Deorâhâ Bâbâ
Harisevak Lalji	Paramhans Yogânandji	Sant Premadâs

Clarification on Time

In India the age and period of a person is not known but accepted as such and such because the people were made to be interested in the date and time when the Moghuls first and the British people later started doubts and clearly wiped out the definite belief that the Indians had. Once doubt crept in their mind then they lost the traditional hold on it. A time came when only the date was important, the life and teachings were thrown away. As a result, for the last three hundred years or so, the Indian scholars have wasted their most valuable time in searching out, discussing, proving or disproving the dates of important figures. It is wasted because the original important persons have not said anything about their birth and there is no record of their death. It is our greatest strength. As a result we have always thought of and accepted time of a person in our Time Frame of Manu, Manwanta, and the circle of four Yugas (Satyuga, Dwâpar, Tretâ and Kaliyug as 32,000 years; 48,000 years; 64,000 years and 1,28,000 years respectively). One circle of the four yugas is called a Manu and six such Manus have elapsed and we are living in the 7th Manu. This calculation was totally rejected by both the rulers during the last one thousand years for the obvious reason that their known existence is only around 2,000 years old. If they accept the cycle of Indian Yuga, then the primitiveness of Indian Culture, Civilization and Knowledge will be proved existing since millions of years ago when the western Sapiens had not taken birth even in imagination.

Our great and learned men have wasted a lot of time in the process of establishing a time of one or the other. That is the reason that I gave the least time to it and wasted none. In my opinion, what the Indian tradition says is true; and they are either fools or big liars that claim the Mahâbhârat to have been written some 5,000 years BC. "BC' is not, has never been and can not be the scale, measure or frame of Indian time span because of its short life, short sightedness and numerous prejudices. At least the time before 18th century BC should be calculated only in terms of Manus and Manwantar. If it is thousands of time bigger than their existence, let it be so because it is actually so. If the world will not see through Indian Calculation of Time then will never know the remote past because the Modern Scientists say that "between 10 to 20 Billion years ago there was the Big Bang and the universe came into being". For them the difference of 10 Billion years seems to be like ten days. They mention millions and billions as if they are months or years. One must feel that one hundred thousand years is a million; and hundred million is a billion. These are very big span, far greater than the mind can perceive; these are not jokes; and should never be used lightly.

In the shorter version of time, particularly in lifetime dates and time have some importance but in the longer version of thousand, myriads or million years; days, dates and years have no significance.

So, an approximate date has been mentioned in this book but there is neither any guarantee of that time nor any rigidity. It is better to ignore the time given in it. It is given here only because it is given somewhere else too, particularly in the books by distinguished writers. Otherwise, in the case of the Sants of India no time frame is needed. All the Indian Sants are beyond Time and Space.

In this context, this may also be mentioned that they can provide a neatly arranged list of dates and events that have only a few centuries at their back and a few hundred names to mention. It's really a very tough work for an Indian that has millions of years at his back and thousands of Super Human Beings in every Yuga (era). Europeans have prepared many Encyclopedias of one, five, ten to thirty volumes which are very much in demand but all of them are crammed up with only information and they give least knowledge. That is the reason that Encyclopedias are bought and possessed but not read. *I bet (though, it is the most foolish thing to do) there was or is not a single person in the world that has completely read a single Encyclopedia, the editors and proofreaders included.* The Indians preferred knowledge to information. They like to add to human knowledge and not to waste the papers on insignificant everyday details.

❑❑❑

5

Different Sants

When most of the things are in the unknown, what should be the place to look into the life of different Sants? Gaudapâda was the ultimate choice. In the matter of time he is perhaps very far away from Veda Vyâsa and his son Shukadeva but in geographical terms he was very close to Shukadeva. The Time of both Shukadeva and Gaudpâda is unknown and the places of both are known. It is intriguing to know whether there is some spiritual similarity between them or not. It was the sole reason that the analysis of a little known life, deeds, words and ideas of Indian Sants and Sages began with Gaudapâda.

1. Gaudapâda

There was a village called Bhoopâla near the âshram (hermitage) of Shukadeva Muni. (Although, it is not very clear where he was the Shukadeva Muni or some other Shukadeva.) A Brâhmin couple named Vishnudeva and Gunawati, rich in wealth, knowledge and culture, lived in the village. They loved worshipping Gods and entertaining guests. They helped others as much as they could. But they had an anxiety. They were growing old but they had no son. Their worry grew and ond day they went to the hermitage of Shukadeva and kept on chanting

Gâyatri Mantra for seven days without taking food or water. On the seventh day, a sound came from the cave of Shukadeva; "O Brâhmin! You would get a brilliant son. He would know all *shâshtras* and achieve perfection. He would be an accomplished man and will be endowed with supernatural powers. All the sages, mendicants and hermits will respect him.

The happy couple returned: pleased and enriched. In due course they got a bright son that glowed in the lap of his mother. After the *jâtakarma Samskâr* he was named Shukadatta (one given by Shuka). He learnt the Vedas at an early age. Then, one day he decided to go to Shukadeva. He went up to the cave but he was not called in. He stood there for almost twenty-four hours when a sound came from the cave, "O Child! Go to Gaur and meet Jishnu Sharmâ, a preceptor of my tradition. He will give you essential lessons in Ethics and philosophy. You will be accepted as my disciple. After completing your study there you may find me everywhere."

Shukadatta returned back and narrated the whole incident to his parents, and expressed his desire to go to Gaur to meet the preceptor and get the needed knowledge. The parents were aggrieved. They did not like the separation. He was the only child that they got in the later half of their life. The boy started his journey. The parents followed him but he requested them to return back. He would get a brother soon. The sad parents returned back.

Shukadatta covered the long distance traveling only on foot and reached the place of Jishnu Sharmâ, his designated preceptor. He met him and narrated the whole incident and his story. He accepted him as his disciple and taught him, *Vedânta; Vedânga; Yoga*; and the secret *Mantras*. Because he had traveled up to Gaur on foot so he was named (or became popular as) Gaudapâda.

Because of his dedication, devotion and learning Shukadeva was very kind to him. Whenever he remembered him, Shukadeva used to appear before him. He kept the word that he gave to a child.

Gaudapâda wrote a commentary on *Mândukya Upanishid.* There are different stories why and how he wrote the commentary. Many anecdotes are really very popular. The fact is that he made *Mândukya Upanishad* available and perceivable to all. That book is famous as *'Kârikâ on Mândukya Upanishad'*. The Shankarâchârya has written a commentary on his 'Kârikâ'. There are two other books that are also claimed to be written by Gaudapâda. They are Commentary on *Sânkhya* and Commentary on *Uttar Gitâ.*

There is an anecdote that once Gaudapâda went to meet Shankarâchârya. He asked him to show the Commentary. He saw it and was pleased enough to bless Shankarâchârya.

(The time element is not digestible. He is claimed to be a Sant that came centuries before the Buddha, how can he be there at the time of Shankrâchârya who was definitely born centuries after the Buddha. But in our country many are treated as immortal, many have the age of thousands of years. They are all accepted as 'beyond Time and Space.' There is no need of any guesswork. Dates of the past will not improve our life or living, only our positive thinking and wholesome deeds can help us in peaceful, pleasant, prosperous and complete life; achieving and accomplishing all the great pursuits of *Dharma, Artha, Kâma* and *Moksha.*)

2. Vishnu Swâmi

Around three thousand years ago, in the Dravidian region there was a king that had a Brâhmin Minister who was learned, wise and religious. The Brâhmin Minister had a wife but no children. The couple performed many rituals, prayed for many years and then got Vishnu Swâmi as their son. (Vishnu has been a very common name. Most of the Vishnu named persons are very famous so, often they get mixed. This Vishnu Swâmi usually gets mixed with Vishnu Sharmâ that he was not. Vishnu Sharmâ must have come centuries after him.

May be because Vishnu Swâmi was a gift of God or he may have carried over the *Samskârs* of his previous life or it may have been the parental effect, Vishnu Swâmi showed brilliance and religious spirit at very early age. After the sacred thread ceremony he learnt the prevalent sixteen branches of learning in a very short time. It included Vedas, Vedânga, Vedânta and Purânas. So, on the accepted ritualistic pattern that the person that has completed his education should devote his life in knowing the Brahman by worshipping Him: *yo yandashah sa tam bhajet*, Vishnu Swâmi turned towards the Brahman. He turned towards Upanishads. It is mentioned at places that he read the description of God in *Brihadâranyaka Upanishad* and went all out to get that form of the Brahman:

Brahman is known through the self. ... ... He that knows Brahman becomes all.

Vishnu Swâmi went all out to know that God. He envisaged the form of Lord Krishna, went for penance and sat in meditation. He had completely surrendered to that God so, he had full faith to know, see and meet his Lord. With utmost devotion his penance continued for many years but of no avail. His devotion and the process of worshipping continued but he stopped taking food and water. His condition worsened with every passing day but the spirit remained the same. On the seventh day, he decided to die in the pain of separation, as it was unbearable. Then his heart and mind was filled up with celestial light. He lost himself in that light. When he regained consciousness he found Lord Krishna with Râdhâ and Rukmini before him. The condition of the devotee to see the God can only be imagined. He got everything that he needed. From then on he started chanting, "*Shrikrishna tawâsmi*!" "O Krishna I'm you." He got numerous disciples and there are as many as seven hundred Âchâryas in his tradition. Ballabhâchârya also propounded his theory on his principles. It is said that one Vilwa Mangal, different from other famous Vilwa Mangals was among his descendents.

3. The Âlwâr Sants

The Ancient Vaishnava Sants of South are called Âlwâr Sants. Âlwâr means the person that has dived deep in the Ocean of Spirituality. The Âlwârs are known for their love and pleasure or the physical form of *Sat, Chit* and *Ânand*. The Âlwârs based their philosophy and spirituality on the Gita and the Upanishadas. They were great devotees and performed *poojâ* and rituals in detail irrespective of the fact that they are at their place or at a strange place. So, often they are called temples.

The Âlwârs were born in different castes and communities but their castes are hardly ever mentioned. They are all Sants and that is all for the general people that are not interested in gaining political favour and power through Sants.

The verses composed by the Âlwârs were made popular by a learned devotee Shrinâth Muni. It was later on made a Path by Shri Râmânujâchârya. He named the path as *Prapati Mârga*. He gave them fame and the popularity that they enjoy.

The four thousand verses of these devotee Sant poets are collected in a book named "*Divya Prabandha*'. The verses are treasure house of self-realization and self-revelation through knowledge, love, beauty, equality and pleasure. In most of the verses the Âlwârs have described the Gods: particularly Nârâyan, Râma and Krishna. They were so engrossed in their songs that they did not care for the popularity of the verses. They sang at a place, moved and repeated the same at another place and so on. The verses flowed from them easily and naturally like a genuine eternal fountain. Their verses are really sublime for they saw the god in each thing. They were completely united with Nârâyan and believed in '*soaham.*' They have composed verses in praise of all the 108 types of idol that are worshipped in different Vaishanava temples of the country.

It is believed among the Vaishanavas that Âlwârs were actually Sri Vatsa; Kaustubha; Vaijyanti; Vanmâla; Shri-bhoo lilâ deities; Anant; Garuda; Viswaksena; Sudarshan Chakra; Panchjanya Conch; Kaumodaki Gadâ; Nandak Sword; and Shârang Bow that were sent on to the earth to popularize devotion and worshipping when it had started fading out.

In the South *Tiruwâyamori* is very popular as an epic. It is in Tamil and it means the 'the sublime speech that came out of the pious Sants'. The priests and the people sing the verses from it invariably at homes and in the temples.

There were twelve Âlwâr Sants. They are the following:

(a) Vishnu Chitta (Peri Ālwār)	(b) Shri Āndāḷa (Rangnāyaki)
(c) Kulashekar Ālwār	(d) Vipra Nārāyan (Bhaktapadarenu)
(e) Muniwāhan (Tiruppanā Ālwār)	(f) Poyagai Ālwār
(g) Bhutatta Ālwār	(h) Peyā Ālwār
(i) Bhaktisār (Tirumarisai Ālwār)	(j) Neelan (Tirumangaiya Ālwār)
(k) Madhur Kavi Ālwār	(l) Namma Ālwār (Shathakopāchārya)

(a) Vishnu Chitta (Peri Âlwâr)

Vishnu Chitta, the great Âlwâr or Peri Âlwâr was the incarnation of Garuda. He was born in a Brâhmin family at a pious village Villiputura in the Tinnevelli district in Tamilnâdu to Mukundâchârya and Padmâ. They had worshipped Lord Vishnu and visited his temple daily for many years. He was born on *Ekâdashi* and Sunday in *Swâti* Constellation. It is said that at the time of birth his mother felt no delivery pain. The child was different from the others. All his Samskârs were performed in right religious spirit and in time. Without going to the temple the boy worshipped Bhagwân Vishnu, as a true devotee so he was name Vishnu Chitta, whose mind is engrossed in Vishnu. Later on, he spent most of his time in the temple and chant *Vishnusahastranâma*, thousand names of Vishnu. He taught people that Vishnu or Nârâyan was the Absolute God. '*Aum Namo Nârâyan*' was his Mantra.

Guru mukham adhinatya prâha vedân sheshân;
Narapati parikalpatam shulkam âdâtu kâmah;
Swasuram amar vandyam rangnâthasya sâkshâda;
Dwijakulatilakam tam vishnuchittam namâmi.

An incident about him is popularly narrated. One night Lord Vishnu appeared in his dream and ordered him to go to Madurai in the congregation of religious leaders called by king Baldeva and to teach them the way to get real bliss. He prayed to God and went to Madurai. Although, he was not well versed in the Scriptures but he knew God and the bliss. He opened his heart in the congregation. The king was impressed by the plain and true ideas of the Sant. He was given a lot of gold and a procession was arranged to felicitate him. From there he went to Villiputur and spent the rest of his life there in composing hymns to God Nârâyan.

(b) Shri Ândâla (Rangnâyaki)

Shri Ândâla popularaly known as Rangnâyaki was the fostered daughter of Vishnu Chitta Peri Âlwâr. Her original name was Kodai, tender as flowers. He got her when he was plucking flower for poojâ. She was a newly born child then. He brought her and fostered her as own daughter. Ândâla dedicated her life to the Lord. From the very childhood she talked only of Nârâyan, composed songs in praise of her Lord and sang them usually in trance. She thought to be doing everything for Lord Krishna and in his presence and among the Gopes and Gopikâs. The people started calling her Ândâla. She is accepted as the incarnation of Bhoo Devi.

Karkate purvaphâgunyâm talasi kânana udabhawam;
Pandey viswam varâm kodâm bande shri ranganâyakiyam.

There is a story that she was actually married to Rangnâth who appeared in the dreams of both Vishnu Chitta and Ândâla and asked them to arrange the marriage. It is said that while the sacred mantras of marriage were being chanted suddenly the light brightened thousand fold and Ândâla became one with the light.

(c) Kula Shekar Âlwâr

Kula Shekhar Âlwâr was born as a son to a religious king of Kollinagar, Kerala by the grace of Nârâyan on *Dwâdashi* in *Punarvasu* constellation. His study started in a very organized manner. He studied both Samskrit and Tamil, the ancient languages and finished all the books available to him. After finishing the study of Vedas, Vedânga and Vedânta, he turned towards arts and learnt all the 64 shâshtras including Politics; Science of war; Archery; Âyurveda; Music and Dancing (Gandarbhaveda and Nritya Kalâ). At the right time he was made the king. He showed great administrative capacity, brought everything on the track, forced all to learn, work and earn. As a result there was neither unemployment nor poverty in his kingdom. It was the golden period for the place. He was wise, pragmatic and a true religious king. He had health and happiness of the people in his mind and the devotion towards Bhagwân Vishnu at heart. He coordinated the two and maintained a strange balance. His verses show both his longing for the Lord and eagerness to improve the life and lot of the people.

His devotion to Shri Ram grew to the extreme when he saw him in his dream. Once, while listening to the epic Râmâyana, he totally identified his self with the time of Râm and when Râm was going to fight against Khar-Dushan alone then he orderd his army to march ahead in support of Râm. He was pacified only when he heard the storyteller's announcement that Râm has killed Khar-Dushan all alone.

Kula Shekhar started giving more time to religious congregations, chanting of mantras, and recitations and singing of devotional songs and hymns. There were always some devotees in the palace. There is a tale that once a diamond was stolen from the palace, the courtiers suspected the devotees but the king had firm faith in the purity of the devotees. In order to show their innocence he put his own hand into the pot with a very poisonous cobra but was not harmed. Later on, the diamond was searched out.

Along with the devotees, he started visiting places of pilgrimages singing the songs and hymns all the way to and from. He stayed for a few years in Shri Rangnâth Region and completed his poetic creation *Mukundamâlâ*, lilting strotras. Then he moved on to Tirupati and composed many devotional songs. After that he took the long tour of the pilgrimages in the northern region including Mathaurâ, Vrindâvan, Ayodhyâ and all the time he composed strotras and hymns, that are a treat to heart and mind; and sang them with other devotees.

Kula Shekhar is known to be the incarnation of the Kaustubha Mani.

Kumbhe punarvasau jâtam chopapattane;
Kaustubhânsha dharâdheesham kulashekharam âshraye.

(d) Vipra Nârâyan (Bhaktapadarenu)

The life of Vipra Nârâyan is like the tidal wave, of high tide and low ebb and high tide again. He fell from the height of total devotion to surrender to a Devadâsi and again achieved that height but this time with his changed name as 'Bhaktpadarenu'. The change in life forced him to change his name. It's a rare example that a Nârâyan bhakt, a devotee of the Lord, changed his own name otherwise most of the 2nd or 3rd names were given either by pandits or kings or the people. Vipra Nârâyan is said to be the incarnation of Vanmâlâ:

Kodande jyeshtanajshatre mandangudipur udabhawam;
Choloh vyâm vanmâlânsham bhaktpadrenum âshraye.

Vipra Nârâyan was born in a Brahmin family. He studied the Vedas and devoted his time and surrenered the spirit to Shri Ranganâth. He was fascinated by the posture of Lord Vishnu half reclined on the great snake Sheshanâga in the Ksheersâgar, the milky ocean. He planted an orchard of fruit trees and flowers around the temple and spent his days in preparing garlands for his lord and singing devotional songs in His praise.

But he was seduced by a Devadâsi; and her beauty infatuated him so that he became a regular visitor of her place. But when she was tired of him he was thrown out. Yet he could not regain his 'self composure'. There is a long story of how the golden dish of the temple reached her place and how both of them were arrested and how they were released and again turned towards devotion. She also changed her mental inhibitions and became a devotee of the Lord. Their last days were spent in total devotion to Shri Ranganâth and in composing and singing stotras, hymns and songs but only after becoming Bhaktpadrenu.

(e) Muniwâhan (Tiruppanâ Âlwâr)

The parentage of Muniwâhan is not known, as he was found in a paddy field and fostered and brought up by a Shudra in Nishulâpuri. He is the incarnation of Shri Vatsa. His fostered father was an expert in his type of songs and music. Muniwâhana easily got accomplished in music and learnt playing *Veenâ*. He used to sing only the name and praise of God on the accompaniment of *Veenâ*. He wished to see Shri Ranganâth but was not permitted to enter the temple.

Muniwâhan came to the bank of Cauveri and started living in a hut. He concentrated on the form of his beloved God and sang in His praise. The *Veenâ* helped him. During the celebrations he used to see the Lord keeping distance when the idol was taken out as procession. He used to weep for Him. He did not like anything else. He explained his pain in his expressive songs.

One day, Sârangamâ Muni entered his hut and announced that the Lord has ordered him to carry you up to him on the shoulders. He refused on many grounds, that Sârangamâ was a Brâhmin; that he has no right to enter the temple, that he can't board the shoulders of another human being; and that it will be a sin to be carried up to the Lord. But it was Lord's order. The Muni had to obey him. He put Muniwâhan on his shoulders and carried him up to the temple to Shri Rangnâth. From there on he was called Muniwâhan, the person that used a Muni as a vehicle.

On the shoulders of the Muni he got the heavenly pleasure as he was going to his Lord. He was in a blissful state. It has been described by others in many songs.

On the shoulders Muniwâhan started singing in a trance that his life has achieved its grand success. It is said that the brightness of light started inside the temple and changed into blazing light and Muniwâhan became one with the light.

(f) Poyagai Âlwâr; Bhutatta Âlwâr; Peyâ Âlwâr

Poyagai Âlwâr; Bhutatta Âlwâr; and Peyâ Âlwâr are three different persons that were born and brought up at three different places but they are always mentioned together as they saw, met and talked to Shri Ranganâth in a hut when chance or the Lord brought them together. The incident occurred in a very simple way.

Once per chance, the three sants, Poyagai Âlwâr; Bhutatta Âlwâr; and Peyâ Âlwâr, went to Tirukkoilura. They reached the place one after another. They knew nothing about each other.

Saroyogi reached there, performed poojâ in the temple went to a disciple and got a place for sleeping in a small hut of the disciple. He was meditating upon the God when he heard, "Who is there inside the hut? Can I come inside to spend the night?"

Saroyogi answered, "Yes, you can definitely get space here. There is enough space in the hut for one person to sleep and for two persons to sit. We can sit and spend the night." The man came inside. They sat there and talked about Nârâyan. After sometime another man called from outside:

"Who is there inside the hut? Can I come inside to spend the night?"

Saroyogi answered, "Yes, you too can come inside. There is enough space in the hut for one person to sleep, for two persons to sit and for three persons to remain in standing position. We can keep standing and spend the night."

He too came inside. All the three were standing in the hut and joyfully talking about Shri Ranganâth. They came to know of each other. They were Poyagai Âlwâr; Bhutatta Âlwâr; and Peyâ Âlwâr.

In the dark hut, suddenly the light started growing; it grew brighter and brighter. They meditated on it and saw through there inner eyes. It was the bright glow of their *Param Ârâdhya*, the Absolute God, Mahâvishnu. They heard God saying, "Ask for blessings". They bowed, prayed and cried, "It is enough, bless us that our devotion in you keeps on growing till our end." The God blessed them and slowly the light faded out.

Each of these three Âlwârs composed one hundred verses in praise of Lord Vishnu that are said to be the Light of Knowledge, *Gyâna Pradeep.*

Poyagai Âlwâr was born in Kânchinagari that was a principal center of education. He is known as the incarnation of *Pânchajanya.* He is also called Saroyogi.

Bhutatta Âlwâr was born in Mahâbalipur and people adore him as the incarnation of the Lord's *Gadâ*, (Mace).

Peyâ Âlwâr was born at Mailâpur in Chennai. He is the incarnation of the Lord's *Khang*, the sword.

They are known as Sants since their birth. They led a very pious life. They were well versed in the Vedas and other Scriptures and had accumulated a lot of knowledge and had achieved inner union with the Lord. Throughout their life they moved from place to place, from pilgrimage to pilgrimage showing the right path to the people to come closer to Lord Vishnu.

(g) Bhaktisâr (Tirumarisai Âlwâr)

Tirumarisai Âlwâr was born to Bhârgava, a great devotee of Lord Vishnu. He lived in Mahisarpur, a place of pilgrimage. It is also known as Tirumarisai. Because the child was born at this place so he was named Tirumarisai Âlwâr.

The boy was once lost in the forest of reeds. He survived. It chanced that a hunter Tiruwâran and his wife Pankajwalli came for cutting reeds. They found the boy and happily brought him home, as they had no child. They called him Bhaktisâr.

There is a story that since the boy did not like others' milk so an old couple started giving him cow-milk. The boy would not drink all the milk. Everyday, he would leave some milk in the bowl. The old couple will drink that. It is said that with the effect of that milk the couple got a son. They named him Kanikannan. Kanikannan is famous as the most favourite disciple of Bhaktisâr.

Bhaktisâr got the revelation at a very early age as he finished the Shâshtras including philosophy very early in his life and went out for *dhyâna yoga* where he was interrupted and hurdles were created for his failure but he was such a determined devotee of Lord Vishnu that he easily crossed over all the hurdles and avoided all the distractions to get united with the Lord. He was blessed and wrote many *Granthas*.

It is said that he threw all the *Granthas* in the Cauveri river. Two of them came towards the shore. Only those two books are available. Rest of them were drowned.

(h) Neelan (Tirumangaiya Âlwâr)

Neelan, Tirumangaiya Âlwâr, was born in a village of Chola Region as the son of a warrior who taught him the art and science of warfare and trained him in fighting with different weapons. He became expert in horse riding and in leading an army. The Chola Naresh (the king of Chola) was so pleased with him and impressed with his skill that he appointed him the Commander of his army. When he attacked, it was the guarantee of victory.

The life of Neelan was one of ups and downs; from power and richness to poverty and jail to richness and again to poverty to robbery and blessings to richness again, irreligious-religious-irreligious and again religious.

Once, Neelan heard of a beautiful dame in Tiruvâlli Region. She was Kumuda Valli, a fostered child of a devotee of Lord Vishnu. She was extremely beautiful and like her father a true devotee of Nârâyan. When Neelan approached her father for her hands, the father consulted her and she declared that she could marry only a devotee of Lord Vishnu. So, Neelan immediately met a Vaishanava Âchârya and made him his preceptor. As his disciple he became a Vaishanava but Kumuda Valli wanted a real devotee. She declared that she could marry him on only one condition that he fed one thousand Vishanavas everyday to ensure that he was a true devotee of Lord Vishnu. Neelan agreed.

They were married. Neelan started feeding 1,000 Vishanavites everyday. In due course, he spent all his wealth on it. Slowly, he spent the tax that he had collected for the king. He became poor and could not get the tax deposited to the Treasure of the King. He was arrested and jailed. In jail he saw Lord Vishnu who suggested him to dig out the wealth lying at the bank of Vegawati River in Kânch Nagar. His requested to the King to go to Kânchi to repay the tax. It was granted and he was sent along with some officers and soldiers. He did as directed and paid back the tax with interest and again started feeding 1,000 Vishanavites everyday. In Kânchi Bhagawân Varadrâja appeared before Neelan. The Chola King was satisfied that Neelan had some supernatural powers. He returned the tax money and asked him to use in feeding the Vaishanavas.

When Neelan spent out this wealth also on feeding the Vaishanavas then he started robbing people for fulfilling the word that he had given to his wife Kumuda Valli.

It is said that once Nârâyan Himself passed through his way as rich merchant couple. Neelan robbed him but when his men tried to pick the loot up and carry it home the tiny loot of ornaments was so heavy that they could not pick it up. Neelan was suspicious. He asked for the mantra that can make the load light. The merchant said in his ears: Aum Namo Nârâyanâya. This worked as miracle. When he looked around, the merchant couple had vanished. When he saw up he saw Mahâ Vishnu and Mahâ Laxmi flying away on Garuda. He bowed to them and cried out in repentance. He was blessed. He was ordered to get the temple of Shri Ranganâth repaired.

It was that 'Aum Namo Nârâyanâya" the pious Mantra, taught by Nârâyan Himself that finally rescued the man from sins and elevated him to the reverend status of Sant.

What Neelan wrote at the end of his life while getting the temple of Shri Ranganâth renovated, is known as *Mahâvâkya*.

They are all verses in praise of Mahâ Vishnu. He is deemed to be the incarnation of the *Shârangdhar* Bow of Lord Vishnu. That may be the reason that he was born in a family of warrior and started his career as general of a King's army. But the final renunciation and salvation is the most important aspect of his life that was possible because of deep devotion to Lord Vishnu.

(i) Madhur Kavi Âlwâr

Madhur Kavi Âlwâr, the incarnation of *Garuda*, was born in Brâhmin family of Sâmveda tradition at Tirukkolar. He decided to go for spiritual revelation as without revelation, love and devotion knowledge was meaningless and useless. He visited the pilgrimages of Ayodhyâ, Mathurâ and Kâshi and lived at the bank of river Gangâ. One day, he saw brilliant celestial light in the southern sky. He followed it and eventually reached Kurukura. He could not find the light any more. After enquiry he came to know that there was an accomplished Yogi, Shathakopâchârya. He went to him. He was sitting in the hollow of a tamarind tree. He tried his best to draw the attention of the Yogi in meditation but of no avail. At last, he went close to him and asked: "O Yogi! I have a question. What should it do if subtle pure consciousness comes to an innate object? Where will it reside, take rest and what will it eat?"

Shathakopâchârya answered: "He will eat that object and reside in it." Madhur Kavi had realized the immortal consciousness in this mortal body. He got his preceptor and Shathakopâchârya got an able disciple. He bowed to his guru and praised him. He promised to work throughout his life to spread the ideas and theories propounded by his teacher, that he did.

(j) Namma Âlwâr (Shathakopâchârya)

The Guru of Madhur Kavi Âlwâr was Namma Âlwâr, better known as Shathakopâchârya. He was born in Tirukurukur also known as Shri Nagari. It is a place on the bank of Tâmraparni River in the Tinnavelli district. Kârimâran was his father; and his mother was Urainangai, one who is loving to Lord. Kârimâran worked on a high post with Pândya Naresh, the king of Pândya Kingdom. Later on he became the king of a small kingdom called Kurugainâdu.

His parents gifted him to the temple immediately after his birth as he did not take meal for ten days after the birth. The most wonderful thing that the moment he entered the temple he stood up and started moving. It is not clear when but it is said that he went to a tamarind tree (in Âyurveda tamarind is not treated as a hygienic tree) in the temple complex and sat in meditation in the hollow of the tree. It remained his favourite place. He sat there for sixteen years and became famous. It is at this place that Vishnu gave him the mantra of *'Aum Namo Nârâyanâya'*. He had no care for his body. That is the reason that he was called Shathkopa. Madhur Kavi also found him there. He lived for thirty-five years then left this body.

Shathakopâchârya composed many verses that are accepted as the precise essence of Sâmaveda. He recited them to the members of Tamil Sangham who applauded it and praised them. It had great influence on the religious and spiritual literature of the time and the later periods. His important books are *Tiruviruttam*; *Tiruwâshiriyam*; *Periya Tiruwantâti*; and *Tiruwâya Moli*. The last one has more than one thousand verses. These four are treated as four Veda Samhitâs of Tamil Literature though they all describe and praise only Lord Vishnu.

It is said that when Kamban brought his Râmâyan to offer it to Shri Ranganâth, he heard a sound, "have you sung the life of Shathakopa?" He denied as he had not mentioned him. But he added the eulogy of Namma Âlwâr, Shathakopâchârya, in the very beginning and praised him in the superlative.

4. The Shaiva Sants

When we are talking of Shaiva Sants, actually we are not talking of the Rishis that originally established Shiva Bhakti. Probably, they were led by Agastya Rishi. In fact, we are talking only of the Sants that came after the Transition Period. Although, there is no Transition Period in the eyes of the Indians, because the whole of the Sanâtana Dharma (Eternal Religion) has one unbroken tradition and chain; yet we are talking of it simply to open the eyes of the people across the globe that the Rishis belonged to a remote past; and they had a lot of spiritual and supernatural powers. As such power is no longer seen in man so they are treated as mythical figures. We are unable to conceive and perceive the reality. So, their period and presence is left out though accepted and believed in. They have been discussed separately in the book **"Rishis and Rishikâs"**.

Then there appeared many Sants whom people claim to have born after Buddha, Vikram and Christ. In between these two groups there are many great Sants, Preceptors; Âchâryas whose time is just a guess work. That is the period of transition. *The Period of Transition is a necessity in Indian History, Culture and Religion because at every place we face four Yugas: Satyuga; Tretâ; Dwâpar and Kaliyuga. It is very significant. Indian life can't be understood by ignoring these yugas.* We can know the complete tradition and fill the gaps and feel the continuity of tradition only when we accept, read and analyze the historical books written by the ancient Indians and modern Indian Religious Leaders. We can't know or feel it by reading the history of India written by Europeans or on European pattern.

One notable fact about Indian Sants is that all of them were singers and they composed verses. The reason may be the fact that while it is difficult to memorize exact words and lines of prose, it is very easy to memorize verses and all the more easier if they are tuned in as songs. The reason behind the availability of such vast wealth of songs and verses is the reason that all of them are sung accompanied by different musical instruments.

The attraction of theme and ideas is different to the musical attraction.

The worshipping of Lord Shiva, known as Shivopâsanâ, is in vogue since primitive period, an unknown time. The most ancient among the Shaiva Sants is Agastya but there are proofs that he was not the first Shaiva Sant. He is the brightest among them. He was followed by many known and unknown Sants. Among the known Sants 'Sant Nakkira'; 'Sant Kannapa' and Sant Tirumular' are very famous.

The Sants of Shaiva sect follow four Paths called *Charchâ, Kriyâ, Yoga* and *Gyâna*. These are also called *Dâsa Mârga; Satputra Mârga; Sahamârga* and *Sanmârga*. There are 64 Shaiva Sants from south only but only four of them are truly famous. They are: **Sant Mânikka Wâchaka; Sambandha; Wâgeesh**; and **Sunder Murti**. It is said that they established the above-mentioned four ways of worshipping Shiva.

(a) Sant Mânikka Wâchaka

Sant Mânikka Wâchaka is a pioneer in Shaiva Tradition. He declared that 'Love' is the only way to get revelation, learning, study of Vedas and Scriptures, turning towards penance, or yoga or meditation are not enough for revelation and salvation. Love is the only way but it should be pure, *sâttvika* and *niskâma* (detached).

Mânikka Wâchaka was born in a Brâhmin family in Vadâur near Madurâi. His brilliance and fame spread so much and impressed the people in such a way that at the age of only ten Pândya Naresh appointed him as his Chief Minister. Though, of a very tender age yet he proved his mettle and intelligence. He was the right-hand-man of the king.

But his life changed when the king gave him money and asked him to purchase horses from Tiruperandurai. There he met Shri Gurudeva and in place of purchasing the horses he spent the money on getting a temple constructed for him. The king was angry. He was punished and ousted from the service. It pleased Mânikka Wâchana. Now, he was free from the responsibilities and the worldly affairs. From there on he only visited different places, composed verses and sang in the praise of Shiva. He worshipped the Natarâja form of Lord Shiva.

(b) Sant Appâra

Sant Appâra was born in a rich Wekâla family in South Arcott district. His parents died when he was only a child. He was fostered by his elder sister. He first came into contact with Jain Scholars and studied the Jain Literature.

It is said that once he got intense pain. On the advice of his sister he went to a Shiva Temple and prayed to Lord Shiva in lilting verses. He got immediate relief and he was given a boon that Saraswati will reside in his tongue and songs. It was the order of his sister to 'serve Shiva with body, to meditate on Shiva with mind and to sing in His praise with speech'. He followed the instructions till the end of his life. The Pândya Naresh wanted to baptize him into Jainism because of his talent and enchanting voice but he refused. As a result he was tortured in many ways but he did never deviate. Once, a huge stone was tied with his body and he was thrown into a river but to the wonder to all the stone floated in place of going down deep.

Sant Sambandha met him in Chadamabaram. He called him 'Appâra', father. From there on he became Sant Appâra. He led a very simple life. He carried a broomstick and used to sweep the temples. He moved on foot mostly along with Sant Sambandha. It is said that he composed forty-nine thousand verses but only eleven thousand are available at present.

(c) Sant Sambandha

Sant Sambandha enjoys the privilege of being the best among the early Shaiva Sants from South.

There is a famous tale about his revelation. Once he went to a river with his father. The father entered the river to take a bath but he remained at the bank, as he was only four years old at the time. In the meantime, it is said, that Lord Shiva and Umâ came through aerial route and Mâtâ Umâ gave him milk to drink in a golden plate. He got spiritual power, the moment he drank it. When the father came out he noticed milk on his mouth. He asked about it and he indicated towards the sky. He forced him to tell and he started singing hymns and shlokas. He became 'Gyâna Sambandha'. He described Shiva and Pârvati in detail. They were his parents. He took Pârvati to be Shakti, the eternal power.

At that very tender age he started moving from place to place singing songs in praise of Shankar-Pârvati. His reputation spread far and wide. It was unbearable to many others. They set his cottage afire. Though, the cottage was burnt to ashes but the fire did not touch his belongings. He married at the age of sixteen at the suggestion of the gurus but kept on composing and singing verses.

(d) Sant Sunder Murti

Sant Sunder Murti led both a *sunder* and *kurup* life, a pleasant and painful life. As mentioned in the books Sant Sunder Murti was born at the place where Sant Appâra lived some hundred years before him. His ancestors were the worshippers of Lord Shiva.

There are many tales associated with him and Lord Shiva. It is said that at the time of his marriage, Lord Shiva came as an old Brahmin and claimed that his wife was his slave and took her away. He decided not to marry again.

During that period a rich man invited him and gifted his two daughters to him. He accepted them as father and fulfilled the responsibilities, as a wise and religious father should.

He married at a later stage on the condition that he would not cross the frontiers of the village. She was a girl from the north of Chennai. She had taken a vow to marry only a Sant or to remain unmarried throughout the life. Fortunately, Sunder Murti reached there and inspired by some spiritual power he married her on the above mentioned condition. One day, unknowingly he crossed over the border of the village and paid the penalty in the form of both his eyes. After a great deal of the prayer to the Lord he got one eye back at Kânchi and another at Tiruvaru.

It is said that Sant Sunder Murti, composed 38 thousand verses but only 700 are available at present.

(e) Woman Sants in Shaiva Tradition

There are many woman Sants in Shaiva Tradition but two from south are very famous. One is **Kâraikkâla Ammaiyer** and the other is **Avvai** whose teachings and verses are sung in south with devotion and reverence. The verses are in chaste Tamil and have literal, symbolic and spiritual meanings.

Kâraikkâla Ammaiyer was the daughter of a rich merchant. From the very childhood she loved to perform poojâ and sing before the idol of Lord Shiva. She was married at the right time but she showed least interest in household affairs. She remained engrossed mostly in spiritual thinking and worshipping the Lord. Her husband married another lady and she became free to move out and teach people Shaiva Philosophy. Once she went to meet her husband. He prostrated on her feet and treated her as mother. Her songs express the beautiful and the sweet.

The Beginning of Shaiva Tradition:

The Five Ganâdhishwars: The following Âchâryas and Pandits established Shaiva tradition and spread the Doctrine of Non-duality of the Original (Special) Power called Shakti

Vishishtha Advait. It is also known as *Lingâng* (inseparable state of ling and ang) *Sâmarasya*; *Shivâdvait* and *Veera Shaiva* Doctrine. It stands for both the physical form of consciousness and energy, represented by the living beings; and the subtle conscious energy represented by Shiva. Advait or Non-duality relates it to the other half of Shiva known as Shakti that proves non-separation in Brahman's energy and entity. The Creation, Distribution and Posession of Shakti by Shiva and their co-ordination and co-existence *(samarastâ, sâmanjasya)* make them inseparable and yet two known entity. It is something special *Vishishtha Advait*. For example many things are cited as: moon and light; brilliance and sun; sugar and sweetness; flowers and fragrance. From *Panchâkshar*, **Aum Namah Shivâya** to **Shivam Bhuyât**, they had many Mantras to please Bhagwâna Shiva and to take His Grace and Blessings.

S.N.	Ganādhishwar	Region and Work
1.	Shri Renukāchārya, Came out of Shri Someshwar Ling	He established a Dharmapeetha in **Rambhāpuri**, in Wālehollura Region. It is known as **Veera Singhāsan**.
2.	Shri Dārukāchārya came from Shri Siddheshwar Linga in Vatakshetra.	He established a Dharmapeetha in **Ujjaini**. It is called **Sat Dharma Singhāsan**.
3.	Shri Ekorāma Ārādhya was born out of Shri Rāmanāth Ling in Drākshārāma Region.	He established a Dharmapeetha in **Himwat Kedār Region**. It is called **Vairāgya Singhāsan**.
4.	Shripati Pandit Ārādhya came out of Mallikārjuna Ling in Shailkshetra.	He established a Dharmapeetha in **Shailkshetra**. It is called **Surya Singhāsan**.
5.	Shri Viswa Ārādhya was born out of the Viswanāth Ling of Kāshi.	He established a Dharmapeetha in **Kāshi**. It is called **Gyāna (Jnāna) Singhāsan**.

VEERA SHAIVA SANTS

(f) Shri Renukâchârya

The story goes like it that once Lord Shiva called his Renuka Ganâdhishwar and odered him to appear in the world through Somanâth Ling in the Kulyapâka Kshetra and teach the people the profound theory of *Shivâdvait*. Accordingly he took the incarnation in *Tretâ Yuga*, went to Agastya, took lessons in *Shiva Advait* Philosophy. That book is perhaps available as it is mentioned at different places. It is known as *"Sidhânt Shikhâmani"* and *"Renukâ-Agastya Samvâda"*. After learning the philosophy from him he went to Lankâ where Vibhishana was the ruler. Vibhishana welcomed him and placed his unique problem of fulfilling the last wish of his brother Râvana. Râvana had taken a vow to establish nine lakhs (at certain places it is nine crores) Shivalings. During his life time he could establish only six lakhs Shivalings. He asked his brother Vibhishana to establish the rest. Vibhishana was not getting three lakhs able pandits to establish them on one particular *tithi* (date). It is said that Renukâ Ganâdhishwar multiplied himself into three lakhs Âchâryas and the wish was fulfilled. This happened in Tretâyuga.

It is also claimed that he took two incarnations during Kaliyuga also and in one incarnation he reached Ujjaini. He is known as Shri Renukâchârya and often called Jagadguru. There is a story that when he was in Malayâchjala Shri Shankarâchârya met him, took a Shivling named *Chandra Mauliswar* and worshipped it. This Shivling is still worshipped in the Peetha of Shri Shankarâchârya.

There is a miracle associated with Shri Renukâchârya. He was asked by some sound from the sky to worship Eka Âmreshwar Idol and pray to it; and to think of a great Âchârya and touch the earth near it. He did so and a tall brilliant glowing figure came out of the earth with Bhasma and Rudrâksha. He was named Shri Rudra Muni. After teaching him Shivâdvait philosophy he returned back to Somanâtha Ling.

(g) Shri Sadânand Shiva Yogi

According to Skand Purâna he belongs to Dwâper. He is described in its 85th Chapter under Shankar Samhitâ. It is claimed that he resided in *Shailkshetra*. In fact, he was the Swâmi of Veera Shaiva Guru Peetha of that region. According to the description given there he had absolute command over the essentials of both Nigam and Âgam. He meditated on Shiva, used to wear Bhasma and Rudrâksha and carry Shivaling. He is addressed as Jagad Guru.

A Brahmin named Harpriya sent another pious Brâhmin named Sweta with his sinful son, named Pingal for relief from painful diseases. It is claimed that he cured him and they became his disciples when he preached them the essential elements of Shiva.

(h) Shri Shiva Yogi Shivâchârya

Shiva Yogi Shivâchârya was a famous Veera Shaiva Sant of Karnâtaka. Out of his many books *'Siddhânta Shikhâ Mani'* is very popular. The followers of Veera Shaiva Philosophy take him as the partial incarnation of Renukâchârya.

(i) Shri Mallikârjuna Shivâchârya

Mallikârjuna Shivâchârya was the Swâmi of Viswa Ârâdhya Peetha. He had achieved many supernatural powers and it is said that he traveled through air route. Shri Jainandan Deva, the then Ruler of K ârâdhyashi had given him 800 parags of land between Kardameshwar and the middle of the Gangâ. The Gift Paper is still available. It was written in Vikram Samvat 631 on *Kârtika Shukla Ekâdasi.*

He got Veera Shaiva Mathas constructed in Prayâga, Nepâla and Dilli (Delhi). He went to Nepâla and preached Shaivite Philosophy to Viswa Malla, the then king of Nepâla. He gifted

300 Mooribhulâ land. That land is still there in the Jangambâri Matha in Bhâta Gaon (village). The Gift Paper was written on Jyeshtha Shukla Ashtami in Vikram Samvat 692.

(j) Shripati Pandit Ârâdhya

Shripati Pandit Ârâdhya, a very popular and accomplished Sant of Veer Shaiva Mata showed his presence in Andhra Pradesh in 1060 AD. He was well versed in Vedas and Vedânga. He wrote a commentary *Shrikar Bhâshya* on *Brahmasutra (Vedânta)* on the pattern of his philosophy. It is very popular and praised in the superlative. He had supernatural powers also.

Once in a debate on Scriptures (*Shâshtrârtha*) he announced that *Prasâda* (offering) is more important than *Agni* (Fire). It created a furore. Others were not ready to accept it. In anger he collected Agni, folded in a cloth and tied in the *Shami* (a sacred tree whose dried out branches are offered to Agni and the flowers to Mâ Shakti.) tree. All the fire of the area extinguished, and the cooking of the complete village stopped. The people gathered, repeatedly prayed to him and accepted the greatness of *Prasâda*. Only then he released Fire.

(k) Shri Nijaguna Shiva Yogi

Shri Nijaguna Shiva Yogi was a very respected Brahmin Sant of Shaiva Sect. He was born in Karnâtaka. Earlier on he was the king of Shambhu Lingan Vetta of Kollegâla Tâluka of Koyimaturu District of Tamilnâdu.As king he studied the Scriptures. He lost interest in kingship, left it and went to the mountains of the area for penance. During the penance he concentrated on Shivlinga, meditated on Shiva, and wrote books. Out of six, his two books commentary on Vedânta and Paramârtha Gitâ is very popular.

Shri Nijaguna Shiva Yogi is claimed to be a sub-incarnation of Shankar.

(l) Shri Mallikârjuna Shivayogi

Shri Mallikârjuna Shivayogi was the Swâmi of Shri Jagadguru Viswa Ârâdhya Peetha of Kâshi during the time of Aurangzeb. He spent most of his time in Jangambâri Matha in deep Meditation on Shiva. One day, while he was in meditation Aurangzeb came and destroyed the Matha. When he came out of the trance he was informed about the destruction. He came up to the gate and showed such an anger that the army dispersed and Aurangzeb fell down and started behaving like a mad man. On requests he forgave him. Then he came to him and begged for shelter and as expiation for the destruction caused by his army he gifted land to the Matha. The Gift Paper is safe in the Jangambâri Matha of Kâshi. It says: "The moment I reached Jangambâri the idol seemed to be standing before me. The idol was black and the eyes were like devastating fire. On the head the hair was like goats'. It was small in shape but has covered the land and the sky. I saw it and out of fear I have come to take shelter and with devotion I gift land."

Out of respect to Shri Mallikârjuna Shivayogi, the king of Reewân Shri Bhâva Singh Deva and Shri Awadh Singhju Deva gave a village as gift for the management of the Matha. The gift paper is also in the safe custody of the Matha. It is dated *Vaishâkha Jyeshtha Dvitiyâ, Vikram Samvat* 1740.

(m) Shri Siddhalinga Shivâchârya Mahâswâmi

Shri Siddhalinga Shivâchârya Mahâswâmi was born in a village named Bangâr Nâyakan Halli in Chitradurga district of Mysore State in 1890 AD in the family of the controllers of the Gurusthal Matha. He glowed as a child and showed exceptional qualities. Some men from Ujjaini Peetha saw him and took him from his father as the would-be Peethâdhipati.

He became Jagadguru in 1903 AD. He invited great scholars of Samskrit to his Peetha and read all the Scriptures. He traveled throughout the country. He preferred to sit in samâdhi for many days at a stretch. He departed to Shivaloka in 1936 AD.

5. Sant Tirumular

While talking about Sant Tirumular many epithets are used as 'Bhagawân,' 'Shri Yogiswar', 'Paramhans,' 'Swâmi', Siddha', 'Mahâtmâ' and 'Sant'. He knew the science to become a spirit and to enter the body of others. Himalayas was his natural abode but once in a while he would visit the places of his liking.

The people of south came to know of him when something strange occurred and when he declared that he was someone from the Himalayas.

One day, a herdsman Moolan, a person that belonged to Yaidayars of Sathnoor, and keeping cow was his profession returned home very late, tied the cows at their places but when his worried wife went to meet him he admonished her from touching a stranger's body. It was in itself a strange thing. Moolan went to a Matha and sat in meditation. His wife followed him there but he was in a trance. He did not open his eyes. She returned back but in the morning she came there with the villagers but Moolan was sitting in the same posture. The brilliant light that his body emitted forced the villagers to keep back. They did not do anything awkward. They waited. They talked to him when he opened his eyes and requested to return home. He refused. They returned back. From Sathnoor he went to Tiruwâva Duthurai. But his wife was much aggrieved. With many villagers she went there too. She wept bitterly. She had none to look after her. It was then that the yogishwar told about the death of her husband and that he had entered his dead body, that the cows led him to his house and that he had hid his own body. The body was not there when he went there again. So, he decided that it was the wish of the Lord.

He told them that he had come from the Himalayas to meet Maharishi Agastya. He had covered a long distance and visited many places on the way including Kâshi, Nepâl, Tirukkadâram, Tiruparupattam, Shri Kalâti and Kânchi. Now, the villagers realized the meaning behind hisstrange behaviour. They were satisfied and returned back. The Sant remained there and translated the books of Shaivâgam into Tamil. Then he returned back to Himalayas. It is said that while he was there he composed about three thousand verses that are collected in "Tirumular Mantra". It has 3047 verses.

6. The Vaishanava Sants

(a) Shri Shankarâchârya

Shri Shankarâchârya and personalities like him are never the past, never a history; they are always the present, shaping the future. They are the roots, the main roots on which the society stands, grows and survives, and men live by and prosper.

Shri Shankarâchârya is the strongest root, the main root that grew up out of the Gods, Rishis and Vedas, just in time to give strength, to re-strengthen, to revive, revitalize and rejuvenate Indian people, mind and society to stand erect against, to endure and survive during the regular, tremendous, and heartless attacks from all sides on life, wealth, literature, culture and civilization. *We are because Shri Shankarâchârya was and is and we would survive and prosper if we keep him with us and within us.*

Shri Shankarâchârya was a force, a cause, effect, and the sole element that became four strong pillars and stood at four critical zones in four directions to bear out and wear out the tempestuous blows from all sides. He became the inner life being, the energizing and always running oxygenated blood of the Indians; and India survived because it created numerous hair-roots in the form of veins and artilleries for timely supply of energy in the form of the Âchâryas, Sants, Sâdhus, Scholars, Kings, Ministers, Pandits, Mahâtmas, Swâmis, Revolutionaries, Sacrificing Soldiers, Fighting People and the weapons of Peace, Character, Religion, Spirituality and Divinity. He made all the Chauhâns, Pratâps, Shivâjies, Paramahans', and Vivekânands possible. India lost a lot yet it saved a lot, enough to re-emerge as world guru and world power. Many Shankarâchâryas are still and incessantly coming out and working positively and in right direction despite the growing threat of the west. *We need them as we need him. We must realize and keep in mind that not the deeds but the lasting effects of the deeds are important because that sustains the present and becomes the strength of the future*. The past is important because it gives that strength. Indians would weaken and lose their ground if they are cut off from the past. Their past is wealth and holds the key. Shri Shankarâchârya is the brightest, golden key.

There are thousands in the process of the creation of a strong, eternal Indian Religion, Culture, Civilization and philosophy. There are thousands behind its long life and survival but Shri Shankarâchârya is the lone figure that binds all, carries all, gives all and hence, influenced it in such a way and to such an extent that whatever is said from his Peethas or Mathas is accepted as the only truth and followed without a shred of doubt thousand of years after his departure.

Shri Shankarâchârya is rich, varied, illuminated and eternal like Rishis and like Indian life, religion, culture and spirituality. It was possible because he was a great Yogi, Philosopher, Scholar and Devotee.

Life and Works

The period of Shri Shankarâchârya is not as debatable as it has been painted; and the guesswork of Indian and Western scholars has distorted it. One thing is clear that he was born after Bhagawâ Buddha and at the time when Buddhism in India was at its peak. It is all the more evident because he was junior and contemporary to Kumârila Bhatta.

Shri Shankarâchârya was born to Shri Sheoguruji and Mâtâ Subhadra after a lot of worshipping of Lord Shiva very late in their life. Many have firm faith that Âshutosh Shankar had come as Shri Shankarâchârya. His life and deeds are proofs that he was an illumined soul in his previous birth and had carried on his achievements of that life into this life.

Shri Shankarâchârya was born on *Vaishâkh Shukla Panchami* a few centuries before Christ; at a village called Kalâdi at the bank of Purnâ River in Kerala. He spoke his mother tongue correctly when he was only a year old; memorized whatever he heard from his mother including the Purâns when he was only two years of age but his father died when he was only three years old. His sacred thread ceremony was performed at the age of 5 and only at the age of 7 he asked his mother to allow him to become a Samyâsi. Mâtâ Subhadrâ was a widow and Shankar her only child. She refused and she would never have given him permission so, one day when the mother was taking bath in a river a crocodile caught the leg of Shankar. He called his mother and said, "If you allow me to become a Samyâsi the crocodile will leave me otherwise I have to die." The loving mother needed the life of the child. She granted him the permission and the Shankar Bhakt crocodile left his leg. The mother added, "But return to me at the time of my death." Only an Indian mother can think and say like that.

Shri Shankar came to the bank of River Narmadâ and became a disciple of Swâmi Bhâgwatpâda Govindâchârya who was the younger brother of the Veda-Bhâshyâkâr Shri Sâyanâchârya. Shri Shankar became Bhagawat Pujyapâd Âchârya as he was the Âchârya of Yogashâshtra only at the age of eight. The crocodile was the illusory creation of his Yoga-Mâyâ. In no time, Shri Shankarâchârya perfected Yoga. Once his guru called him. He was on the other side of the lotus pond. He ran towards his guru through the mid pond placing his racing feet on lotus leaves. He came the other side. It was a wonder for his guru and other disciples. It is said that he knew the science to enter the body of others. When his study was over his guru ordered him to write a commentary on Brhama-Sutra (Vedânta) by Veda Vyâsa.

Shri Shankarâchârya came to Kâshi, the seat of learning. His first disciple was Sanandan who became Padma Pâdâchârya and lived with the Âchârya like a shadow. In Kâshi Lord Shiva came to him as a *chândâl* but Shri Shankarâchârya recognized him and saluted him then Lord Shiva appeared before him in His original form.

Shri Shankarâchârya completed the Commentary on Brahmasutra in Kâshi at the age of fifteen. It was praised by many scholars there but an old Brahmin came and raised doubts on the analysis of some of the Sutras. Shri Shankar and the old Brahmin got engaged in prolonged debate that lasted for more than eight hours (at many places it is written that the discussion continued for eight days.). Padma Pâdâchârya got suspicious. He meditated over the identity of the Brahmin. In meditation he realized that he was Veda Vyâsa. So, he said:

शंकरः शंकरः साक्षाद् व्यासो नारायणः स्वयम् ।
तयोर्विवादे सम्प्राप्ते न जाने किं करोम्यहम् ॥

Shankarah shankarah sâkshâd vyâso nârâyanam swayam;
Tayorvivâde samprâpte na jâne kim karomyaham.

Veda Vyâsa showed his self and blessed him: "You had the age of only sixteen that is coming to its end, I add sixteen and double it." It was his blessing that he could live for 32 years. Next year he completed the commentary on 'Prasthân Trai'.

There is a story regarding his sacrifice. Once, a Kâpâlika requested him that he needed the head of a learned man to complete his Sâdhanâ. He agreed and said, "Keep it secret. If others will come to know of the incidence it will become a problem for you." He went to the burning ghât and sat in meditation. The Kâpâlika duly completed his rituals but in the meantime Nrisingh Bhagawân, the favourite God of Padma Pâdâchârya informed him about the happening. He came at the right time and killed the Kâpâlika. Shri Shankarâchârya was saved.

Shri Shankarâchârya took on the great work of spreading Sanâtana Dharma, the Eternal Religion propounded by the Vedas, Scriptures and Brahma Sutra. The scholars of different sects rose against him and he answered them logically. They felt defeated and accepted him as guru and they also came forward in favour of the Eternal Religion. He traveled the whole country First he went to Kurkshetra, Badarikâshram and then up to Rameshwaram. For the next sixteen years he traveled through out the country and established Sanâtana Dharma. Almost at every place he had to entertain debate that is popularly known in India as **Shâshtrârtha**.

(In Samskrit **Dharma** stands for Sanâtana Dharma, so in every book it is written that he established Dharma. He did it in a different way. He brought together all the divided and warring sects together under Dharma or Sanâtana Dharma. At many places Hindu Dharma is mentioned. The people from other countries called us Hindus and made the word so popular that we became Hindus. As Hindus we may get divided. Actually, we are the followers of Sanâtana Dharma, the Eternal Religion; and in that sense and way we can never get divided because that is the only religion that was before the development of known civilization and has continued and since it is the Original and Eternal Religion so it will continue for ever.)

As a result of his endeavour both the scholars and the kings accepted it and all the people from bottom to the top accepted it and Sanâtana Dharma was established beyond doubt. In order to keep that spirit and to guide the people he established four Peethas at key points: **Puri**; **Dwârkâ**; **Shringeri** and **Badarinâth** (Jyotirmatha) and appointed a disciple at each place for saving the Religion as he believed in the traditional declaration: *dharmo rakshati raksjitah*. Shri Shankarâchârya left this world at the age of 32 near Kedârnâth after establishing the Sanâtana Dharma and a great tradition of Advait Gyân.

His Books:

(*i*) Swâtmaprakâshikâ

(*ii*) Viveka Chudâmani

(*iii*) Prabodha Sudhâkar

(*iv*) Mani Ratna Mâlâ

(*v*) Prasnottar Mâlâ

(*vi*) Commentary on Brahmasutra

(*vii*) Commentary on Prasthân Trai

(*viii*) Commentary on 11 Upanishads and many other commentaries.

His Teachings

Shri Shankarâchârya wrote a 'Swâtmaprakâshikâ', a small but very popular book. The following three quotations have been taken from that book: 6; 14; and 17.

सर्पादौ रज्जुसतेव ब्रह्मस्तैव केवलम् ।
प्रपंचाधार रूपेण वर्तते तद् जगन्न हि ॥

Sarpâdau rajjuh stteva brahma sttaiva kewalam;
Prapanch âdhâr rupena vartate tad jaganna hi.

In the false snake as there is only the existence of rope, so there is only the existence of Brahman in the universe that we see.

घटाव भासको भानुः घटनाशे न नश्यति ।
देहाव भासकः साक्षी देहनाशे न नश्यंति ॥

Ghatâwa bhâsako bhânuh ghatnâshe na nashyanti;
Dehâwa bhâsakah sâkshi deha nâshe na nashyanti.

The sun shines on the earthen pot but as the sun is not destroyed when the earthen pot is destroyed; in the same way the soul gives light to body and the soul is also not destroyed when the body is dead.

न हि प्रपंचो न हि भूतजातं
न च इन्द्रियं प्राणगणो न देहः ।
न बुद्धि चित्तं न मनो न कर्त्ता
ब्रह्मैव सत्यं परमात्म रूपम् ॥

Na hi prapancho na hi bhuta jâtam
Na cha indriyam prâna gano na dehah;
Na buddhi chittam na mano na kartâ
Brahma yeva satyam param âtma rupam.

The world is not true; the living beings are not true; the essence organs are not true; neither body nor conscience, neither mind nor ego; only Brahman is true in absolute form of the self.

Shri Shankarâchârya wrote another great book 'Vivek Chudâmani' which is perhaps his most talked about book. The following three quotations have been taken from that book: 17; 30; and 32.

विवेकिनो विरक्तस्य शमादि गुण शालिनः ।
मुमुक्षोरेव हि ब्रह्मजिज्ञासा योग्यता मता ॥

Vivekino viraktasya sham âdi guna shâlinah;
Mumukshoreva hi brahma jigyâsâ yogyatâ matâ.

Only he has the ability to know the Brahman that has pure conscience, detached, six wealth of sham dam etc, the desire to get salvation and is conscious.

वैराग्यं च मुमुक्षत्वं तीव्रं यस्य तू विद्यते ।
तस्मिन एव अर्थवन्तः स्युः फलवन्तः शमादयः ॥

Vairâgyam cha mumukshatwam tivram yasya tu vidyate;
Tasmin yeva arthwantah syuh phalawantah shamâdayah.

The shama-dama yogic qualities are useful only in him who has intense feeling of detachment and desire for salvation.

The following are the meanings of some of the questions with answers from **Maniratna Mâlâ** and **Prasnottar Mâlâ** written by Shri Shankarâchârya in a unique style of **Questions** and **Answers**.

Who is a slave? *He is a slave who indulges in physical pleasure.* What is salvation? *Detachment from all physical longing is salvation.* What is the worst hell? *Longing for body is the worst hell.* What is heaven? *The state of no lust is heaven.*

What cuts off the worldly bondage? *Self-revelation according to the dictates of Shruti cuts off the worldly bondage.* What is the purpose of salvation? *The purpose of salvation is self-revelation.* Where is the entrance to hell? *The entrance to hell is woman and sex.* How is heaven achieved? *Heaven is achieved only through non-violence; by saving and not killing other living beings.*

Who sleeps in peace? *He sleeps in peace who meditates on God.* Who is awakened? *He is awakened who knows the good and bad.* Who are enemies? *Our own sense organs are enemies but if won over, they turn to be friends.*

Who is a pauper? *He is a pauper who has uncontrolled lust.* Who is rich? *He is rich who is fully contented.* Though alive who has died? *He is dead who does not work.* Who is living? *He is living who is aloof from physical pleasures.*

What strangles? *Fascination and ego strangle.* What intoxicates like wine? *Women intoxicate like wine.* Who is completely blind? *He is completely blind who has intense desire for sex.* What is death? *Self-notoriety is death.*

Who is a preceptor? *He is a preceptor who guides for betterment.* Who is a disciple? *He is a disciple who is devoted to the preceptor.* What is a lasting disease? *The disease of worldly longing is a lasting disease.* What is the panacea for it? *The sense of good and bad is the panacea for it.*

What is the best ornament among the ornament? *Good character is the best ornament.* What is the greatest pilgrimage? *One's own pure mind is the best pilgrimage.* What things should be despised at? *Gold and woman should be despised at.* What should one always listen to? *One should always listen to the teachings of the guru and Vedas.* What are the ways of union with the Brahman? *Companionship of Sants; Charity, Thoughtfulness and Contentment are the ways of getting united to Brahman.* Who is a Sant? *He is a Sant who is completely detached and is devoted to Brahman as Shiva.* What is fever in living beings? *Anxiety is the fever in human beings.* Who is a fool? *He is a fool who has lost his reasoning.* With whom one should cultivate friendship? *One should cultivate friendship with a devotee of Lord Shiva.* What is a good life? *An error-free life is a good life.*

What is knowledge? *That is knowledge that helps in getting united to the Brahman.* What is wisdom? That is wisdom that facilitates salvation. What is profit? *Self-revelation is profit.* Who has won the world? *He has won the world who has won his mind.*

Who is the greatest warrior among the warriors? *He is the greatest warrior who is not affected by enticement of sex.* Who has equanimity, patience and wisdom? *He has equanimity, patience and wisdom and is not enchanted by the winks of a coquette woman.*

What is the poison of sensual earning? *All the sensuous elements are poison.* Who is always aggrieved? *He is always aggrieved who is licentious and indulges in sensual pleasure.* Who is lucky? *He is lucky who helps others.* Who is respectable? *A devotee of Lord Shiva is respectable.*

What one should not do in all the circumstances? *One should not show lust for sensual pleasure and one should not commit sin in all the circumstances.* What should the wise men do diligently? *The wise men should study Scriptures and classics and perform religious deeds diligently.* What is at the root of the universe? *Anxiety is at the root of the universe.*

Whom we should not accompany and with whom we should not live? *We should not accompany or live with fools, sinful, wicked and malignant people.* What should the persons do immediately who wish to get salvation? *The persons with a wish for salvation should be in the company of Sants; be extremely cruel to longings and be totally devoted to God.*

What is the reason of poverty? *'Asking from others' is the reason of poverty.* What is the root of importance? *The root of importance is non-asking from others.* Whose life is ideal? *His life is ideal who won't take birth again.* Who is immortal? *He is immortal who does not die again.*

What is the worst enemy among the enemies? *Sex, Anger, Falsehood, Desire and Lust are the worst enemies.* Who is never satisfied even after excessive indulgence in sensual pleasure? *Desire never gets satisfied.* What is the cause of pain? *Affection is the cause of pain.*

What a wise man should do when the death is very close? *The wise man finding death very close should meditate on Him who takes off the fear of Death with complete devotion and dedication (with body, mind and speech).*

What is the purpose of day and night? *The ephemeral quality of the world and Self-like Shiva are the purpose of day and night.* What are good deeds? *They are good deeds that Lord Shri Krishna loves.* In whom one should doubt? *One should doubt the oceanic world.*

What are the provisions for the journey? *Religion is the provision for the journey.* Who is a scholar? *He is a scholar who has learning and reasoning.* What is poison? *Insult to elders is the poison.*

What is enchanting like wine? *Affection enchants like wine.* Who is a robber? *The sensuous group is the robber.* What is the creeper that lives on others? *Lust for sensuousness is the creeper that depends always on others.* Who is an enemy? *Lack of endeavour is enemy.*

What is instable like drops of water on lotus leaves? *Youth, Wealth and age are instable like the drops of water on lotus leaves.* Who is as clean as the rays of moon? *The Sants are as clean as the rays of moon.*

What is hell? *Slavery is hell.* What is pleasure? *Renunciation of all companies is pleasure.* What is truth? *Truth is that which helps the living beings.* What does the living beings love? *All Living being love life.*

What is real charity? *The charity without expectations is the real charity.* Who is a friend? *He is a friend that stops one from committing a sin.* What is ornament? *Moral character is ornament.* What is the ornament of speech? *Truth is the ornament of speech.*

What is destructive? *Pride is destructive.* What gives pleasure? *The friendship of gentlemen gives pleasure.* Who succeeds in destroying all bad habits? *He succeeds who has relinquished everything.*

Who is blind? *He is blind who is indulged in bad deeds.* Who is deaf? *He is deaf who does not listen to good advice.* Who is dumb? *He is dumb who does not speak sweetly at right time.*

What is deadly? *Foolishness is deadly.* What is precious? *The charity at right time is precious.* What pinches till the death? *Secret sins pinch till the death.* Who is a sage? *He is a sage who has good moral character.* Who is vile? *He is vile who has lost his character.* Who is able to win the world? *He is able to win the world who speaks the truth and has tolerance and forgiveness.* What is grievous and sorrowful? *Miserliness of wealthy is grievous and sorrowful.* What is praiseworthy? *Benevolence is praiseworthy.* Who is worthy of respect among the scholars? *He is worthy of respect among the scholars who is gentle by nature.*

What are the four gentle qualities that good men usually praise? *Charity with sweet words, knowledge without pride, valour with forgiveness, and wealth with sacrifice are the four gentle qualities that good men often praise.*

What should be the aim of day and night? *Chanting the hymns to God should be the aim of day and night.* Who are blind with eyes? *The atheists are blind with eyes.*

Whom should all remember? *All should always remember the God.* What should the wise men not say? *The wise men should not say scandalous and false things.*

How does one get salvation? *One gets salvation only through devotion to God.* Who is God? *He is God that releases from ignorance.* What is ignorance? *The inaction of soul is ignorance.*

Who is illusory? *God is illusory.* What is magical? *The things of the world are magical.* What is dream-like? *The awakened actions are dream-like.* What is truth? *Brahman is the Truth.*

Who is the God present before us? *Mother is the God present before us.* Who is respectable and like teacher? *Father is respectable and like a teacher.* What is like all the gods? *The active and wise Brahmin is like all the gods.*

What is the gain from devotion to God? *Realisation of God and union with Him or getting His abode are the gains from devotion to God.* What is salvation? *The annihilation of ignorance is salvation.* What is most important in the Vedas? *Omkâr is the most important in the Vedas.*

7. The Sants in the Tradition of Advait Gyân

(a) Shri Gaurpâdâchârya

He is the most famous among the Sants of that tradition. His disciple Âchârya Govind Bhagawatpâda was the Guru of Shri Shankarâchârya. His *Mândukyopanishad Kârikâ* is very famous.

(b) Padmapâdâchârya

His original name was Sunandan. He was the first disciple of Shri Shankarâchârya.

(c) Sureshwarâchârya

Sureshwarâchârya is the name given to Mandan Mishra whom he defeated by the order of Kumârila Bhatta. He became his disciple and was given this name. He is the one that wrote maximum number of books in this philosophical tradition.

(d) Sarvagyâtma Muni

He wrote *Samkshepa Shâriraka*

(e) Vâchaspati Mishra

He wrote *'Bhâmati'*, the most valuable bookof that tradition.

(f) Shri Harsha

He wrote *'Khandankhandkhâdya'*

(g) Swâmi Vidyâranya

He is also known as Vidyâranya Mahâmuni. He wrote Kâla Mâdhava and Parâshar Mâdhava as Mâdhavâchârya; and 'Panchdasikâr' as Vidyâranya. He wrote many other books. The important among them are: *Veda Bhâshya* (all four Samhitâs);*Brâhman Bhâsya* (four); *AnubhutiPrakâsh; Manusmriti Vyâkhyâ; Sarva-Darshan-Sangrah; Ahri* Shankar Digvijay etc.

The other famous Sants are: Shri Chitsukhâhârya; Âchârya Bhârati Teertha; Âchârya Shankar Âchâryanand; Shri Ânand Giri; Appaya Dikshit; Swâmi Madhusudan Saraswati etc.

8. Shri Yâmunâchârya

Shri Yâmunâchârya was the grand son of Âchârya Nâth Muni, one of the principal Âchârya of the Vaishanava Sect. His only son Ishwar Muni died at an early age. Sri Yâmunâchârya was the son of Ishwar Muni. He was born on Vikram Samvat 1010 in either Veera Nârâyanpur or Madurâ. He was fostered by his mother and grandmother. He showed brilliance at study and had a wonderful memory. He was taught by Shrimad Bhâshyâchârya and completed the Shâshtras within a few years. He developed an individualistic pattern of thinking. It was different from the process of thinking of the others. He showed it at an early age of 12 years. The story related to it is the most interesting story about the Sants and Âchâryas.

There was an egoist scholar named Kolâhal (Noise). He was brilliant at debate and had evolved different ways of defeating the scholars. As a punishment the scholar was forced to pay tax to the victorious Kolâhal. Sadly enough, the guru of Yâmunâchârya, Shrimad Bhâshyâchârya used to pay tax to Kolâhal. It so happened that he could not pay the tax for a few years. One day, a disciple of Kolâhal came to take the tax from the guru and used rough language. 12 years old blooming scholar could not tolerate the insult of the guru and challenged Kolâhal for a *Shâshtrartha* (Debate). The king wondered at the strange challenge by an immature boy. He sent his own servant for confirmation. Yâmunâchârya confirmed it and asked through the messenger to send a royal coach to take him to the court.

Meanwhile there was a debate in the court about this imbalanced debate. The queen had the motherly instinct and announced that the boy would win but the king had seen the performance of Kolâhal. He was sure of his win. The queen vowed in the court that if the young scholar is defeated she would work under the maid of the maid of the queen. In the same spirit the king announced that if the child scholar wins he would give half of his king to him.

The messenger returned and as requisitioned the king sent a chariot. When the guru returned he heard of the challenge, he was worried. But his young disciple was confident. He touched the feet of his guru and boarded the chariot and went to the court to face Kolâhal. When Kolâhal saw the child he asked to the queen: "Will this boy defeat me?" The queen replied confidently, "Yes, this boy will defeat you."

The debate started and Yâmunâchârya put three very cunning questions whose answer would crucify Kolâhal. The three questions were:

(a) Refute (Deny) the fact that your mother is not sterile.
(b) Refute (Deny) the fact that the King (Pândya Naresh) is religious.
(c) Refute (Deny) the fact that the Queen is as chaste as Sati Sâvitri.

Kolâhal had no way out but to keep silent. He could not answer a single of them. When Yâmunâchârya asked to answer the questions, he logically developed his answer to a very convincing conclusion.

He was declared victorious. The queen congratulated the boy by saying, "Âlwandâr!" Bravo! Well Done! From then on Yâmunâchârya got another name Âlwandâr. The King kept his vow. He gave half of his kingdom to Yâmunâchârya. As a ruler he proved that he was a great administrator and had a lot of foresight.

Though, he had taken Samyâs yet his grand father Nâth Muni was worried about his only grand child. He asked his disciple Râma Mishra to keep an eye on him that he should not forget his responsibilities after becoming a king."

So, when Yâmunâchârya was 35 years old, Râma Mishra brought him to Shri Ranganâth Temple and turned him towards his religious and spiritual duties.

Yâmunâchvrya relinquished the kingdom and devoted all his time in worshipping and in writing books. It was this period that Shri Râmânujâchârya became his disciple and followed him throughout his life; and completed the deeds that he left unfinished. During the rest of his life he completed four books: *Strotra Ratna*; *Âgamprâmânya*; *Siddhitraya* and *Gitârtha Sangrah*. *Strotra Ratna* is a *champu kâvya*, written both in poetry and prose. It is treated as the best among the four.

9. Shri Râmânujâchârya

Shri Râmânujâchârya was the son of Keshava Bhatta and resided in Terunkudura region. His father died during his childhood. He was *prgyâwâna*, one that knows the past, present and future, from his childhood. He went to study at Kânchi to a teacher named Yâdava Prakâsh. He would point out the mistakes in the lessons imparted by the guru. The guru was both angry and jealous and hatched a conspiracy to get him killed in a forest through his another disciple Govinda Bhatta but he was saved by a hunter couple.

Râmânujâchârya was exceptional in knowledge, character, devotion and super natural power. He not only cured a princess but also searched out a very ancient temple which he got renovated with the help of King Bhittideva of Shâlagrâma of Mysore. There was a very decent idol of Râma with the Sultân of Delhi. His daughter loved that idol. Using his supernatural powers Râmânujâchârya forced the Sultân to give the idol. That idol is still there in the temple. The temple is still there. In the beginning it was named 'Tirunârâyanpur' but later on he allowed the Shudras to enter the temple and renamed it as Tirukkulattar.

Shri Râmânujâchârya belongs to the tradition of Yâmunâchârya and fulfilled the three wishes of his Guru indicated through three folded fingers. When on death bed, Yâmunâchârya sent a message to Râmânujâchârya to come immediately. He tried his best but he reached there a few hours after the death of his mentor. He saw the three folded fingers of his preceptor. He knew its meaning. He may have indicated it earlier. He promised to get commentary on three books written. He announced the names of the book: *Brahmasutra*; *Vishnushahasranâma* and *Divya-prabandham* by the Âlwârs. The moment he said that the folded fingers straightened. He himself wrote the commentary on *Vedânta, Brahmsutra*; and it is famous as *Shri Bhâshya*. He asked the two sons of his principal disciple Kurt Âlawâr to write the other two commentaries. Parâshar wrote the commentary to *Vishnusahasranâma* and Pillan completed the commentary on *'Divyaprabandham'*.

Shri Râmânujâchârya was so great and loving to his disciples that one of his disciple, his principal disciple Kurt Âlwâr sacrificed his eyes to save him from the cruelty of the Chola Naresh Kulotunga. When called he went to his court in the guise of his guru and like him he established Vaishanava philosophy. As punishment one of his eyes was taken off by the king. The disciple was pleased to save his guru.

During that period he traveled extensively and taught Vaishanava Philosophy that accepts Nârâyan as the Absolute God. He taught the people to surrender to Him after throwing the ego away. Laxmi and Nârâyan are the parents and the living beings are their children. One must chant *'Aum Namo Nârâyanâya'*. For making this mantra popular he was first punished and then rewarded by his preceptor Shri Nâmbi. When Shri Nâmbi gave him this mantra he asked him to keep it secret but one day Râmânujâchârya went at the top of the temple and calling all the people present there announced the mantra *'Aum Namo Nârâyanâya'*, and asked them to chant it for salvation. Shri Nâmbi was angry and cursed him to get the hell-like pain. With folded hands he said, "I accept the hell-like pain if this mantra is to give pleasure and bliss to thousands of people. It opened the eyes of the guru and he blessed his disciple.

After the death of Chola Naresh Kulotunga, he returned back to Shri Rangam and got a new temple constructed in which the idols of Âlwâr Sants were kept. He got the temple of Tirupati renovated and re-established the idol of Bhagawân Govindarâja Perumal. He left this world at the age of 120.

10. Shri Nimbârkâchârya

It is interesting to note the controversy regarding the time of Shri Nimbârkâchârya. His disciples claim that he belonged to Dwâper Yuga and cite the presence of Nârad in his sacred thread ceremony to prove it. It is said that Devarishi Nârad gave him Gopâl Mantra at the time of his *Upanayan Samskâr.*

The European Scholars declared that he was born in 5th century AD. Others claim that he belongs to 500 BC. Some neo-scholars have come up with proofs that Shri Nimârkârchârya was born in the 11th century AD.

Whatever the truth may be Shri Nimbârkâchârya belongs to the tradition of Sanak-Sankâdi munies and re-established the old belief of *Dvaitâdvait*. It means that the Creator and the Beings are both One and Separate: i.e. Dvait means Dual; and advait means non-dual. In his Bhâshya he has mentioned both Nârad and Sanat Kumâr. That is in itself a proof of his time.

Earlier on, he was called Niyamânand; and he is known as the son of Aruna Muni and his wife Jayanti Devi. They lived in at the bank of Godâvari River near Vaidurya Pattan in the hermitage called *Arunâshram*. Some take him to be the incarnation of *Surya*, other claim him to be the incarnation of *Sudarshan Chakra* of Lord Krishna.

He had a lot of Supernatural powers. Once he brought the sun after the sunset. It so happened that a Sant came to him. They talked and talked and forgot about the time. The sun went down. When there was deep darkness then they realized that it was too late. He requested the Sant to take food but he refused as he had the rule to eat till the sun is there. He won't eat after the sunset. It was a problem for the Âchârya. How can he allow a guest to return hungry. And lo! There was a miracle. The light improved and the sun peeped through the *Neem* trees. He gave food to the Sant. He took the meal and then the sun went down again. From then on he was called Nimbâditya and Nimbârkâchârya. For him it was the kind act of Krishna but for his disciples it was his *Yoga-Siddhi*.

Only one book of Shri Nimârkâchârya is available. It is the commentary on Vedânta Sutras known a *Vedânta Pârijâta Saurabh*. He had two famous disciples: one was **Keshava Bhatta** who was detached and his disciples are Samyâsi; the other was grihastha **Harivyâsa** and his disciples are men of the world.

The Sants that were Disciples of Nimbârkâchârya

11. Shri Shrikeshavajee Bhatta

Shri Keshavajee Bhatta was born in a Brâhmin family in Kashmir in around 12th century. He lived for about two hundred years and met Shri Râmânandâchârya and Shri Chaitanya Mahâprabhu. He gave the sacred thread to the latter. He was a disciple of Shri Nimbârkâchârya and fought tooth and nail against the *Vâma Mârga* and to establish *Bhâgawat Dharma* that is the *Santâtan Dharma*, the Eternal Religion. He had many divine qualities and traits and worked for the welfare of mankind. That is the reason that a shloka is recited in his praise:

वगीशा यस्य वचने हृत्कब्जे श्रीहरिः स्वयम् ।
यस्य आदेशकरा देवा मन्त्रराज प्रसादतः ॥

Wâgishâ yasya vachane hritkabje shri harih swayam;
Yasya âdeshkarâ devâ mantra râja prasâdatah.

(Saraswati is on his mouth and lips; and in his lotus heart the God Shri Hari; and he has control over the gods as he has perfected *Mantra Râja Siddhi.*)

Shri Nâbhâjee also praised him. He acquired fame for his laudable efforts to write commentaries on the Gitâ and Vedânta during his long stay at Vrindâvan.

12. Shri Shribhatta

Shribhatta was the favourite disciple of Shri Keshavajee Bhatta. The teacher stood of exemplary excellence and dignified richness and the disciple stood for sweetness and delight. He composed '*Yugal Shat*' in 1352 in which he described the life and relation of Râdhâ-Krishn-Gope-Gopikâ. He has presented himself as a character in their *Râsa-Leelâ* and has described it as an eyewitness. He spent most of his years in and around Vraj Bhumi.

13. Shri Shrihari Vyâs Deva

Shri Harivyâs Deva was born in a Gaur Brâhmin family in 1300. He was a disciple of Shri Bhatta. He waited for thirty-six years and lived in Vrindâvan taking rounds of it for becoming the disciple of Shri Bhatta.

There is a story about him that makes it clear that he stopped the killing of animals for worshipping the deity. Once, he was in Panjab at Garhyâwal when he saw hundred of goats tied to be sacrificed the next day before the deity. He wept to see the condition and the ultimate end of the goats. It was arranged by the king of that region.

During the night the deity came into the dream of the king and admonished the king from sacrificing the innocent goats. She asked him to free them and to ask for forgiveness from the Sant whose heart was aggrieved at the cruel sight.

The king obeyed. He freed the goats in the morning and went to the Sant and became his disciple. It is said that there is still a temple there where sacrifice is strictly prohibited and the *prasâd* of flowers and *vatâsâ* is distributed.

He had a great influence on the people and the Sants. He stared a tradition which is known as *Rasik Sampradâya* (Sect).

14. Shri Shriparashurâm Devâchârya

Shri Parashurâm Devâchârya belonged to a Gaur Brâhmin family of Nârnaul. He was the son of Sudevaji. He had a younger brother named Bâsudeva. He was born in 1444 AD. He became an orphan during childhood and took *dikshâ* at the age of 15. He was given the responsibility of looking after the idol in the temple. He was very close to his preceptor Shri Hari Vyâs Devajee. After his demise he became his heir.

For the rights of the Hindus he had to fight against the Muslims. He fought against Saleem at Ajmer. He accepted his defeat. The people were not safe there so he got a temple constructed there and place the idol of the Absolute Lord and lived there for a long time.

When he finally returned to Vrindâvan he met Sant Tulasidas many times. The *Samâdhi* of the Preceptor and Disciple are still intact.

15. Shri Shriswâmi Haridâsjee

Shri Swâmi Haridâsjee belongs to Nimbârka Sect and is the disciple of Âshdheerji. He was born in a pious Brâhmin family that was known for sacrifice, detachment, love and sweetness. He had many distinctive qualities.

Haridâs is the greatest devotee and musician of his time. He is the guru of famous Tânasen, a Ratna of Akbar and Baiju Bâwarâ his competitor. He refused riches and luxury. There is a tale that Akbar went with Tânsena to his hut to listen to his singing and waited for the Guru to sing on his own volition, as he won't take orders from a living creature. He was obedient of and responsible to only the Absolute God. He remained engrossed in Râdhâ-

Krishna all the time and had perfected *sahaj-yoga*. He could go in trance at any time and any place. It was very natural to him and never a mental or taxing exercise. When he used to sing often there was celestial light in his hut and the people believed that Lord Krishna had come to listen to Haridâs.

There is one very interesting incidence. Once a merchant brought a bottle of fragrance for the Guru. He was singing in excitement. He took the bottle and poured out all the content on the soil. The merchant looked amazed. 'Why did you pour it on the soil?' He slowly asked.

'I was playing Holi with my Krishna' – Haridâs answered but there was doubt in his eyes so he added, 'If you don't believe then go to the temple and see.'

Many people went with him to verify and lo! All the clothes of Krishna were wet in the same fragrance that had filled the temple and outer area.

His *Samâdhi* is still intact in Nidhi-Van.

16. Shri Madhwâchârya

Shri Mâdhwâchârya said:

"Vedas have three meanings; Mahâbhârat has ten meanings and Vishnu Sahasra Nâma has hundred meanings."

"Remember the God everyday and incessantly so that you may not forget him at the last hour. At the time of death *vâta*, *pitta* and *kaff* give pain equal to the stings of hundred scorpions. The dying man is afraid of everything. It would be difficult to keep God in memory at such hour."

"Everyone has to feel pain and pleasure because it comes according to the deeds of man. So, don't forget the God even when happy; and don't curse in pain."

"Act according to the teachings of Scriptures. Remember the God with all humility while doing something. God is the Supreme; the Guru of all and the Creator of the universe. Offer all your deeds to Him."

"Don't waste your time in the worldly anxiety. Get absorbed in God."

That Mâdhwâchârya traveled the whole country and discussed many things with the scholars and Sants at every place with certain definite intentions in mind: to make the people religious and devotees of the God; to establish the authenticity of the Vedas; to clarify the illusory notions and to teach moral; to prove his points with arguments and ethical values.

He showed his supernatural power, placed idols at different places that became temples that are still at their respective places.

What is un-digestible about Mâdhwâchârya is the fact that in one side people claim that Vyâsa gave him three idols of Shâligram that he placed at Subrahmanya; Udupi and Madhyatal on the other hand they say that he was born in Vikram Samvat 1295 to Nârâyan Bhatta and Vedavati on Mâgha Shukla Saptami in Velali in Udupi region. There is no balanced reasoning behind it.

It is said that once a merchant's ship going to Malâbâr from Dwârkâ sank in the sea near Tuluba. It had a beautiful idol of Lord Krishna that was covered by sandalwood. He came to know of it and brought out the idol. He placed that idol in Udupi. From there on Udupi became a place of pilgrimage for his followers. In Udupi alone he established 8 temples and placed 8 idols.

Once he saved the ship of another merchant who tried to give half of the wealth, but he refused. After his departure his disciples also established numerous Mathas all over the country. They declared him to be the incarnation of Vâyu Deva.

17. Shri Vallabhâchârya

It is our traditional and religious belief that the family that completes hundred *Soma Yagyas*, the God takes birth in that family. Shri Vallabhâchârya was born after his ancestors had completed 100 *Soma Yagyas*. He is accepted as the incarnation of Fire God. He was born to Laxman Bhatta and Ilammâ; in Champâranya near Raipur on *Vaishâkh Krishna Ekâdasi* in Vikram Samvat 1535. He was the second son. They were Uttar Tailang Brahmins and *Soma Yagya* was a tradition in the family. They belonged to Bhârdwâja Gotra and their Sutra (thread) is related to Âpastamba. The three parwars of their sacred thread are Bhârdwâja, Ayâsya and Ângirasa. All his Samskârs were performed in time.

He studied at Vârânasi better known as Kâsi. After finishing the study at the age of 11 he went to Vrindâvana. Visiting the places of worship he came to Vijay Nagar and defeated many scholars in the court of Râjâ Krishna Deva. He was felicitated with *"Vaishnavâchârya"*. In the presence of all the scholars and the courtiers and the people Vallabhâchârya was given a Golden

Throne to sit and a lot of gold. He took a part of the gold and distributed the rest among the scholars present there. Wherever he sat during his journey it became a religious place; for example: The Ghât of Mathurâ; the Banyan tree at the bank of River Shiprâ; Chunâr etc.

It is said that Lord Krishna with Râdhâ came to him on many occasions. And the people saw him going up into the sky with his body at Hanumân Ghât in Kâsi. A temple in his name is there as witness.

18. Shri Râmânandâchârya

Shri Râmânandâchârya was the Jagad Guru in the true sense of the term. Neither he asked anyone, nor his disciples, to change religion. He welcomed everyone from all religions and satisfied his religious and spiritual longings. He was popular not only in India but Arab countries and western world also. Sants and Religious Leaders from different countries used to come to him with different questions and returned with satisfactory answers.

Shri Râmânandâchârya had hold not only on Religious and Social set-up but also on the political atmosphere. He attracted and influenced all.

Shri Râmânandâchârya was the Sant that cooled the heat of the attacks of Muslims, in general and Muslim Rulers in particular, on Hindus. It was he that stood in the way, as a result one of the most cruel Sultân of Delhi Md. Tughlak, had to send a messenger and beg for forgiveness. Tughlak had to sign a treaty and accept all his 12 conditions regarding 'Safeguarding the Interests of Hindu Religion'.

Shri Râmânandâchârya was the Sant that deeply felt the division of Hindus in different sects and growing enmity among them. It was the most dangerous trend for the whole Arya Community. He freed them from jealously and internal clashes. He brought peace in the name of *Sanâtana Dharma, Bhâgawat Dharma* or Sâttavika Dharma; the essential qualities of Eternal Religion. Happily enough, that tradition is still alive and active.

The whole life of Shri Râmânandâchârya is full of sublime thoughts and deeds. His life was as divine as his actions: *janma karma cha mey divyam.*

Shri Râmânandâchârya represented the sound of the famous conch *Pânchjanya* of Shri Krishna that awoke and united the whole country and gave one universal aim to save Indian wisdom, culture, civilization and life. He saved India from becoming a Muslim country.

The Important Disciple
Sants of Shri Râmânandâchârya

1.	Anantânand	7.	Pipâ
2.	Kabir	8.	Bhâwânand
3.	Sukhânand	9.	Raidâs
4.	Surasurânand	10.	Dhanâ
5.	Padmâwati	11.	Sena
6.	Narharyânand	12.	Surasuri

The Important Books by Shri Râmânandâchârya

1.	Shri Vaishnava Matābja Bhāshkar	8.	Yoga Chintāmani
2.	Shri Rāmārchana Paddhati	9.	Rāmārādhanam
3.	Gitā Bhāshya	10.	Vedānta Vichār
4.	Upanishad Bhāshya	11.	Rāmānandādesh
5.	Ānand Bhāshya	12.	Gyān Tilak
6.	Siddhānta Patal	13.	Gyān Lilā
7.	Rāmarakshā Strotram	14.	Ātmabodha Rāmamantra Yoga Grantha

19. Shri Chaitanya Mahâprabhu

Shri Chaitanya Mahâprabhu, the incarnation of Râdhâ, was born in Navadweep village of Bengâl in Shak-Samvat 1407 on *Phâlguna (Shukla 15) Purnimâ.* Shri Jagannâth Mishra and Shachi Devi were his parents. The Vaishanavas of Bengâl worship him as Purna Brahman, Absolute God.

Shri Chaitanya Mahâprabhu remained a grihastha till the age of 24; married 2nd time after the death of the first wife; then, took Samyâsa under Sant Keshava Bhârti. It is said that Lord Krishna appeared before him many times in different garbs. In

Shri Khand in South India he changed a pond completely into honey. It is still called: *Madhu Pushkarani*. There are many other miracles associated with Shri Chaitanya Mahâprabhu.

Shri Chaitanya Mahâprabhu was an incomparable devotee of Shri Krishna. He is unique and strange, and a solitary figure in his way and manner. He metamorphosed the self completely into Râdhâ and the last six years of life were spent as Râdhâ. He would get extremely excited and passionate for Lord Krishna and would behave, sing, dance and act like an intoxicated maniac that had forgotten all else and remembers only Krishna. His life was that of extreme devotion to Shri Krishna.

Shri Chaitanya Mahâprabhu gave eight very plain teachings known as *Shikshâshtakam*:

Men should spend maximum of their time in singing sweetly the Name of the Lord. It is the best and the easiest way to get purged.

One should be so engrossed in Him while singing His name that tears may start rolling out of the eyes; speech may grow ecstatic and the body starts feeling spiritual and passionate sensations.

Men chanting the Name of the Lord should think of the self to be smaller than a straw; he should be more tolerant than a tree and be humble enough to give honour to all else.

In the chanting of the Name of the Lord there is no barrier of Time and Place. Anyone can chant it any time and anywhere.

The God has filled His Names with sweetness and delight.

While chanting the Name one should earn Divine Wealth that comprises of: kindness; non-violence; lack of lust; truth; equality; equanimity; detachment; stability of mind; control over senses; seriousness; compassion; friendship; brilliance and tolerance etc.

In this way and in this context, Shri Chaitanya Mahâprabhu gave the most popular *Nâm-Samkirtan-Mantra* that is chanted everywhere in India and abroad. It is most lilting and musical; and it can be composed in any tune, *râga* or *uparâga* or *râgini*. It has incomparable elasticity. It is:

Hare Krishnâ Hare Krishnâ Krishnâ Krishnâ Hare Hare!
Hare Râmâ Hare Râmâ Râmâ Râmâ Hare Hare!

Shri Chaitanya Mahâprabhu touched and melted the hearts and affected, purged and altered the mind of the people. As a result of his extreme devotion and pure pleasure and the state of bliss that he lived in, persons like Prakâshânand Saraswati that believed in advait turned to be a devotee of Krishna; the pure criminals like Jagâi and Madhâi became Sants; and that his opponents and critics became his followers, including some famous Sants of the time.

Shri Chaitanya Mahâprabhu had one opinion and one aim that devotion is the greatest aspect of life and that all should turn into devotees. For it there was no need to criticize any religion. He did never do that. There is a chance that he got no time to think of other religions. He was absorbed in either the inner self or Shri Krishna and had forgotten the rest. To him the easiest way to achieve freedom from impurities and the painful cycle of birth and death was *Jap* and *Kirtan*: to try to please the God by reciting, chanting, singing and calling his name; by dedicating the self to the Absolute Entity.

20. Disciples of Shri Chaitanya Mahâprabhu

The following nine disciples of Shri Chaitanya Mahâprabhu became very famous. They are also accepted as Sants. They are:

(a) Shri Nityânand Prabhu

Nityânand Prabhu was born to Harâi Pandit and Padmâwati in Ekachakrâ village in Veerbhuma district of Bengâl in 1473. He became a Samnyâsi at a very tender age under Mâdhavendra Puri. Later on he met Chaitanya Mahâprabhu in Navdweep and instantly accepted him Guru and rose to be the principal disciple of Mahâprabhu. Later on he accepted Grihasthâshram and married Jânhwi Devi.

(b) Shri Advait Prabhu

Shri Advait Prabhu was born in Shântipur Village of Nâdiyâ district of Bengâl. He was 33 years older than Mahâprabhu. His immaculate devotion brought Shri Chaitanya Mahâprabhu into limelight.

(c) Haridâs Sâdhu

Haridâs Sâdhu was also some 30 to 35 years older than Shri Chaitanya Mahâprabhu. He was born in Burhân village of Jassore district in Shak Samvat 1372. He was born in a Muslim family but was enchanted by Hinduism since his childhood.

(d) Raghunâth Dâs (Dâs Goswâmi)

Raghunâth Dâs was the son of a Jamindâr of Saptagrâm near Kolkata. The annual income of that area was 12 lakhs per annum during that period. But Raghunâth Dâs was not attached to the worldly wealth and luxury. He relinquished it and became an ardent follower of Shri Chaitanya Mahâprabhu.

(e) Roop

Roop was the son of Kumâr Deva and Mâtâ Rewati. He was born in 1489 AD and died in 1563. He worked on a high post with Nawâb Hussain Khân of Gaur. He was called 'Dabirkhâs'. He left his job and home and became one of the principal disciples of Shri Chaitanya Mahâprabhu.He wrote many books in which he propounded and established the theory and principles of *Gauriya Vaishanava* Philosophy.

(f) Sanâtan

Sanâtan was the son of Kumâr Deva and Mâtâ Rewati. He was born in 1487 AD and died in 1558. He worked on a high post with Nawâb Hussain Khân of Gaur. He was called 'Sâkar Mullick'. He left his job and home and became one of the principal disciples of Shri Chaitanya Mahâprabhu.He wrote many books in which he propounded and established the theory and principles of *Gauriya Vaishanava* Philosophy.

(g) Jiva Goswâmi

He was a great Sant of Gauriya Sect. He was related to Roop and Sanâtan. He wrote a philosophical treatise '*Shat Samdarbh*' in which he explained and illustrated the philosophical theories of Shri Chaitanya Mahâprabhu.

(h) Râi Râmânand

Rai Râmânand worked for some king and tried to create balance between the worldly life and spiritual life. Very late in his life, he took Samyâs but he was leading a saintly life while working with the king.

(i) Narhari Sarkâr Thâkur

The son of Nara Nârâyan Thâkur, Sant Narhari Sarkâr Thâkur remained a celibate throughout his life. He was born in Shrikhand village of Wardmân district in Bengâl in 1478 AD and departed in 1570. He enjoyed supernatural powers. It is said that when Shri Chaitanya Mahâprabhu reached his village there were no flowers to offer him. He requested a Kadamb Tree and it instantly gave two flowers and kept on giving two flowers everyday for three long years till Mahâprabhu remained in the village.Most of these Sants worshipped 'Râdhâ-form' while Narahari worshipped the form of Shri Krishna.

21. Shridhar Swâmi

Shridhar Swâmi enjoyed a life of blessings, grace and luck on the one hand and that of ignorance, problems and attachment on the other. He was an orphan. As a result he could neither get proper food and training nor education. His mind could not develop. He became a case of mental retardation.

But strange are the ways of life. One day, when he was carrying oil in some improper container that obviously was causing waste to it, the king and his minister were passing by that place and talking about devotion and its effect.

The minister said, "Simply by devotion, an unskilled grows into a skilled person, an ignorant into wise and a demon into godly."

Some unknown power made the king ask, "Can this foolish boy grow into a wise one only with devotion?" He showed Shridhar Swâmi.

The minister was confident, "Sure!"

The boy was brought to the court, given initial training into *Nrishnha Mantra,* ways of worshipping, *prânâyâm* etc and was placed in a temple as a case study. Actually, the boy was not on test, devotion was being tested. The grace of God was such that the boy got the benefit. Whatever he was asked to do he did it without hesitation and with all purity. His ignorance had kept his purity intact. He gave to the Lord whatever he had; and his possessions were not very significant.

His simplicity, truthfulness, un-mutilated devotion and consistency and regularity bore fruits. God appeared before him and taught him all the Vedas and blessed him. He showed his knowledge, used it and participated in kingly debates in different courts and became famous as a learned man. And, the awards that he was given made him rich. He was married. That was the thing that he could neither resist nor stop, neither he liked nor relished. It was a burden on his head. He wanted to devote all the time in worshipping the Lord.

Either luck favoured him or the blessings bore fruit. While giving birth to a child his wife died. He was free from the wife but the child was a burden on him. He gave many logical reasons for leaving the child on its fate. One was the Krishna's statement of the Gitâ, *'Yogakshemam wahâmyaham'*, I give health to all and protect all and the other came as practical example.

One day, an egg of a bird fell and broke up before him. An unhealthy sibling came out. It could not move for some time but it started with a doddering movement. A fly came and sat on the broken egg. The sibling gulped it. Its organs were strengthened and it started moving. He felt complete detachment, left everything behind and came to Kâshi for further study and worshipping. He wrote many commentaries. His commentaries on Gitâ, Bhâgawat and Vishnu Purâna are still available. It was accepted by the God, the critic were also forced to accept them and Shri Chaitanya Mahâprabhu praised his commentary loudly. A retarded brain grew into a scholar with devotion and the grace of god and that life was well utilized.

22. Buddhist Sants

(a) Awalokiteshwar

Sant Awalokiteshwar is such a great Sant that rose to the height of God and added meaning and substance to Sants and Sainthood. It is difficult to find a peer for him as his achievements and status have kept on growing after his departure and with the passage of time. He has been shown in the following different forms from time to time:

Awalokiteshwar	Got a place among gods.
	Called Lokeshwar/ Loknāth by the Buddhists.
	Became Shakti for the Shāktas.
	Shown with a lotus in one hand and the other raised up as in blessing.
	Shown as Chaturbhuja with two folded hands and lotus and a garland in the other two.
	Shown as Shiva with deerskin, kamandal, snake and skull.
	2nd to Buddha in Buddhism.
	The greatest among the Boddhisattavas.
	Equal to the third Ratna as leader of Sangh in Buddhism.

(b) Manjushree

Manjushree	The oldest idol of Manjushree has two hands; the sign of wisdom and is sitting on lotus.
	He is mentioned in six Tantra-Granthas.
	He is the symbol of the essence of wisdom.
	'Nāma Sangiti' mentions him as Brahmā and Saraswati as his Shakti.
	He is a Boddhisattava.
	He is the founder of culture in Nepāl.
	He is said to be a prince.
	He wrote *Pragyā-Pārmitā Granthas*.
	He belongs to Mahāyān Sect.

(c) Sâriputra

Sāriputra	One of the two principal disciples of Lord Buddha; the other is Maudgalāyan/ Moggallān.
	His first name was either Upatishya or Upatissa.
	He is known as Shāriputa, Shāliputra, Sharadwatiputra also.
	Buddha declared that after his departure Sāriputra would conduct 'Dharmachakra'.
	There are many stories about him.
	He is said to have written the Granthas of Mahāyān.
	He was like Dharma Senāpati.
	Sāriputra used to teach the children.
	'Sutra-Nipāt' says a lot about him.

(d) Maudgalâyan/ Moggallân

Maudgalāyan/ Moggallān	One of the two principal disciples of Lord Buddha; the other is Sāriputra.
	He was the son of a Brahmin lady named Bhadra Kanyā.
	He was perfect in both Worldly (*laukika*) and Spiritual (*Pārlaukika*) control
	He could walk on water, go through a wall, reappear at a different place, and meet the gods.
	He could enrich one with inner power and could give inner peace.
	He could move things with his toe.
	He used to teach the elders.
	Both he and Sāriputra departed at about the same time and cremated at the same place.

(e) Dhammapâla

Dhammapāla	He was the presiding authority (*Dharmādhyaksha*) at Nālandā University.
	He was the preceptor of Huen-sang.
	He was a very learned scholar.
	Dhammapāla has explained the verses of Buddhism in 14 volumes.
	It is debatable whether he was a Boddhisattava or not.

(f) Kanak Muni

Kanak Muni	Kanak Muni is called Konāgaman' in Pāli.
	He was born in Nepāla.
	Ashok the great got a pillar raised in his memory at his birthplace.
	He has a lot of historical importance.
	His deeds and achievements are only in stories otherwise they are not available.

(g) Sant Padma Sambhava/ Padmâkar

Sant Padma Sambhava/ Padmākar	He went to Tibbat with his disciple. He was specially invited by the Rāja Mātā.
	He was the first one to teach Buddhism there.
	He was the first āchārya of Buddhism.
	He started *Lāmā Dharma* which is a Tibbatan synonym of Buddhism.
	He taught Samskrit to local people.
	He usually concentrated on the Mantras and Magi.
	He established a Dharmasangh called 'Samyās'.
	He also fixed the dress for the Lāmās.

23. Jain Sants

(a) Maharishi Metârya

Maharshi Metârya was a follower of Bhagawân Mahâvir. He

was born in a Shudra family but from childhood he kept on roaming from forest to forest in search of something that he had no idea and at last he got the *Siddhi*. He followed the teachings of Bhagawân Mahâvir with meticulous ease and dedication and taught the people his five great teachings of non-violence; truth; non-stealing; sacrifice and celibacy:

पंचैतानि पवित्राणि सर्वेशां धार्मचारिणाम् ।
अहिंसा सत्यमस्तेयं त्यागो मैथुन वर्जनम् ॥

Panchaitâni pavitrâni sarveshâm dharmachârinâm;
Ahimsâ satyam asteyam tyâgo maithuna varjanam.

There is a tale very popular about Metârya that a goldsmith punished him by mistake while his gold balls were eaten away by a bird. He endured the hard punishment to save the life of the bird. It would have mounted to violence had he revealed the fact about the bird. The bird would have been killed. Like other Sants he too had great patience and tolerance.

(b) Vidyuchchar

Vidyuchchar was the eldest son of the king of Hastinâpur but he turned to be a robber. He could not keep the great tradition of his parents. The king was aggrieved and angry and declared him dethroned. It made no difference to Vidyuchchar. He raised his great band of 500 robbers.

The Prince of Râjgriha changed his life. He became a Sant along with the complete band. They all knowingly died in a natural calamity, although they were in a position to avoid it.

(c) Seth Sudarshan

Seth Sudarshan was a merchant and very handsome. His health, personality and look justified his name Sudarshan, one who is handsome to look at. He lived a very regular and pious life of a householder and performed his duties well. He followed the Scriptures, performed yagyas and on every *chaturdashi* went to the place of cremation and spent the night in *dhyân*.

The young queen of the place saw him and was enchanted by him. She tried hard to mold him but she failed, as Seth Sudarshan was a man of determination and strong character. With the help of the maid the queen did something nefarious. Seth Sudarshan was lifted in the position of Dhyân from the *Smashân* and brought to the bed of the queen. She tried hard to break his concentration but failed and it was morning. It would have been deadly for her if another person was found in her bedroom. She acted devilishly and blamed Seth Sudarshan of immoral act. The king was informed and ordered that Seth Sudarshan be killed. Seth Sudarshan was still in *Yoga-Samâdhi*.

Everything was ready to kill him. But when the butcher raised his hand with sword to kill him his hand did not come down. An uproar was raised and the reality came out. At his usual time, Seth Sudarshan returned to his senses and came to know of the whole incident. He was disillusioned and took *pravrajyâ* then and there. He became a very popular Sant.

His *Samâdhi* is still there in Pâtaliputra, the modern Patna, the capital city of Bihar.

24. The Sants of Nâth Sampradâya (Sect)

(a) Matsyendra Nâth and Gorakh Nâth

Although Matsyendra Nâth was the guru of Gorakh Nâth but they are often mentioned together. They are most popular Sants for different reasons. There are numerous and scandalous tales famous among the general people and they like to tell them with interest. Whenever their name is mentioned some tales are invariably told and the greatness of the guru or shishya remains debatable. Neither they decided in their lifetime, which was greater nor the people have decided. Their *hathyoga sâdhna*, merit, achievements and supernatural powers are often discussed in detail and remain inconclusive. The most talked about power is their ability to enter the body of others, *parkâyâpravesh*. This science became popular from the time of Shri Shankrâchârya. The usual belief of the people is that the yogis and Sants enter the dead body of others while Mahâbhârat clarified that the yogishwar may create many body and be present at many places simultaneously. The soul remains one. It is performed only in India. Such things are not even talked about in other countries. With different body one enjoys the luxurious life of a king with one body; delves deep in penance with another body. The ripples are created in the mind of a yogi like the rays of the sun; and like the sun he collects the ripples and sits in some cave in samâdhi:

आत्मनो वै भारीराणि बहूनि भरतर्शभः।
योगी कुर्याद् बलं प्राप्य तैश्च सर्वैर्महीं चरेत् ॥
प्राप्यनुयाद् विशयान् कैश्चित् कैश्चिद् उग्रं तपश्चरेत् ।
संक्षिपेच्च पुनस्तानि सूर्यो रश्मिगणानिव ॥

Âtmano wai sharirâni bahuni bharatarshabhah;
Yogi kuryâd balam prâpya taischa sarvaih mahim charet;

Prânuyâd vishayân kaishchchit kaishid ugram tapah charet;
Sankshipechcha punastâni suryo rashmiganâniva.

It seems that Matsyendra Nâth had the ability to be more than one while Gorakh Nâth had the ability to enter a dead body. Matsyendra Nâth will remain away from his original body for months in a row and Gorakh Nâth had the responsibility for safekeeping the body or corpse. But it is endless.

It is believed that Lord Shiva taught yoga to Matsyendra Nâth and hence in Nâth Sect He is known as Âdinâth, the Creator of all. He is the one that has never changed: Half Moon and Gangâ on the head; snake in the neck; bhashma on the body; deerskin in the lion; long trident with Damaru in the hand. He is Shiva, Bholenâth, Âdinâth: *mahokshah khatwângam parashuh ajinam bhashma phaninah kapâlam cheti.*

As the bubbles are created by themselves in the sea and again mix with the sea, in the same way many living beings come out of the sea-like Shiva and return back to Him:

ब्रह्मादि कीट पर्यनताः प्राणिनो मयि कल्पिताः ।
बुदबुदादि विकारान्तः तरंग सागरे यथा ॥

Brahmâdi kita paryantâh prânino mayi kalpitâh;
Budbudâdi vikârântah tarangah sâgare yathâ.

Matsyendra Nâth is known and talked by different names. It is a wonder that in the Purânas he has been referred to by many names. He is Matasya Nâth; Matsyendra Nâth; Meen Nâth; Siddha Nâth; Akhilsiddha Nâth; Bâbâ Machhender etc. His most popular name is Machhender Nâth.

Matsyendra Nâth and Gorakh Nâth had a peculiar call pronounced in a very high pitch: **Alakh Niranjan**. Whether they belong to his tradition or not but all the similar sâdhus and nâgâs prefer to repeat "*Alakh Niranjan*".

Gorakh Nâth propounded a theory of his own and he showed the results by following that theory. His disciples are numerous and they rightly and proudly call themselves Gorakh Panthi. His followers get their ears torn and wear different things so they are called: *Kân Pharawâ*; *Kâna Phatâ*; *Bhâkat Phatâ* etc.

His Yogi Sampradâya is divided in 12 divisions so it is called *Bârah Panthi* also. It is believed and declared that the first six of them were propounded by Lord Shiva; and the other six by Gorakh Nâth. They are:

1. Bhuja ke Kanthar Nâth
2. Pâgal Nâth
3. Râwal
4. Panka or Pankha: Satanâth, Garibnâth, Dharam Nâth, and Hâri Bharang are associated with him.
5. Bana
6. Gopâl or Râm Sampradâya.
7. Chând Nâth Kapilâni: Gangâ Nâth; Mâya Nâth; Kapilâni; Neema Nâth; Pâras Nâth are associated with him.
8. Hetha Nâth: Laxman Nâth; Kâla Nâth; Dariyânâth; Nataseri; are associated with it.
9. Âi Pantha's Choli Nâth: Masta Nâth is associated with it.
10. Vairâga Pantha: Bhai Nâth; Prem Nâth; Ratan Nâth are associated with it.
11. Pâwa Nâth of Jaipur: Pâpantha; Kâniyâ; Bâmâraga are associated with it.
12. Ghaja Nâth.

The last one is claimed to be propounded by Shri Hanumân. It seems that in *Gorakh Nâth Sampradâya* many ancient Sects have amalgamated as for example Yoga Mârha of Kapil; Lakuli Shamata; Kâpâlika Mata; Wâma Mârga etc.

So many things inculcated in the theory of Gorakh Panth are different to the traditional Yoga Sâdhnâ.

a. In place of Ashtânga Yoga the Yoga by Gorakh Nâth is called Shadâng Yoga.
b. The most important parts of Ashtânga Yoga the first two Yama and Niyam are insignificant in Gorakh's Yoga.
c. Its process is called Hath Yoga.
d. It lays a lot of stress on the contol of breath and Prânâyâm, Âsan and Bandha.
e. The books by Gorakh Nâth elucidate and explain this process.
f. It aims at Sahaj Samâdhi.

If one Sant enjoys the popularity and has disciples from the seas in South to the Himalayas in the North, then he is Gorakh Nâth. He got immense popularity. Nepâl is his kingdom and he had a rest house in Mahârâshtra. He is given numerous epithets but two in Marâthi are very important: **Vishaya Vidhwansaik Veera** and **Yogâbjini Sarovar**. On the other hand Matsyendra Nâth enjoys popularity of a bit different sort. It is said that on Saptashringi Mountain in Nâsik a Sant was lying with hands and feet separated from his body. Matsyendra Nâth gave all his organs back. There is a famous cave of Gorakh Nâth in the back of Trayambakeshwar on Brahmgiri Mountain near Nâsik. On the round about of this mountain there is a Math, the hermitage of his disciple Gaininâth. There is a samâdhi of Gorakh Nâth on Newâsâ Mountain and in the Sâtârâ district there is the samâdhi of Matsyendra Nâth. A yâtrâ called Matsyendra-yâtrâ is held every year on *Vaishâkh Krishna Panchami*. On this Garh (mound) there is a tamarind tree famous as *Gorakh-Imli*. In Kanhâd the tide is called Matsyendra Shawl. What a grand popularity that these two enjoyed!

Gorakh Nâth or Goraksha Nâth was far more active than Matsyendra Nâth. These two along with Jalandhar Nâth and

Kânaphi or Krishna Pâda or Kânha Pâda or Kânhapâ are accepted as the original founders of Nâth Sampradâya. But Gorakh Nâth excelled with his theorization and practical approach. One book in Prâkrit, 27 books in Samskrit and 40 books in Hindi written by Gorakh Nâth are available. They are:

Books by Gorakh Nâth in Samskrit:

1.	Amawask	15.	Gyân Shatak
2.	Awarodha Shâshanam	16.	Gyân Amrit Yoga
3.	Awadhuta Gitâ	17.	Nari-gyân-Pradipikâ
4.	Goraksha Kâla	18.	Mahârth Manjari (Prâkrit)
5.	Goraksha Kaumudi	19.	Yoga Chintâmani
6.	Goraksha Gitâ	20.	Yoga Mârtand
7.	Goraksha Chikitsâ	21.	Yoga Beeja
8.	Goraksha Panchaya	22.	Yoga Shâshtra
9.	Goraksha Paddhati	23.	Yoga Siddhâsan Paddhati
10.	Goraksha Shatak	24.	Viveka Mârtand
11.	Goraksha Shâshtra	25.	Shrinâth Sutra
12.	Goraksha Samhitâ	26.	Siddha Siddhânt Paddhati
13.	Chaturshit Âsan	27.	Hath Yoga
14.	Gyân Prakâsh Shatak	28.	Hath Samhitâ

Books by Gorakh Nâth in Hindi:

1.	Sabadi	21.	Nava Grah
2.	Pada	22.	Nava Râtra
3.	Sishyâdarsan	23.	Ashta Pârchhayâ
4.	Prân Sankali	24.	Raharâsa

5.	Narawe Bodha	25.	Gyân Mâla
6.	Âtam Bodha I	26.	Âtam Bodha II
7.	Abhai Mâtrâ Yoga	27.	Vrat
8.	Pandrah Tithi	28.	Niranjan Purân
9.	Sapnavâda	29.	Gorakh Vachan
10.	Machhindra-Gorakh Bodha	30.	Indri Devatâ
11.	Româwali	31.	Moola Garmâwati
12.	Gyân Tilak	32.	Khâna Vâruni
13.	Gyân Chautish	33.	Gorakh Sata
14.	Panch Mâtrâ	34.	Ashta Mudrâ
15.	Gorakh-Ganesh Goshti	35.	Chaubi Sidhi
16.	Gorâwadatta Goshti	36.	Dakshari
17.	Mahâdeva Gorakh Gushta	37.	Panch Agni
18.	Sista Purân	38.	Ashta Chakra
19.	Dayâ Bodha	39.	Awali Siluka
20.	Jâti Bhaurâwali	40.	Kâphir Bodha

Gorakh Nâth spent a lot of time in Mahârâshtra and was very popular there. He wrote two books in Mârâthi also: **Amarnâth Samvâd** and **Goraksha Gitâ**.

(b) Other Important Sants of Nâth Sect

In the 12th Century AD Gorakh Nâth gave the mantras to **Trayambak Pant**. He was the great grand father of Gyâneshwar. There is a long tradition of Gorakh Panthi Sants. The grand father of Gyâneshwar was taught by **Gaini Nâth**, another disciple of Gorakh Nâth. Gaini Nâth also gave Dikshâ to **Nibriti Nâth**, the elder brother of Gyâneshwar. **Gyâneshwar**, another Sant, wrote a book called 'Gyâneshwari' which deals with all the events in detail.

Once, while taking a round of the Brahmagiri Mountain at Nâsik a tiger came and the family of Nibritinâth ran helter and skelter for safety. Nibritinâth took refuse in the cave of Gaini Nâth. He remained there for seven days and returned as his disciple after taking the Mantra of Mahâvâkya. He said, 'Even if the sky break into pieces and Meru Mountain turns into splinters yet never back out from the inner pleasure of the self.' Nibritinâth followed the Guru and composed 400 *Abhangs*, some deal with yoga and others with Advait and Shri Krishna.

Nibriti Nâth had two other brothers and one sister: Nibriti Nâth; Gyâneshwar, Sopân Deva and Muktâbai. They all became great Sants in the tradition of Gorakh Nâth. Only their short life can complete a book on Indian Sants or on the Sants of Nâth Pantha.

25. Sant Gyâneshwar

When their parents Vitthal Pant and Rukmini Bai took Jala Samâdhi at Triveni, Prayâga their four children, Nibriti Nâth was 7 years old; Gyâneshwar was 5 years old; Sopân Deva was four years old and the youngest Muktâ was 3 years old. They were dependent on begging. Whatever raw grain they got they prepared their food with that and spent the rest of their time in singing songs in praise of the lord. They did it even while begging.

The first real problem that they faced was that of their Sacred-thread ceremony. The death of their parents in spiritual fashion had a deep impression on the people and pandits of the place. They were ashamed of what they had done and really wanted to help them. They suggested them to go to Paithan, and promoissed to abide by the decisions of the pandits there. They accepted it and all the four walked on foot up to Paithan. They consulted the scholars. A meeting was held and the scholars announced that the way described in Shri Madbhâgawat is the only way for them:

Visrijya smayamânân swân drisham vridâm cha laukikam;
Praname dandwad bhumâ vâshywa chândâl gokharam.

They should prostrate before the persons that laugh on them, the dogs, chândâls and cows. This way they can show devotion in God. Then they can be saved. Nibritinâth accepted it. Sopân and Muktâ said, "It's a pleasure'. Gyâneshwar said seriously, "Whatever you say is right for us."

When they were about to return back from the place some people started teasing them. One of them asked, "What is your name?"

Gyâneshwar said politely, "My name is Gyân Deva."

There was a buffalo there. Indicating the buffalo that man said again, "Here, this buffalo is Gyân Deva. Throughout the day it carries the load of gyân. Say, Deva, are you a similar Gyân Deva."

Gyâneshwar promptly replied, "Yes, yes, there is no doubt about it. It is my soul. There is no difference in this buffalo and me."

Some one else teased him by twice beating the buffalo with a stick, and said, "You must have felt the pain of the sticks?"

Gyâneshwar said in the same polite tone, "Yes." He opened his back and the people wondered to see the red mark of the sticks on his back.

There was some change in the attitude. A scholar came forward and said, "If the buffalo is like you then he must be knowing what you know. Make the buffalo speak like a similar wise man."

Gyâneshwar went to the buffalo and placed his hand on its back and Lo! The buffalo started with Aum and chanted Mantras like Gyâneshwar. The whole milieu changed in a moment. The scholars realized that he is not an ordinary boy. He is some rare soul that has taken birth for some definite purpose. They prostrated before the children, washed the feet of Gyâneshwar and announced victory for them.

Gyâneshwar was still polite. He said, "It is your grace. I'm only a child."

They were invited for meal at the shrâddha in a Brâhmin family. Gyvneshwar called his ancestors. "*Âgantavyam*, " and his dead ancestors took body, appeared before them and took meal.

The whole Paithan was enchanted by them and worshipped them. The Scholars humbly gave him the certificate of purification. They had no burden and anxiety over mind. So they remained in Paithan for a long time. They used to take bath in Godâvari, study books, discuss spirituality and show people the right path. During their stay there Gyâneshwar studied the Commentaries by Shri Shankaracharya, Shrimad Bhâgawad, Yoga Vashishtha and others. Only then they retuned back to Newâse, near Âpegaon, their birthplace. From there they went to Âlindi where they were heartily welcomed. Again they came back to Newâse and this time, Gyâneshwar, at the age of fifteen, delivered the commentary on Gitâ as lectures to 17 year-old Sadguru, Nibriti Nâth. Sachchidânand wrote it. It is famous as Gyâneshwari Grantha.

After that Sant Gyâneshwar started his journey to places of pilgrimage. His sister and brothers were with him. But the group kept on growing as more and more Sants joined it. Visobhâ Khechar; Gorâ Kumbhahâr; Chokhâ Melâ; Narhari Sonâr; Shri Nâmadeva; and others joined them. There fame had reached the places before they went there. They visited Ujjain; Prayâga; Kâsi; Gayâ; Ayodhyâ; Gokul; Vrindâvan; Dwârkâ; and Girnâr and returned to Pandhârpur. They were famous and respected at all the places. They sang the hymns; chanted the mantras and taught the people. He completed '*Gyâneshwari*' or *Bhâwârtha Dipikâ*; *Amritânubhava*; *Haripath's Abhangs* and *Chângdeva Pâsathi*.

1,500 years old Sant Chângadeva came to them and became a disciple of 15 years old Muktâ Bai.

At the age 21 years, 3 months and 5 days **Sant Gyâneshar** took **Alive-Samâdhi (jivita Samâdhi)** on Mârgashirsha Terasa in Vikram Samvat 1353.

The same year **Sant Nibriti Nâth**, his elder brother, **took Alive-Samâdhi** but he left his body on . Âshâdh Krishna Dwâdasi Vikram Samvat 1354.

Just one month after the samâdhi of Gyâneshwar, his younger brother **Sopân Deva,** left his body while performing Harinâma Samkirtan at Sâswad.

Just five months after the samâdhi of Sant Gyâneshwar, his only sister **Sant Muktâbai,** left her body in Mâna Gâon at the bank of River Tâpti.

But that family of Sants is still alive, singing hymn, chanting mantras and teaching people.

26. Shri Mukund Râj: A Strange Sant

Shri Mukundrâj was born in Vikram Samvat 1185. He was a disciple of Shri Raghunâth who was a disciple of a famous Sant Shri Hari Nâth. His two books: *Vivek Sindhu* and *Param Amrit*: are very famous. He wrote *Vivek Sindhu* at the age of 60. It is treated as the first great book in Marâthi Literature. Both his books are composed in '*obi*' poetic meter. *Vivek Sindhu* has 18 Chapters and 1671 *obies* while *Param Amrit* has 14 Chapters and only 303 obies. Both of them are based on *advait* philosophy.

There is an interesting story behind the creation of this book. The credit is given to king Jayant Paul, the son of Nrisingh Ballâla, who created the situation that eventually gave the concept of the book. King Jayant Paul had only one question: *You people talk of Brahman and the revelation of Brahman, have you ever seen the Brahman. If yes, then can you show me the Brahman?* He was ecstatic about the answer and wanted the correct answer at any cost. In expectation that some day some Sant will give him the correct answer he would call each Sant to his court ask the question and in case of failure in showing him the Brahman he would put them into prison. The number of the Sants in the prison-house kept on increasing and it crossed the 500 mark.

When Mukund Râj heard of the Sants in jail for a different reason, he vowed to free the Sants. He went to the court of the king. The king asked the same question. He said, "Yes, there is Brahman. I have the revelation of Brahman. If you want to see the Brahman, say me I can show Brahman any time anywhere you like as Brahman is everywhere." The king was eager to see Brahman. He expressed his desire to see Brahman then and there.

Mukundrâj asked him to get a horse there. A horse was led into the court. He asked him to ride the horse. When the king settled on the horse Shri Mukund Râj moved his right palm on the head of the king and the king immediately fell into trance and remained seated in the same position for three days and three nights. When he regained his senses he fell on the feet of the Sant and became his disciple. The Sant asked him to free the Sants. The Sants were freed, shown proper respect and worshipped. For the *Purna Bodha*, (complete realization) to the king Shri Mukund Râj wrote the book *'Vivek-Sindhu'*.

27. Shri Chângadeva

Shri Chângadeva is a peculiar figure among Indian Sants and Sages. He had complete education and knew all the sciences. He had such a command on Astrology that he calculated that he would get a real preceptor after 1,400 years. For that he may have to take births and rebirth and again would have to learn everything from the beginning. So, he decided to live in the body that he had. So, whenever his death came closer he would go deep into meditation and control the body. That way he lived for one thousand five hundred years.

Shri Chângadeva, a Shukla Yajurvedi Brâhmin, had his hermitage in Punatâmbe region at the bank of River Godâvari. During this long period he had lakhs of disciples and 1400 disciples lived in his hermitage. Because of his Yoga, accomplishments and long life he had acquired and kept a lot of ego.

Shri Chângadeva was in Samâdhi when Sant Gyâneshwar got the Certificate of Purification and became popular. When his Samâdhi was broken he came to know of their achievements and fame. He calculated and found that he is his preceptor. He was ready to go to them when the disciples said, "Simple by reputation you cannot accept them as your guru. It will belittle your status." He accepted their suggestion and decided to write a letter. But he could not write the letter simply because of his ruling ego. He sent the blank page to Sant Gyâneshra through his disciple.

Sant Gyâneshwar saw the blank paper and on the advice of his elder brother and guru Nibritinâth wrote the reply. It is famous as *"Chângadeva Paisathi"*, in which he declared that despite living for so many centuries he was blank. Shri Chângadeva read and re-read the book but could not understand the essence. He decided to go to him. Along with his one thousand and four hundred disciples he was ready to go to them. He called a tiger to take him to the place. He used a snake as a whip to drive the tiger.

When Chângadeva reached at their place all the four were sitting on a square mound. Sant Gyâneshwar saw him on the tiger and ordered the mound to move. When Chângadeva saw the mound moving up and towards him as a welcome gesture he came down and prostrated in the feet of Sant Gyâneshwar and asked for the meaning of the answer. Sant Gyâneshwar said that he would reveal the meaning provided that one of your disciples gets ready to sacrifice his life but no one was ready. Chângadeva declared that he would sacrifice his life. At this the fifteen-year old preceptor explained the omnipresent form of the God without quality (*triguna rahit*). Muktâbai moved her right palm on the head of Chângadeva to make him feel 'perfection'. He is known as the disciple of Muktâbai. From then on the four became five including Chângadeva. When Sant Gyâneswar took Samâdhi alive then Chângadeva also departed from the world.

28. The Sants of Gyâneshwar Tradition

(a) Gorâ Kumbhâr

After Govindji Gorâ Kumbhâr is the only Sant that was called 'Châchâ' by many Sants. He was born at Teradho in Vikram Samvat 1324. He had two wives but once his first wife Santi admonished him not to touch her. He obeyed till the end of his life. She forced him to marry her sister and asked him to behave with her as if she was like Santi. As a result he did not touch her also. His wife repented but she could do nothing to a Sant who had complete control over his senses. Once, both the sister forcibly put his hand on their body. He thought the hands to be sinners and cut both the hands off. He was the one to declare that Nâmdeva was in need of a guru who accepted Visobâ Khechar as his guru. His works, mostly *abhangs* include *'Satarahawin kâ Udaka'* and *'Khechari Mudrâ'*

(b) Visobâ Khechar

Visobâ Khechar, a Yajurvedi Brâhmin, belonged to the Audiâ Nâganâth, a very ancient region of Lord Shiva, famous for one of the Twelve Jyotirlingas. It is 150 km away from Pandhârpur. He used to dye the clothes and was expert in Yoga. He was a disciple of Sant Gyâneshwar and has praised him in his *abhangs*. Once, Nâmdeva came to meet him. He was lying on the ground with his feet on the Shivaling. Nâmdeva raised hue and cry. Khechar asked him, "I'm old and tired. Do move my feet at a place where there is no Shiva or Shivaling." He picked his legs up and placed away from the Shivling. Another Shivling came out under his feet. He repeated the act eight times and every time there was a new Shivling under his feet. The miracle forced Nâmdeva to accept him as his Guru. He helped him in the revelation of Lord Shiva.

(c) Shri Nâmadeva

Shri Nâmdeva was born at Narasi Brâhmani in Samvat 1327 on *Kârtika Shukla Ekâdasi* on Sunday in the morning to Dâmâsheta and Gonâi. It was a tailor family and traditionally a devotee of Bhagwân Vitthal. When he was asked to read and write he used to write only Vitthal. He used to play and run with Vitthal on his tongue. He got a very big family and shifted to Pandhârpur. That was the best place for him in the world. Whenever he went on pilgrimage he used to praise his place and like to return back soon. As mentioned earlier, he accepted Visobâ Khechar as his guru but he spent most of his days with Gyâneshar etc. Once, they could not get drinking water. They saw a dry well. With his yoga Gyâneshwar went to bottom of the well, broke up the land and drank water. When he came up, Nâmdeva called his Lord and asked for water.

Within minutes the well was filled up with water. Lord Vitthal was so pleased with him that once the pandits forced him out of the temple. He went in the back of the temple and started singing kirtan. Bhagwân Vitthal turned towards him. He spent 18 years in Panjab and his sixty abhangs have been included in *Shri Guru Grantha Sahib.*

(d) Rânkâ-Bânkâ

Rânkâ was born to Laxmidatta and Rupâdevi, a Rigvedi Brahmin of Pandhârpur, as a partial incarnation of Bhagwân Vishnu; and Bânkâ was born to a Brahmin, Harideva of Pandhârpur, as a partial incarnation of Goddess Laxmi. In due course, they were married. They were very poor but had no desire to get wealth. They would collect dry firewood and sell it for livelihood. On the request of Nâmdeva, Bhagwân Vitthal threw a cloth with gold and jewel on their way to the forest. Rânkâ saw it and started covering it with dust, so that his wife may not wish to take the wealth home. She came and asked. He said the truth. Bânkâ said 'You are only covering dust with dust.' Once, the Lord collected many bundles of dry wood in the forest so that they can easily take it away but they did not touch it thinking that it belonged to some one else. They did not get dry wood that day and slept without taking meal. God appeared before them. They spent more than hundred years on the earth.

(e) Sâwatâ Mâli

Sâwatâ Mâli was born in Aranbheri near Pandhârpur in 1172 Shak Samvad to Parsuwâ and Nângitâ; and took Samâdhi in 1217. He chanted the Name and praised Him in his *abhangs*. He was so adapt in yoga that the Lord would often call on him. Once, He came and asked him to hide Him, as some persons were following him. He hurriedly cut off his abdomen with *khurapi* (weeding instrument) and covered it with a shawl. Gyâneshwar with others reached there. He knew that the God is with Sâwatâ. They requested and he showed them.

(f) Senâ Nâi

Senâ Nâi was a barber and had a decent habit. In place of working silently he would keep on chanting 'Vitthal' while pruning the hair or shaving the beard. He also served a king. The king was also a devotee of Bhagwân Vitthal. Once, when he was shaving his beard, the king saw the Lord in His full attire in the mirror. He thought that it was an illusion. He turned the mirror down. Then he saw the Lord in the water. He asked the barber about it and he showed his ignorance. Because of Senâ Nâi the king was able to see the Lord. He was an extraordinary Sant and a disciple of Sant Gyâneshwar. He has composed many *abhangs* and has taught people to work honestly and to perform *nâm-kirtan*. He has taught even the barbers to follow a perfect schedule.

(g) Narahari Sunâr

Narhari Sunâr was a goldsmith and a stout devotee of Lord Shiva. He knew no God other than Devâdideva Mahâdeva. He had a unique way of remembering the Lord. In order to concentrate on his work he would concentrate on Lord Shiva and chant His Name. He was such a strong devotee of Shiva that he never went to the Vitthal Temple and never saw the idol of Bhagwân Vitthal although he lived in Pandhârpur. He did his work and was popular. Once, he was given the gold and ordered to make a *kardhani* (waist-band) for Vitthal Bhagwân. He completed it but it was long by four inches. He worked on it and shortened it. This time it was short by four inches. He did it four times and every time it was either long or short. He decided to take the measurement. To avoid looking at the idol of Vitthal he covered his eyes with manifold cloth. He was led to the idol. He touched thei dol for taking measurement and felt it to be the idol of Lord Shiva. He could not believe his touch. He opened his eyes. It was Vitthal Bhagwan. He closed his eyes and he felt embraced by Lord Shiva. He opened his eyes and it was Vitthal Bhagwân. It happened thrice and then he realized that Lord Shiva and Lord Vitthal are one and the same. From that day, his version changed. He saw the Lord in everything. He has sung His praise in his *abhangs*.

(h) Jaga Mitra Nâgâ

Jagamitra Nâgâ was a Brâhmin from Parli Vidyanâth region. He was a disciple of Nâgesh. He was a simple soul, lived on begging and blessed all for peace and prosperity. He got revelation when his hut was burning and he was saved. He has composed *abhangs* to describe the great deeds of Govind.

(i) Janâ Bâi

Janâ Bâi was a housemaid. She used to work in different houses for a living. She was born at the bank of River Godâvari in Gangâkheda. Her father was called Damâ and her mother Karund. Once, she went to Pandharpur and saw Vitthal Bhagwân in the temple. She decided to serve the Lord. She was left with the father of Shri Nâmdeva. When Nâmdeva was born she fostered him. Whenever she got time she would recite *Gitâ Gyâneshwari*. Once, a jewel was stolen from the neck of the idol. Janâ Bâi was blamed, and she was to be hanged. When she was brought to the hanging place, she cried pathetically to the Lord for help. The hanging triangle melted as water. The people realized their mistake. From then on she became a member of Nâmdeva's family.

(j) Kurma Dâs

Kurma Dâs was a contemporary of Gyâneshwar. From very birth he had no hand and no legs. He was just a mound. He lived in Paithan. He could move only through his abdomen. Someone would come and feed him. He was dependent on others for his food. He had nothing to do, so he would chant the Name of Hari. Once, he heard the sound of Hari Kathâ in the village. He wished to listen to it. It took some time but he reached the place of kathâ in time to listen clearly the great benefits of the journey to Pandharpur to Vitthal Bhagwân on the ekâdashi (eleventh day) of Kârtika. He decided to go to Pandharpur on the Kârtika Ekâdashi. He had four months time at his disposal. He announced his decision and in the morning he was on his way to Pandharpur. It was a painful suffering to move on abdomen on the dusty road. Yet, he covered more than two kilometers every day. He was about ten kilometers away on the Dasami (tenth) of Kârtika. He knew he could not reach there. He wept and wept but had no way out. An idea flashed, he can't go to Vitthal but Vitthal has power, he can come to him. He requested another person who was going there to write a letter on his behalf. He touched the letter with his head and asked him to give it to Vitthal Bhagwân. The pilgrim offered his poojâ and placed the letter of Kurma Dâs at the feet of the Lord.It was ekâdasi. Kurma Dâs was moving ahead and calling the Lord. The Lord had heard him. He was there in person along with Gyâneshwar, Nâmdeva and Sâwatâ Mâli. Kuma Dâs touched His feet with his head. It is said that Kurma Dâs went nowhere from there till he was alive, and a temple came up at that place. It is still there as a proof of the dedication of Kurma Dâs.

(k) Sâdhwi Sakhubâi

The life of Sâdhwi Sakhu Bâi is that of a simple daughter in law and her cruel in laws. What is different is her tolerance and dedication and devotion to Laxmipati. As a last resort she wished to go to Pandharpur to see Vitthal Bhagwân but was stopped and tied hard. She prayed to Lord and the Lord appeared as a lady like her. He freed Sakhu Bâi and asked her to go to her mission and he remained tied there. Sakhu Bâi saw her Lord and took Samâdhi. She died and was cremated. It was a problem for Laxmi. She collected her bones, gave her life and sent home to free Nârâyan. She came and took her place. The milieu had changed. It was a secret. But the Brâhmin that had cremated her came to inform the family. They asked her and the story came out. The whole family turned to be devotees of Bhagwân Vitthal.

(l) Jogâ Permânand

Jogâ Permânand lived in Wârshi. He had a unique way of visiting the temple that he did everyday. His way is known as 'danda'. He used to prostrate on the earth, make a mark of the distance covered, rise up, come to the mark, chant one Shloka of Gitâ, prostrate again and repeat the complete procedure. Every time one Shloka of Gitâ is chanted. He would finish all the 710 shlokas of Gitâ when he reached the temple. Once, a person gave him '*pitâmbar*'. While going to the temple, he was conscious of the new cloth and hence was delayed in reaching the temple. He realized that he had not concentrated on the Lord. He sold the cloth and punished the self by getting tied to the oxen and by mercilessly dragged by them hard and fast. First he lost his skin, then flesh but he kept on chanting the Shlokas. At last, the Lord saved him. He appeared before him and healed up the wounds. It was *Paush Krishna Chaturthi*. Every year on this day a fair is arranged in his memory.

(m) Chokhâ Melâ

Chokhâ Melâ was a Sant in the group of Sant Gyâneshwar and a disciple of Nâmadeva. By profession he used to carry out the dead animals. But he was so engrossed in the devotion of Bhagwân Vitthal that he appeared before him and adorned him with His basil and jewel garlands. Jani Bâi has praised his revelation in her *abhangs*. It is said that a part of a roof crushed down when he was working at a construction work. He died along with other labourers. Shri Nâmdeva went there to collect his bones. He started listening to the bones, the bones that vibrated the sounds of Vitthal were accepted as the bones of Chokhâ Melâ.

(n) Sant Gangânâthjee

The introduction to Sant Gangânâth and his Siddhi in Yoga is established with the story of the Sant and Nawâb Fateh Khân who was jealous of the popularity of the Sant and decided to get a palace constructed in the forest and his residence just at the place where the Sant meditates. The Sant came to know of it and immediately collected in cloths all the burning and inflamed materials from the *dhuni*, and left the place. Fateh Khân was amazed to hear of the fire in cloth. He immediately moved to stop the Sant from living the place. He reached his place and saluted the Sant; and requested him to return to his original place. At first he reused but after repeated request he announced to remain at the place where he was. He untied the cloth and again his burning *dhuni* was ready. The Nawâb was so impressed that he gave many plots of land which the Sant gave away to

Brâhmins. The Nawâb became his disciple. When he took Samâdhi alive at that place; then he got a temple constructed. It is still there.

29. Sant Kabir

The life of Kabir is very popular among the general people and the scholars alike. He was born to a Brâhmin widow who threw him near a pond and a weaver couple picked up the infant, fostered him, he grew up a good weaver, turned towards yoga under the influence of Nâth Sants, then settled at the pond making it his work place, living place, a place for congregations and *satnâm kirtan*. He accepted Shri Râmânand as his preceptor and Râma as his God without qualities. It has now developed into a pilgrimage with memorial, museum, library, and of course a temple. People from all castes, sects and religion became his disciple including the Muslims. It was not acceptable to the Muslim Sikandar Lodi who committed numerous excesses and tried hard to kill him. He was bound as a bundle and thrown before a mad elephant thrice to be crushed to death but the spiritual power in Kabir stopped the mad elephant from touching him. He was saved. He left Kasi and spent his last days in a nearby village Magahar. It too has been developed into a place associated with Kabir. Kabir sang solos and in chorus and the songs are collected to make many books that have been collected in *Kabir Granthâwalis* (Collected Works of Kabir). Kabir had a very long life and departed at the age of 102.

Kabir is refreshed past and herald of future. The first fully bloomed fragrant flower that shows the strength of the plant and gives the hope of the healthy and similar flowers to come.

Kabir is a religion in himself; an amalgamation of religions; like Eternal (Sanâtan) Religion that is the ploughed and prepared field with seeds of religion; religions meet in him; he does not belong to any religion.

Kabir is not the sea that allows all the currents to fall and makes them salty; Kabir is the Sunlit reservoir that takes juicy essence both from inside and outside and maintains the healthy quality of water: clean; pure; cool; oxygenated; mineralized; sweet and healthier. All these adjectives define the life, mind, deeds and works of Kabir.

At his time Kabir ensured the health of society and is still capable of keeping the society healthy provided that one drinks the juice and water that Kabir offers.

Literacy had little value in his time; wisdom and revelation was all that was needed; Kabir possessed both of them. Wealth had little importance in his time; work and skill was all that was needed; Kabir possessed both of them. Degrees had no importance in his time; religiosity and spirituality was all that was needed; Kabir possessed both of them. He had everything: wisdom and insight; purity and religiosity; spirituality and revelation;

We need communion, communication and companionship because we lack it; so we are poor in plenty and luxury; foolish with diplomas and degrees; loveless with dating and marriages.

We possess the body but lack the spirit; we try to heal wounds and pains with medicines and surgery and never by tender soft touch; sweet whispering voice and warm compassionate look. Kabir had that; Kabir used that; Kabir lived; Kabir helped others to live. We are not helping others to live hence we are not living. We are placing obstacles and raising hurdles for others to check their growth and prosperity and we are dwarfed; face and stop at obstacles; turn direction and change post, place or business to see hurdles; run and escape; escape and run; and fail to live.

Kabir had roots, strong main root and numerous tiny hair roots; he absorbed and reflected the strength of the plant. We have rejected the tradition; are rootless; unable to absorb minerals and sap from the past hence there is no projected future before us. We are living for the body, in and with the body hence neither the power is thrusting from behind nor the brightness is pulling ahead.

Kabir was not a revolutionary; not an extremist; he was a balanced and practical man of the world. He tried to stop others from doing excesses that was called revolution. He tried to open the eyes of others by showing the hard realities that were different to their concept; and he was declared to be a revolutionary. He found a path (may be hard, uneven, rough and pinching), showed it and asked others to move on it. The path lacked the luxury, softness and smoothness hence he was rejected as revolutionary.

We too have rejected all Kabirs that show realistic ways and try to check us from excesses because we are unrealistically committing excesses in every field and direction. We are extremists, extreme materialists. We are revolutionaries, have revolted against life and Nature, and the continuity of life and beauty of Nature.

Kabir was not one but many; and in his inner self, as it appears, he was all. Variety is a word that can define Kabir. He wrote all types of songs prevalent during his time or known to him: *Ramaini, Shabad; Dohâ; Pada; Sâkhi; Nirguna; Ulatabânsi.* He used all the languages. Perhaps he did not know the languages but had a rich vocabulary collected from: *Awadhi; Bhojpuri; Maithili; Panjâbi; Râjasthâni; Khari Boli; Purvi; Vrajabhâshâ; and Nepâli* etc. Obviously, his language is the language of *Janpada*, some like to say *Purvi Janapada* but it is now true. Kâsi has been and remained a rare place. People are noe talking of metropolitan city, world citizenship etc. Since many millenniums Kâsi has been a true metro city. It is the only surviving city of the ancient world or primitive world. People from different areas came, sat near him, listened to him, discussed religion, yoga, morality, philosophy and ethics with him. While doing so they carried away a lot from there and in return they left a lot there in the forms of both words and ideas. Kabir used them well and in a very impressive and meaningful way and context.

God for him was father, mother, friend, husband, king, master: *hari more pew main râm ki bahuria*; or *hari janani, main bâlak torâ*. His relation with God is very simple, natural, pure, close and deep. Kabir absorbed and expressed all the religious trends in vogue during his time: Nâth Sampradâya; Sufism; Advait of Vedânta; Ramânand's Râma and other Sagun Gods; Nirguna Brahman Hari. They are all one in Kabir. Kabir abused all the abuses that he did not appreciate; he chided all the men that led artificial life: pseudo pandits and pseudo-kajis; blind faith; wrong concept;

As Kabir had least knowledge of the books so he preferred knowledge through love and experience. Yoga has meaning and substance but devotion is the greatest thing for him. He was sure that even Yoga needs devotion.

Kabir established a relation with God as the Husband. The moment it was done the soul became His beloved. The relation deepens. From it the mysticism of Kabir takes birth. He described God not as incarnation but as Symbol. His inner love, mental relation needs no physical action. The meeting is bliss, the separation a curse and an unbearable agony: *hari bin rahai na sake merâ jiva*. Without any meeting or resolution, only on the basis of popularity and mass appeal and convincing quality of ideas expressed that it conceived, created and established a different sect, very famous both as *Sant Sampradâya* and *Sant Kâvya*.

Kabir did not knowingly used figures of speech, they appeared in his expressions in a natural way, as a part of natural language. There is no deliberation for them. The most interesting and mystic creations are *'Ulatbânsi'* in which meaning is derived from opposition: *pahale puta, pichhaire bhâi*; or *barase kambal bhinje pâni*. The unique nature, function and presentation of the coordinates, mostly out of the ordinary and difficult to comprehend on its face value made him a mystic poet; and lulled both the common people and intelligentsia to think and concentrated on his sayings for understanding and appreciation. Naturally, Kabir attracted, attracted and influenced more people than other Sants. It was the real reason, that Kabir was translated in more languages than any other Sant.

As a result of variety and colourful presentation, all the nine *Rasas* (the ways of aesthetic expressions) including *Shânt Rasa* and *Adbhuta Rasa* are found in Kabir. With it Kabir becomes a unique Sant, Teacher and Poet who presented the truth and realities of life in crude fashion, refined way and aesthetically satisfying manner. His religion lies in natural activities, acts and performance and in purity of self and intentions.

30. Sant Raidâs

Sant Raidâs was a great Mahâtmâ of his time. By announcing *santani mein ravidâs sant*, (among the sants he preferred Sant Raidâs) Kabir has accepted and declared the supremacy and great qualities of Sant Raidâs. There is a borrowed tradition of declaring the caste while in India from the primitive time Sâdhus and Sants have no caste. Sadly enough, it is always reminded that Raidâs belonged to Shudras. He was a cobbler by profession. By caste and by spirit he was a Sant, and should be mentioned like that.

Meeâ Bâi, another great Sant was a disciple of Sant Raidâs. It is really a great achievement to be praised by the contemporaries. Sant Nâbhâdâs and Sant Priyâdâs have also regarded him as a great saint who had great supernatural powers but lived on the traditional profession asking for nothing from the God. He had the bliss, peace, and love, what else he could have asked for? Riches were burden for him. He did never like to be separated from his God, the only possession that he needed.

The philosophy, ideas, expressions, diction and poetic meter in Sant Raidâs are all in keeping with the great tradition of the Sants. Sant Raidâs has announced complete renunciation essential for Santhood. Truth is the Supreme Truth and is inexpressible because of the numerous forms and ever changing form so, *jasa hari kahiye tasa hari nâhi*; whatever you say of the Brahman, He is not like that. He is everywhere and the same but different according to the time, place, thing or being: *hai aisâ jasu kachhu taisâ*: He is like that where He is. He pervades all as the living self. He is *Akshar* and *Abinashwar*. It is all in accordance with *Ashtânga Bhakti Yoga*.

It is tragedy that Sant Raidâs, and many other Sants are called *unpadh*, illiterate. What is the need of literacy for the man that knows the hidden reality and can compose such lilting, mellifluous hymns in the praise of the Unseen and Unknown? Literacy is needed for a clerk or an officer to create a huge pile of files, packed and stored after a few years or destroyed after a few decades. The Sants are immortal. Literacy may have made him a servant, not a Sant. He would not have been remembered centuries after his death. Sainthood gives bliss and beatitude, the ultimate aim of all living beings.

It is enough that hand written Manuscripts of the works of Sant Raidâs are found in Râjasthâni, his more than 60 verses have been collected in *Shri Guru Grantha Sahib* in *Gurumukhi*, a collection of his poems has come up in Hindi and most of his works have been translated into other languages. He is included in '*Bhaktamâla*' and has been immensely praised. Like Kabir he had literate disciples to write the songs; and the worth of the songs can be appreciated by the fact that they have survived the rough weather that India has faced during the last few centuries.

Sant Raidâs was popular in Gujarât, Panjab, Râjasthân, and the whole of central India, from east to west. He made the life easier and relations among people cordial.

What the critics have failed to realize that the simple language that Sant Raidâs has used can come only from a purged heart, *nirmal hridya*. He had thrown away all the impurities from heart and mind. This can be easily and well appreciated in the modern world when all the metros of the world are fighting against garbage and the huge pile of garbage looks at them in a challenging way. The cities are spending million dollars on the cleanliness. They clean the main highways and collect the garbage in the backyard or dump it in the seas polluting the most important life element. With impurities one can't lead a happy life. Purities, like Sainhood, ensure bliss and beatitude. That is the sole aim of living beings. It is our fault that we have forgotten it. We can't throw the responsibilities of our misdeeds on immortal Sants that worked hard to purify the heart of all that came to them or tried to avoid them. Meerâ's acceptance that Sant Guru Raidâs gave her eyes to see the inner reality is for the blind modern man who are living and working for only material gain and physical pleasure, the most temporal things. Meerâ said:

Guru Raidâs mile mohi pure, dhur se kalam bhiri;
Sat guru sain dai jab âke, antar jota lari.

The modern scholars and critics are searching the influence of other languages and religions on Sant Raidâs and other Sants they should be content to show what influence he had on the living human beings of the time, and those that followed. It should satisfy them that a tradition was established called *Raidâs*

Pantha; and even these days, many people happily call themselves '*Raidâsi*' and use the word in their names as their title.

In India, people of 80 years or more, including the Shudras, are respected and revered. Sant Raidâs lived for 120 years. The Brâhmins saluted him with respect. One can be jealous of but can't achieve the height that Sant Raidâs achieved and the popularity that he enjoyed.

31. The Shaiva Sants of the Middle Ages

Among many philosophical branches in India *Shaiva Darshan* is also a rich and illuminating philosophy. In theory it takes *Pati* (God); *Pashu* (Living Beings); and *Pâsh* (Cyclical Chain). Most of the things have been explained through these three that form yet another eternal triangle. (Incidentally, there are numerous eternal triangles in India created by Tri.) It declares that if the living beings, *Pashu* loves, worships and follows sincerely the God, *Pati* then he/she can be freed from *Pâsh*, the cyclical chain of birth-death-rebirth. It is based on the cause and effect theory.

The God is the essence and has both the forms: with quality and without quality. He is the emblem of love and kindness. *Sat*, *chit* and *ânand* is his basic form. He is the Creator and Soul of the universe. This philosophy was created in the primitive period in the *Shaivâgam Granthas*; and revived many times; the latest during the Middle Ages by the following Sants.

(a) Sant Arun Giri Nâth

Some 500 years ago, he was born in Tiruwannamale. He composed many poetical works including '*Kandarantâdi*'. It was completed in one sitting in a meeting.

(b) Tâyumânyavar

His father Kediliyappa belonged to Vedâranyam; he left the job at the palace and came to Râmnâd. He got a son but his wife died and he opted for Samyâsa. He composed many poetic works.

(c) Shri Râmlinga Swâmi

He was born in Marudar near 4Chidambaram to Râmayya Pillai and Chinnammala. He established a '*Gyân-Sabhâ* at Badalur. Though, a householder, he dedicated his life to Bhagawân Subramanyam i.e. Lord Shiva. He composed nice devotional poems. '*samarasa sanmârgam*' is the essence of his teachings that includes only two things: tolerance and good moral character. '*Tiruvarutyâ*' is the collection of his works.

(d) Meyakand

The son of a rich man Kâlappâlan was baptized in Shaiva Sect and given the name Meyakand by Paramjyoti Munivar. He organized and gave a philosophical base to Shaiva thinking and worshipping through his recognized and worshipped work '*Meyakand-Shâshtra*'. In his tradition, Umâpati Shivâchârya wrote, a big and great book on Shaiva-Darshan named "*Shiva-Prakâsh*".

(e) Chidamber Swâmi

Chidamber Swâmi belongs to the tradition of Sangam Poets. He became a disciple of Kumârdeva when he failed to explain some words from Vedânta. Later on he wrote commentaries on many Vedânta Granthas in Tamil. Once he was ordered in dream by celestial peacock to renovate the Tiruporur Temple. He went for that. Four thieves stole away his belongings. They became blind. They prayed and he asked them to offer all of their belongings to the temple. They obeyed and got their eyes back. He has many poetical works in Tamil including: *Tiruporur Sanniddhi Murai* and *Vairâgyashatak*.

(f) Kachiappa Shivâchârya

Shivâchârya was born in Kanchi to the Pujâri of Kumârgoshta Temple, Kâlathiappa Shivâchârya. Later on he took the post after the death of his father. He translated *Skandpurânain* Tamil in ten thousand verses.

(g) Kumâr Gurupar Swâmi

Gurupar Swâmi was born to Shanmunashikhâ Mani Kaviyya in Ahawar Tirunagari. He got revelation in Tiruchandur. And he recited to God *"Kandar Kalivenwâ"* which is hymn to Lord Subramanyam. His other poetical workd include: *Minâkshi Ammo Pillai Tamil; Kovai; Kalambakam; Nannendi and Niti Nari Vilakkam.* He went to Kashi and established his hermitage in Vanârasa. He was the disciple of Mâshilâ Mani Deshikar.

Among the others are: Tewâram; Tiruwâchakam; Tiruwâyurmoli; Tiruppugal; Arula Nandi; Marai Gyân Sambandh; Umâpati Shivâchârya;

32. Guru Nânak Devaji

Guru, Âchârya, Preceptor Sant Nânak Deva was born to Bedi Kâluchand Patwâri at Talwandi of Raibhoi, the present Nânakânâ Sâhib on Vaishâkh Sudi Dwitiyâ Samvat 1526. He gave the concept of Sikhism and became the light for millions of people with his practical teaching.

The greatness of the great Sant lies in the fact that he combined the four *Varnas, Brâhmin, Kshatriya, Vaishya*, and *Shudra* in one *Sikh*, (Disciple) and created one society out of the various smaller divisions. He declared One God, and called him with different names: *Ek Omkâr*, *Wâhe Guru, Sat-Guru, Hari, Râma*, and others. He worshipped the *Nirguna* Form of the Brahman, the God without Qualities.

Guru Nânak led a saintly life. He taught the people in unique way with songs and example and won them with inner moral character and pious deeds. He said that the power of ethical earning and moral deeds helps one in distinguishing between good and bad; virtue and vice; and agreeable and disagreeable. He ordered his disciples to prefer **Nâm-Jap**; *binu harinâm kou mukuti na pâwasi dubi muye bin pâni* (None can get salvation without chanting the Name of the Lord, Harinâm.) to spend a reasonable part of their life in serving others, and to depend on truth and earning through right means for livelihood and fostering the family. He advised them to spend a part of their earning in charity.

He arranged *Langers* (free-food), and advised others to do so and made it compulsory for all to eat together wiping out the ego; and the feeling of rich and poor; high and low; and young and old. It was his clear advice to nip in the bud the sins that tried to raise their head; to feel that the height of success on the strength of character; and to wipe out lust and such feelings.

His teachings united the people and gave them immense power that a few people were able to complete the works of many with ease, pleasure and in time. That is the beauty of inner strength and confidence. One reason behind his immediate acceptance was the fact that he taught the people in their language. It had instantaneous mass appeal.

Nânak had the sublime spiritual element in his mind since his birth that showed during his childhood and got complete expression in many ways and at many places. They are interesting stories and all the places related to those incidents have become places of Pilgrimage for all in general and for the Sikhs in particular.

Nânak could not get to these facts easily. He took four long journeys both in terms of time and the distance covered. These journeys are known as *Udâsies*. During these journeys Nânak both learnt from others and taught others. It was reciprocal, and hence he was able to make disciples and create many home-like places in distant part of the country.

Like Kabir Guru Nânak also thought a devotee to be a beloved and the God, a Lover or the Husband:

Barasu ghanâ merâ manu meenâ;
Amrit bunda suhâni hiyarai
Guri mori manu Harirasa leenâ.

What a grand description Nânak has presented in one of the verses of celestial *Ârati*; the sky is the dish, the moon and the sun are *Deepa*, the lamp; the stars are the pearls; the fragrant wind is the *Dhoopa*; the blowing air is the fan, and the Cosmic sound is the music. They are readily worshipping the Infinite Lord:

Gagan mai thâli ravi chandu Deepak bane târikâ mandal janak moti;

Dhoopu malayânalo pawanu chawaro kare sagal barâi phulanr joti;

Kaisi ârti hoti bhavakhandanâ teri ârti;
Anhatâ sabad bâjant bheri.

Guru Nânak departed for the Heaven on the Âsoja Sudi Dasami Samvat 1596 at the age of 70 years and four months but his body disappeared replaced by flowers which was divided among his disciples for separately burning and cremation.

33. The Sants of Sikkhism (Shikh-Gurus)

(a) Guru Nânak Devaji

His life and works are given elsewhere.

(b) Guru Angad Devaji

Originally, he was Lahanâ, a businessman. On the way to Jwâladevi Pilgrimage he met Guru Nânak in 1589 and became his disciple. He was made the Guru in Âshâdh samvat 1596.

(c) Guru Amardâsji

At the age of 60 Amardâsji heard a shabad from the wife of his younger brother Amaroji, the daughter of Guru Angaddeva.

He came to him and became his disciple. He was given Guruship on Vaishâkh Tritiyâ, Samvat 1609.

(d) Guru Râmdâsji

Originally called Bhâi Jethâji, Guru Râmdâs was born on Kârtika Vadi Dwitiyâ in Samvat 1592. He was made the Guru in Samvat 1631.

(e) Guru Arjundevaji

The son of the 4th Guru and Bibi Bhâniji, Arjuna Deva became the Guru in 1638 and started the collection of Verses by different Gurus.

(f) Guru Hargovindji

The only son of Guru Arjun Deva and Mâtâ Gangâji was born in Samvat 1652 and became Guru in 1663 after the martyrdom of the fifth Guru.

(g) Guru Harirâiji

Hariraiji was born in 1686 and became the Guru in Samvat 1701. He was the son of Bâbâ Guru Dintâji and Mâtâ Nihâlkuwariji.

(h) Guru Harikrishnaji

The son of the 7th Guru and Mâtâ Krishna Kuwariji,

Harikrishnaji was born in Samvat 1718 and had to become Guru in Samvat 1723, at the age of five years and three months.

(i) Guru Tegbahâdurji

Guru Tegbahâdur was born in Amritsar to Guru Harigovindji and Mâtâ Nânakiji in Samvat 1689 and became the Guru in 1722.

(j) Guru Govindsinghji

The last human Guru, Guru Govindsinghji was the son of Guru Tegabahâdur and Mâtâ Gujariji. He was born in 1723 in Patna and was made the Guru at a tender age of nine at Ânandpur after the martyrdom of his father.

(k) Shri Guru Grantha Sâhib

Guru Givind Singh declared Shri Guru Grantha Sâhib to be the last Guru. From then on the Sikhs treat it to be their reverend Guru. They prostrate before it, sing its songs and follow its teachings. It includes verses composed by all the famous saints of the time.

34. Sant Pipâji

Sant Pipâji was a king in Râjasthân, and an ardent devotee of Shakti. Once, some Vaishanavas stayed with him but they were not treated well. They prayed to Universal Power Mâ Shakti who appeared in the dream of Pipâji to teach him a lesson. She showed him the Oneness of the Creator and the sense of duality and division disappeared from his mind. He decided to go to Kâsi and become a disciple of Shri Râmânandâchârya. He met him but he did not receive him well, instead, he said, "We are *Samyâsis*. We don't need the lustful and luxury loving kings among our fold. We like to see only *sâdhus*."

Pipâji was determined. He returned back to become his disciple as a *sâdhu*. Now the Âchârya was in a fix. In order to test his sincerity he asked him to jump into a well. He would get God there. Pipâji went directly towards a well and was about to jump in when at the instance of the guru his disciples stopped him and brought Pipâji to him. Pipâji was accepted as a disciple. He invited his guru to come to his kingdom Gâgaronagarh in Râjasthân. The guru accepted. After a few years the guru, along with a host of disciples, reached Gâgaronagarh and was given a royal reception. As the news had spread out so people from different parts of the region came to see and listen to him. He stayed there for about a month and when he was to return back Pipâji accompanied him as a Samyâsi. It became a problem when all his one dozen queens also tried to go with them. Eleven of them were pacified and asked to return to the palace but one was rigid to go with them. Âchârya asked her to accompany them naked and she agreed. It is said that the queen remained with Pipâji till the end. She herself became a Sant and a part of all the incidents of his life.

He remained at Dwârakâ for a long time then returned back to his kingdom and started living in a cave. That place is still there. A temple has come up and a fair is held every year. People come there to take holy-bath.

From that place Pipâji taught people, arranged free food, changed the kings to rule according to the scriptures. His life is full of strange incidents. He met Lord Krishna twice: once when the couple jumped into the sea to see him. They remained in the sea for a week. They saw Krishna and Râdhikâ who gave him something like a stamp that had celestial power to purge the people and free them from the worldly ties.

He departed from the world but left his mark as a social reformer.

35. Bâbâ Lâl Dayâluji

Yoga Siddha Sant and Brahman Gyâni, Bâbâ Lâl Dayâluji had his Matha in Gurudâspur district of Panjab near Bâtâlâ at Dhyânpur. It is a pilgrimage and two big fairs are arranged every year one on *Vaishâkhi Dasami* and the other on *Vijayâ Dasami*.

Bâbâ Lâl Dayâluji was born on Mâgha Shukla Dwitiyâ in Vikram Samvat 1412 to a Kshatriya Bholânâth and Krishnâdevi. He lived for three hundred years with the Yogic Science of rejuvenation, and departed from the world in 1712.

Bâbâ Lâl Dayâluji finished his education at the age of 8. Two years later he met Swâmi Chaitnyadevaji and decided to become a Samyâsi. He went to Mathurâ, Vrindâvana and Kâshi in search of a competent guru but was not satisfied; but he met the same Swâmiji at the bank of River Airâvati near Lahore and became his disciple. The guru taught him Siddhies like Animâ etc but he was not satisfied then he was given Brahman-Gyân; and he realized that there is no difference in a living being and Lord Shiva. The God is in the living beings. We all possess Him:

Mana nishchal âtama gati hoi;
Jiva shiva mein bheda na koi.

His guru disappeared after giving him Brahman-gyân and the order:

Ab tum âtamrâm pachhânâ;
Bhakt janon ko dijai dânâ.
Karma, bhakti, gyân bistârahu;
Patit jiva ab sabhi udhârahu.

From then on, Bâbâ Lâl Dayâluji, along with his disciples traveled to Panjâb; Gajani; Peshâwar; Surat; Delhi; Kândhâr etc and taught the mass the right way to live and to get peace and salvation.

It is said that Moghal Prince Dârâ Shikoh was impressed by Bâbâ Lâl Dayâluji. He invited him and arranged a grand public meeting when Bâbâ Lâl Dayâluji reached Lahore. There were long sessions of discussions between Dârâ and Bâbâ Lâl Dayâluji. It is published as '*Asarâre Mârphat*'.

Bâbâ Lâl Dayâluji could fly in air; appear at desired place and disappear when liked and he gave life back to dead persons also.

36. Sarvânand Thâkur

Sarvânand Thâkur is a rare Sant that got all the knowledge and siddhies at a very early age, and is claimed by Indian and Foreign Scholars to be still living as he was seen in Champâran about a decade ago. We get a lot of information by two books: *Sarvânand Tarangani* by Shri Shivanâth Bhattâchârya and the other *Shakti and Shâkta* by John Wooddruff. They analyse his early success as the successes of his previous lives and had left his body for meeting Bhagawati at Neelânchala; Vindhyâchala;

Badarikâshram; Gangâsâgar; Kâshi and Kâmkhyâ. It was then that he got everything that he desired in his life as Sarvânand Thâkur.

Sarvânand Thâkur wrote many books but all are not available. Most of his books were related to Tantra-Shâshtra. His book *Sarvollâsa* is available. Two other books the hand written manuscript, *'Nawânha Poojâ Paddhati'* kept in the Raghunâth Matha in Kashmir and *'Tripurârchana Dipikâ'* are said to be written by him.

It is said that a Tapi Brâhmin Vâsudeva left his body and was born as his own grandson as Sarvânand who was given the Mahâmantra and Sâdhnâ-Paddhati by a Tântrik that helped him to see the Devi as blazing light who accepted him as her son and declared that he would get whatever he wished for:

Adyârambh mam twameva niyatah putrah pratigyâ kritâ;
Yasmin yanmanasi twameva kurushe sampâdaniyam mayâ.

The Goddess was pleased enough to show her all the ten forms at his request and created moonlight with her nail and disappeared. From then on, he became quite dumb and moved wherever and whenever he liked but during that period he presented many miracles.

Later on Sarvânand Thâkur came to Kâshi and lived in the Shârdâmatha in Ganesh-gali as Awadhuta. It is also claimed that he visited many pilgrim places and settled in some cave in the Himalayas, unknown to the outer world.

37. Shri Nrisingh Saraswati

Shri Nrisingh Saraswati was born to Mâdhava and Ambâ Bhawâni in Samvat 1465. He was an uncommon child who pronounced AUM just after birth and said nothing other AUM till his Upanayan *Samskâr* (Sacred Thread Ceremony) when he silently repeated the Gâyatri Mantra and then Chanted four Mantras one each from Four Vedas:

Agnimile purohitam.	अग्निमीले पुरोहितम् ।
Ishe twâ.	इशो त्वा ।
Agna â âhi.	अग्न आ आहि ।
Ye trishaptâh.	ये त्रिशप्ताः ।

Much before this wonderful happening, once, he picked up an iron rod that changed into gold. He was accepted as an incarnation of some great Sant and treated like that since his childhood.

Shri Nrisingh Saraswati wanted to leave the house but because of the parents he waited and when his mother gave birth to a twin, he showed his Datâtreya Form to his mother and left home.

Shri Nrisingh Saraswati first went to Kâshi and was baptized into Samyâsa by a very old and able Samyâsi Shri Krishna Saraswati. After that he moved from place to place and showed some miracles.

In Bhilawandi, an ignorant and foolish Brâhmin child was sitting in the Bhuwaneshwari Devi Temple for knowledge. Shri Nrisingh Saraswati gave him *Buddhi Yoga* and wisdom with it.

Shri Nrisingh Saraswati remained for 12 years at the Pancha-Sangam of Shivâ, Bhadrâ, Kumbhi, Bhogâwati and Saraswati rivers, at the garden of Narsovâ. To free a poor Brâhmin from the curse of poverty he pulled out with roots a creeper from his hut and he got immense wealth from under it.

In Shirol he freed a Brahmarâkshas who used to kill the children of a lady near his abode. From there on her children survived.

The list of the miracles shown by Shri Nrisingh Saraswati is long and includes making a dried buffalo give milk; giving life to a husband of a sincere wife; curing diseases; to give son to a sixty year old lady; to make a pauper feed one thousand persons;

to show the *teerthas* without going there; and to beg from different houses at one time are all described in detail in the book named '*Shri Guru Charitra*'.

Shri Nrisingh Saraswati left this word in Samvat 1515.

38. Sant Narasi Mehtâ

Sant Narasi Mehtâ was born at Junâgarh in Kâthiwâr state in a family of Nâgar Brâhmin. He is honoured as the greatest devotee of Lord Krishna from Gujarât region. His verses are sung with honour everywhere in the country. One of his verses: *Vaishanava jan to tene kahiye je peera parâi jâne re*; was the favouite *bhajan* of Mahâtma Gandhi and is sung everywhere. The song is a touchstone of *Vaishanavism*.

During his childhood, Narasi Mehtâ got associated with some sâdhus and turned towards Shri Krishna and started giving more time to bhajan-kiratan and less time to domestic affairs. One day, the wife of his elder brother challenged him to go to Lord Krishna and meet him. It pinched him sharply. He felt intense pain and went to the temple of Mahâdevaji and started worshipping him. Shivaji was pleased. He appeared before him and as wished by Narasi Mehtâ he took him to the abode of Krishna and showed him the *râsa-lilâ*. He had met his Lord, so he returned home and started living separately. But there was no change in his routine.

Sant Narasi Mehtâ had firm faith in Krishna and was sure that the Lord will fulfill all his needs and desires. The Lord reciprocated.

At the time of the marriage of the daughter of Sant Narasi Mehtâ Lord Krishna brought everything needed and stood near the *mandap* to supervise everything.

Again at the time of the marriage of the son of Sant Narasi Mehtâ the Lord did everything and it was completed without any problem.

The people of his caste ordered him to perform the Shrâddha of his father and arrange a feast at that time. Sant Narasi Mehtâ agreed but had nothing for the ritual or the feast. He prayed to his Lord and everything was fulfilled. At the time when the feast started, shortage of ghee, refined butter, was detected. The sant took a pot and went towards the market to purchase ghee. On the way, he met sâdhus who requested him to sing bhajans. He started singing bhajans and forgot ghee. The feast started. Lord knew where was Narsi Mehtâ and what was he doing? He came up with ghee in the guise of his devotee and served the people.

The Sant returned very late with the ghee and begged his wive's forgiveness. She looked at him in bewilderment as she had seen him serving the people.

Once, Rao Mândalika of Junâgarh challenged Narasi Mehtâ "If you are a true devotee then place a garland to Lord Krishna and ask him to garland you with it." He accepted the challenge, placed the garland on the neck of the idol of Lord Krishna, sat down and started singing his devotional songs. In the presence of thousands of people, after a few hours, the still idol started moving, came up to Narasi Mehtâ and garlanded him.

After the deaths of his wife and the son, he started teaching people devotion towards the Lord. The people from distant places used to come to listen to him. He was popular and honoured.

The following is his most popular Bhajan, devotional song:

Vaishanava jana to tene kahiye je peera parâi jâne re;

Par dukhe upakâr kare to ye, mana abhimân na âne re. (Refrain)

Sakal loka mâ sahune bande, nindâ na kare keni re;

Vâcha kâchha mana nischal râkhe, dhana-dhana janani teri re. (Refrain)

Sama drishti ne trishnâ tyâgi, para stri jene mâta re;

Jihwâ thaki asatya no bole, par dhan nava jhâle hâth re. (Refrain)

Moha-mâyâ vyâpe nahi jene, dridha vairâgya jenâ mana mâ re;

Râma nâm soon tâli lage, sakal teerath tenâ tan mein re. (Refrain)

Vana lobhine kapat rahit chhe, kâma krodha niwâryâ re;

Bhane narasaiyon tenu darasana karatân, kula yekotera târyâ re. (Refrain)

39. Sant Goswâmi Tulasidâs

Indian people and Indian society always boasts of numerous sublime and divine souls that have guided it (them) during crisis and saved the life, society and culture during the past; and that still there are numerous people that are silently, diligently and intelligently; and with pious intentions working hard to keep the culture and tradition intact.

Sant Goswâmi Tulasidâs was one such great, pious and divine soul who along with other bhakt and Sant poets and religious leaders rejuvenated and united the society under One Supreme God, Râma and saved the country from accepting the demonic ways of living and worshipping. Along with other Sant-Poets, Sant-Singers and Sant Teachers he gave faith and confidence to the people, and filled them with the belief that

Râvans are to be killed for establishing peace and equality. The victory of Truth and Pious Deeds over tyranny and oppression is a certainty. It all came with devotion.

What is miraculous about the Sants? It is the fact that they presented all the facts and facets of the Eternal Human Religion at different places and in different ways. It was not an organized effort. They knew that the whole country with different cultural milieu, geographical set, variety of products, food and ways of living cannot be tagged in one particular way. With devotion as the undercurrent uniting force they rose from all corners of the country with one way of devotion or the other to give the lasting impression in the mind of the simple and general public; that Eternal Religion possesses all: Brahman, the Nirgun God, the God without Qualities; Trinity, Brahmâ, Vishnu and Mahesh, the Gods with Qualities; 9 Incarnations of Lord Vishnu; The Goddesses of Power, Energy, Wisdom, Prosperity, and Ganesh, the Lord of Auspiciousness; and left the option on the people to opt for this and that. They clearly indicated that all are one, and all the paths lead to Prosperity, Peace and Salvation. It is the inner strength that counts at the end and survival depends on that inner strength, tolerance, sustenance, contentment, compassion and cooperation. They taught them all and showed everything.

It would never have been possible with One God or one Sant or one way as the attacks were coming in vehemence, on everything and from every direction. Thus, they saved virtually all. The contribution of the Sants and Tulasidâs among them should be analysed, gauged, judged and praised on that line. They gave Faith; Hope; Devotion; Penance; Patience; Tolerance and Morality that proved magical and miraculous panacea. They knew and said with certainty and confidence that without inner strength it is impossible to survive.

Tulasidâs was born and grew in that milieu, watched and read it well, drew his conclusion, grew in strength, became a stern devotee and **shared everything with the Mass in their language, vocabulary and phrases. Side by side, by composing lyrical shlokas and strotras he established his knowledge and scholarship so that the people should realize that the conclusions are coming from a seasoned and mature person of over 70 and not from a nouvice.** Tulasidâs succeeded in his pious effort.

Tulasidâs was born on *Shrâvan Shukla Saptami* in Samvat 1554 in the family of a Saryuparin Brahmin at Râjâpur in Bândâ district. Pt. Âtmârâm Dubey was his father and Hulasi his mother. He was born with all the thirty-two teeth in his mouth in an inauspicious constellation so he was rejected by his parents, as there was danger on them. Tulasidâs departed from this world at the age of 126 years on the same tithi, *Shrâvan Shukla Saptami* in Samvat 1680.

On *Jyeshtha Shukla Trayodashi* he was married to Ratnâ (at certain places the name is given as Buddhimati.) Young Tulasi was inundated in the love of his wife and when she returned to her parents, he went to meet her during a dark night. He caught up a snake, thinking it to be a rope and climbed up to her window. She chided him, "The love that you are showing to this mortal body if you show half of it to Lord Râma, you can get salvation."

Hâra mânsa ko deha mam, tâpar jitani preeti;
Tisu âdho jo râma prati, awasi mitihin bhawabhiti.

It worked like magic on Tulasidâs and he immediately returned back. He left his home, went on pilgrimage, traveled to Jagannâth, Râmeshwaram, Dwârakâ; and Badarinârâyan on foot. He saw the country, came to know of its problems and thought out the solution. He became a disciple of Narahari Dâs.

It is said that after a long time his wife sent him the following couplet and he replied her in the same vain.

Kati ki khini kanak si, rahati sakhin sang soi;
Mohi phate ko daru nahin, anat kate dar hoi.

The reply by Tulasi:

Kate eka raghunâth sang, bândhi jatâ sir kesh;
Hama to châkhâ pema-rasa patni ke upadesh.

It was almost the end of their relation but it is said that at the fake end of his life he reached the place of his in laws by mistake. He did not remember it. But his wife recognized him and came before him next day in the morning. Knowing that he was at a wrong place he immediately left the place.

The spiritual life of Tulasidâs started with the encounter with a Spirit (Preta) that was pleased with him. When he ordered Tulasidâs to ask for something, he used it in the best way possible by asking him to give him an opportunity to see his God, Râma. He did not do that but gave him the way. He said that Hanumân comes to listen to Râma-Kathâ at the temple. He comes first and goes last. With only his grace you can see Râma.

Tulasidâs was pleased and followed the direction. Hanumân was pleased with him and asked him to go to Chitrakut. Tulasidâs went there and after waiting for some time, he saw Râma and Laxman riding on horses.

On a *Mouni Amâwasyâ* Tulasidâs was preparing sandal paste at Chitrakut. Râma appeared there. Tulasidâs lost himself in Râma yet he was conscious enough to anoint him with sandal:

Chitrakut ke ghât par bhaye santan ko bheer;
Tulasidâs prabhu chandan ghisen, tilak leta raghuvira.

Tulasidâs faced many problems while composing the great epic poem; even the manuscript was stolen. It is said that Râma and Laxman stood guard during the nights to protect Tulasi and his work.

He was such a great devotee of Râma that once he refused to bow before and salute Shri Krishna saying:

Kâ baranau chhabi âpa ki, bhale bane ho nâth;
Tulasi mâthâ tab nawe, dhanush bâna lewa hâth.

It was the greatness of God and the success of Tulasi that Krishna appeared before him as Râma.

Tulasidâs first composed hymns, prayers and devotional songs in praise of Shri Râma and completed many books. Then inspired by Hanumân he started composing an epic on the life of Râma, called *'Râma Charit Mânas'* and completed it in two years, seven months, and 26 days. He did it when he was mature and sure enough to complete it. The biggest of Hindi and the most popular book in India: at once, social, political, spiritual and religious in nature, was completed under odds.

Once, Tulasidâs blessed a widow whose only son had died and the boy got his life back. The news came to the Bâdshâh. He called him and asked to show some miracles. Miracles don't occur every time and everywhere, so, they are called miracles. To be rare is the condition of miracles. Tulasidâs declared that he knew no miracle. He was only a devotee of Râma. The Bâdshâh was angry and put him in jail. In the jail, Tulasi prayed to Hanumân. He could do nothing else. Suddenly, hundreds of monkeys attacked the palace and started causing damage everywhere. The Bâdshâh begged his pardon and released him.

Sant poet and one of the nine jewels of Akbar, Rahima Khânkhânâ was very friendly to Tulasidâs. Once, he came with a message of Akbar to join his court as another jewel. Tulasidâs refused on the ground that he was a servant of Râma, he could not accept the service of any one else.

Tulasidâs composed many books; some say 12, others 24 but in the Sâhitya Kosha Volume 2 published by Gyân-Mandal, Vârânasi the following 39 books have been claimed to be written by Sant Tulasidâs, but they too say that only the first 12 have air-tight proofs that they are the creations of Tulasi. The authorship of the rest of the books is debatable though they are popular as the compositions of Tulasidâs.

The fact is, that Tulasi must have written many things in order to have good practice and elaborate grasp of the subject matter before he ventured to compose an epic at the age of more than 70. He completed it within three years but he lived for another fifty years. During that long span he sang in loneliness, before his God, in the congregations and with the Râmalilâs that were being popular at that time. The collected and total effort cannot be less than the thirty-nine books that have been composed by him. He must have composed many things on the demands of the people or the need of the time. In any case, the following is the list of all those 39 books:

S.N.	Granthas	S.N.	Granthas
1.	Râmalalâ Nahachhu	21.	Bharat Milâp
2.	Râmâgyâ Prashna	22.	Vijaya Dohâwali
3.	Jânaki Mangal	23.	Brihaspati Kând
4.	Râmcharit Mânas	24.	Chhandâwali Râmâyana
5.	Pârvati Mangal	25.	Chhappaya Râmâyana
6.	Geetâwali	26.	Dharmarâi ki Gitâ
7.	Krishna Geetâwali	27.	Dhruva Prashnâwali
8.	Vinay Patrikâ	28.	Gitâ Bhâshâ
9.	Barawai Râmâyana	29.	Hanumân Strotra

10.	Dohâwali	30.	Hanumân Châlisâ
11.	Kavitâwali	31.	Hanumân Panchak
12.	Hanumân Bâhuka	32.	Gyân Deepikâ
13.	Vairâgya Sandipani	33.	Râma Muktâwali
14.	Satasai	34.	Pada Bandha Râmâyana
15.	Alkâwali	35.	Rasa Bhushan
16.	Kundaliyâ Râmâyana	36.	Sâkhi Tulasidâs ki
17.	Bajaranga Vâna	37.	Surya Purâna
18.	Bajarang Sâthikâ	38.	Tulasidâs ki Vâni
19.	Sankat Mochan	39.	Upadesh Dohâ
20.	Satbhakt Upadesha		

The place, where Tulasidâs resided at Kâshi is at present famous as Tulasidâs Ghât. The idols of Râma called 'Râmapanchâyatana' and the idol of Hanumâna placed on *Beesâ-yantra* by Tulasi are still there and worshipped. A part of the boat used by Tulasidâs, his wooden slipper called *charan-pâdukâ* and parts of his hand written manuscript are still kept safe for the posterity. Todarmala, another jewel of Akbar was a disciple of Tulasidâs. There is a very ancient painting available in which Todarmala is serving his guru by fanning him. The temple of Hanumân that Tulasidâs got constructed is now famous as '*Sankat Mochan*'.

The works of Sant Goswâmi Tulasidâs are representative creations of a variety of writing. *Râmcharit Mânas* belongs to the '*Chaupâibandha* tradition' in which the *dohâs*, *Sorathâs*, *Harigitikâ* and other meteres are surround or boundeded by a *Chaupâi*, Quartet. All the songbooks related to marriages; for example *Râmlalâ Nahacchu*; *Jânaki Mangal* and *Pârvati Mangal* have been composed in *Sohar*, a method of singing very popular among the ladies even today. *Gitâwali* and *Vinaya Patrikâ* are collections of short lyrics. *Kavitâwali* is presented in *Kavitta* and *Sawaiyâ. Dohâwali* is a collection of couplets; written from time to time and scattered around. *Vinaya Patrikâ* presents both prayers and teachings:

Man pachhitaihen awasar bite.
Duralabha deha pâi hari pada bhaju, karam vachan aru hi te;
Sahasbâhu, dasvadan âdi nripa bache na kâla bali se;
Ham-ham kari dhana-dhâma sawânre, anta chale uthi rite;
Suta vanitâdi jâni swâratharat, na karu neha sabahi te;
Antahi tohe tajenge pâmar! Tu na taje abahi te;
Aba nâthahi anurâga, jâgu jada, tyâgu durâshâ ji te;
Bujhai na kâm agini tulasi kahu, vishaya bhoga bahu ghee te.

Sant Goswâmi Tulasidâs truthfully prayed to Râma that he had no other wish. He wished only for complete devotion towards Him. He knew his heart and by giving extreme devotion He should free his heart from sex and other maladies:

Nânyâ sprihâ raghupate hridaye asmadeeye
Satyam vadâmi cha bhwân akhil antarâtmâ;
Bhaktim prayachha raghupungachha nirbharâm me
Kâmâdi dosha rahitam kuru mânasam cha.

As answer to the questions of Garuda Sant Goswâmi Tulasidâs has given a great piece of advice and in the process clearly indicated the qualities of Sants:

Nar tana sam nahi kawanau dehi;
Jiva charâchar jânchat tehi.
Naraka swarga apbarga niseni;
Gyân virâga bhagati subh deni.
So tan dhari hari bhajahu na je tana;
Hohin vishaya rata mand-mand tara.
Kânch kirisha badale te lehin;
Kar te dâri parasa mani dehin.
Nahin daridra sam dukha jaga mâhin;

Sant Milan sam sukha jaga nâhin.
Para upakâr vachan mana kâyâ;
Sant sahaja subhâva khagarâyâ.
Sant sahahin dukh par hita lâgi;
Par dukha hetu asanta abhâgi.

The greatest quality of Sant Goswâmi Tulasidâs is that he is as interesting to an ignorant person as to a great scholar. He has collected and expressed all sorts of ideas for all types of men in the society. Tulasi has left nothing out and has ignored none.

40. Meerâbai

Even after so many centuries Meerâbai is popular all over the world as the greatest devotee of Shri Krishna and the disciple of Raidâs but very few people know that she was the daughter of Rathore Ratan Singh of Meratâ; the grand daughter of Rao Dudâji and great grand daughter of Jodhâji who laid the foundation of and established a world famous city 'Jodhapur.'

Meerâbai is said to be a very close friend of Shri Krishna in her previous life that took birth in Chokari village in Samvat 1573. The claim holds water, as it seems that Meerâbai was born only to show the intensity of love and explain the meaning of love to the world, though, the world learnt least and turned towards physical pleasure. The world foolishly claims physical pleasure to be the meaning, essence and aim of love. It is not. It can't be so for 'love is not love that changeth when changes find'; it's the pole star that is fixed in the north. The western world has forgotten even this great sonnet by Shakespeare. Perhaps, the modern world has lost its contact with the reality and truth. The men leaving far away from Nature can never perceive the Truth: Temporal or Eternal.

Since Meerâbâi was in spiritual union with the Lord, so, she could not recognize the worldly relations and did not give importance to them. She was married to Prince Bhojarâja, the elder son of Mahârâjâ Sângâ of Udaipur but she had surrendered to her closest friend Lord Krishna. She was given poison in a drink, she was informed of the poison but drank it knowingly and it did not kill Meerâ. So, in a way, Meerâ was not accepted into the royal family and she did not accept the family. A snake was sent to her in a bamboo box but when Meerâ opened the box, it turned into a stone-idol of Shâligrâma. She played with it. The Lord saved her at every step. Nothing could bring her harm. Her husband died and she was free. She left the palace. The Krishna Temples became her home; her friends and she moved with the Sants and Bhakts and composed verses, mostly hymns and love-songs for Krishna. She sang them in ecstasy. It was not an ordinary love and Meerâ was not an ordinary human being: *paga ghungharu bândh meerâ nâchi re.*

She accepted Sant Raidâs as her preceptor, and kept on composing songs for her Lord. They are included in *Narasiji kâ Mâyarâ; Govinda Tikâ; Râma-Govind* and *Râga Soratha.* She saw in her heart and found Krishna there. She has described Krishna from that replica. She clearly stated that though she was bought by her Lord, yet people thought and said that she has lost her way. In one of her verses she has described the hurdles that she crossed over at the palace with the grace of God:

Meerâ magan bhai hari ke guna gâya;
Sânp petârâ unâ bhejyâ meerâ hâth diyo jâya;
Nahâya dhoya jab dekhan lâgi, srâligrâm gai pâya;
Jahar kâ pyâlâ rânâ bhejyâ, amrit dinha banâya;
Nahâya dhoya jab peevan lâgi, ho amar achâya;
Sula seja rânâ ne bheji; dijiyo meerâ sulâya;
Meerâ ke prabhu sadâ sahâi, râkhe bighna hatâya;
Bhajan bhâwa mein magan dolati, girdhar pe bali jâya.

Meerâbâi knew all and perceived all. She was an emblem of love; a living symbol and moving idol of love, dedication, devotion and surrender to the beloved. The presence of or the distance from the beloved had no meaning. Her love lived, it is living; her love was meaningful, it is meaningful. Her love was immortal and spiritual; it is immortal as the spirit of love. The love that Meerâbâi showed never dies; not even centuries after the death of the person and even though, the lover was not a human being but the God:

Baso mere nayanan mein nandlâl.
Mohani murati, sâwari surati nainâ bane vishâl;
Adhar sudhârasa murali râjati, ura vaijyanti mâl;
Chhudra ghantikâ kati tata sobhit, nupur shabda rasâl;
Meerâ prabhu santan sukhadâi, bhakt vatsal gopâl.

Meerâbâi established neither a sect of her own nor joined a particular sect. As a result, she is respected and sung by all the Bhaktas without discrimination. It makes no difference whether they are Krishna Bhakt or Râma Bhakt. She is the emblem of extreme purity and utmost dedication. That is all that the devotees need. She was a lady and free from all traditional and domestic bondage, that is the only reason that she had to bear the tyranny of the royal family.

Meerâbâi announced to her lover Shri Krishna that she had given up everything for him. Now he had to take care of her and save her from worldly disgrace:

Mere to girdhar gopâl dusaro na koi;
Jâ ke sir more-mukut, mero pati soi;
Tât, mât, bhrât, bandhu, apanâ nahin koi;
Chhâr dai kula ki kân, kyâ karegâ koi;
Santan dhiga vaitha-vaitha, loka lâja khoi;
Chunari ke kiye dui tuka, odha linha loi;
Âi main bhakti kâja, jagat dekha mohi;
Dâsi meerâ girdhar prabhu, târe aba mohi.

The verses of Meerâbâi are liquid forms of intense emotions that flow forcefully and beautifully creating devotional ripples and foam continuously. They show concentration and dedication as fully absorbed and submerged in the enormity and infinity of her Master who is the Master of all. Meerâ is often declared as the Râdhâ of the Middle ages but one must keep it in mind that Râdhâ never showed that intensity, and she never broke the social boundaries. Along with the Gopikâs she wept from her place for Krishna but none of them ever stepped out. Meerâ was exceptional and uncontrollable. She was mostly in a state of ecstasy and had love in exuberance. The difference lies in the fact that Râdhâ had spent the years of her childhood with Krishna and knew the pleasure; Meerâ had no such experiences, she only imagined the pleasures.

Meerâbâi knew music. She must have got lessons in music as a princess. All her verses are based on some *râga* or *râgini*, irrespective of the fact whether they are in her mother tongue Râjasthâni or Gujarâti, the language of the place of her exile or in Vrajabhâshâ, the language of the devotional writing on Lord Krishna. They are classical both in appearance and essence. Simplicity, spontaneity, clarity and purity are the qualities of both her self and her songs.

41. Sant Tiruvalluvar

Sant Tiruvalluvar was weaver by profession and resided near Chennai in Mailâpur village. His teachings are called 'Kural' and it is regarded as the Veda in Tamil.

Sant Tiruvalluvar said that:

As there is 'a' (the first letter of Devanâgari Script) among the letters so is the God in the universe.

What is the use of learning? If the learned do not bow to the feet of Sachidânand Bhagawân, and is not blessed by Him.

The devotees of God that reside in the heart of the relatives and friends will always live in Heaven.

Those that sing hymns in praise of the God without attributes, never get pain.

It is impossible to get rid of the anxieties with singing hymns to the Absolute and Incomparable God.

42. Madhusudan Saraswati

Madhusudan Saraswati, whose first name was Kamalaja Nayan, was the third son of Pramodan Purandar of Kotâlpârâ village in the district of Faridapur in West Bengal. He had studied *Nyâya*, Jurisprudence along with a great scholar of Nyâya Shâshtra Gadâdhar Bhatta from Harirâma Tarkawâgish.

Madhusudan Saraswati came to Kâshi and studied Vedânta with Shri Visheshwarâshram daraswati. He did not enter the life of a householder and took Samyâs. He became a great scholar of Advait Philosophy and wrote many book:

Siddhânta Bindu	*Vedânta Kalpa Latikâ*
Sankshepa Shâririka Vyâkhyâ	*Advait Siddhi*
Gurârtha Dipikâ	*Advait Ratna Rakshana*
Prasthân Bheda	*Mahimna Strotra Vyâkhyâ*
Bhakti Rasâyan	*Bhâgwat Vyâkhyâ*

He was not only a scholar but also a devotee of Krishna. It is also evident with his books *Gurârtha Dipikâ* and *Bhakti Rasâyan*. *Gurârtha Dipikâ* is a commentary on Gitâ.

Madhusudan Saraswati composed nice and musical shlokas in praise of Shri Krishna. The following Shloka describes Krishna in all his glory:

Vanshi vibhushita karânnavanih adâbhât
Pitâmber adâruna bimba phala adharoshtathât;
Purnendu sunder mukhâd arvind netrât
Krishnâtparam kimapi tatwam aham na jâne.

Madhusudan Saraswati was an egoist and full of pride. He would prefer to invite debate, defeat the scholars and be pleased with it but the defeated scholars felt pain and were aggrieved. One day, a Paramahans came to him. He welcomed him with respect. When they were alone Paramhans said, "Swâmiji, you feel proud at the defeat of the scholars but with that you commit the sin of giving pain to scholars." It opened his eyes. He became his disciple. He went for penance. After a long and dedicated penance Shri Krishna appeared before him and it is said that he wrote the commentary on Gitâ at the behest of Lord Krishna.

43. Shri Hitâchârya Mahâprabhu

According to the Bhaktmâla written by Shri Nâbhâdâs, Shri Hitâchârya Mahâprabhu was born in a village named 'Bâda' near Gokul in Mathurâ on *Vaishâkha Shukla Ekâdasi* in Samvat 1530 in the morning to Shri Keshava Nâth Mishra alias Vyâsajee and Târâwati; and departed from the world in Samvat 1609 leaving behind a big family with four sons. Every year, even now his birthday is celebrated here ceremoniously.

Shri Hitâchârya Mahâprabhu studied least but showed religious spirit and poetic talent during his childhood. He was declared to be an incarnation of the Flute of Shri Krishna.

Later on he settled at Vrindâvana with his new family and got a temple constructed to establish the idol of Mahâdeva given to him by his father in law. But he remained a true devotee of Shri Krishna and followed the ways dictated by Him.

After getting direct '*darshan*' of Shri Krishna, Shri Hitâchârya Mahâprabhu rejected everything that created a gulf between a *jiva* and the God:

Tanahi râkhu satsang mein, manahi premarasa bheva;
Sukha châhata harinasa hita, Krishna kalpa taru seva.
Sabason hita nishkâma mana, vrindâvana vishrâma;
Râdhâ-vallabha lâla ko, hridaya dhyâna much nâma.

Shri Hitâchârya Mahâprabhu wrote many books. The following books are available:

Shrimad Râdhâsudhânidhi | *Shri Âshâstava*
Chatushloki | *Shri Yamunâshataka Strotra*
Râdhâtantra

Shri Hitâchârya Mahâprabhu propounded the philosophy known as "*Râdhâ-Vâllabhiya Siddhânta.*"

44. Jagannâth Dâs

Jagannâth Dâs was born on *Bhâdrapda Shukla Ashtami* in 1490 AD at Kapileshwar in Orissâ to Shri Bhagawân Dand Padmâwati. It is a very auspicious *tithi* as both Shri Râdhikâ and Bhagawati Durgâ appeared on *Bhâdrapda Shukla Ashtami*. The Vaishanavas treat him as an incarnation of Shri Râdhikâ and the Shâkt treat him as an incarnation of Shri Durgâ.

Jagannâth Dâs showed from the very childhood that *honhâr birwân ke hota chikane pâta*, a strong and healthy tree has smooth and green leaves. His innovative brilliance came to light during his childhood. He finished all the Vedas and Vedângs and other

Scriptures before the age of sixteen. He started reading and telling the stories of the Râmâyana and the Mahâbhârat at that tender age and people from distant places used to come to listen to the stories and discourses that Jagannâth Dâs presented.

Jagannâth Dâs first major work was the translation of Shrimad Bhâgawat into Oriyâ. Once the king Purushottam Devaji called him and made nice arrangement for Jagannâth Dâs to tell the religious and lilting tales of Shrimad Bhâgawat in the southern flank of the Jagadish temple. He took many months to finish the book.

The people realized his revelation when he asked the currents of the sea to remain seven blows away from his hermitage that was in the seabed. It was named '*Sâta Lahari*' from then on. The Prince, Pratâp Rudra Deva became the king and a new hermitage was constructed for him called Oriyâ Matha. It is still there in Neelânchal region.

Shri Chaitanya Mahâprabhu also used to come to listen to the story-sessions and discourses of Jagannâth Dâs, whom he gave all due respect. Once the king requested him to be the guru of the Queen but Mahâprabhu suggested the name of Jagannâth Dâs as the Guru.

Once, the king presented him sandal paste of a very high quality. Jagannâth Dâs immediately started anointing a wall. When asked what was he doing? He innocently replied. "Anointing my Lord Shri Krishna", and lo, the same sandal paste was found smeared on the idol of Shri Krishna.

The king himself announced that once when he was listening to the stories Sant Jagannâth Dâs appeared as Krishna with eight arms.

Shri Jagannâth Dâs wrote many books in Samskrit and many books in Oriyâ. The following are the two lists:

The List of Books in Samskrit:

Krishna bhakti kalpa latâ mâlâ	*Nitya Gupta Mâlâ*
Upâsanâ Shataka	*Prem Sudhâ Ambudhi*
Nitya âchâr âdi dikshopâsanâ Vidhi	*Shri râdhâ rasa Manjari*
Neelâdri Shataka	*Jagannâth Charit Ambudhi Sârani*

The List of books in Oriyâ:

Sholo Cahupothi	*Shaivâgam Bhâgawat*
Shatasanga Varnan	*Gunducha Vijaya*
Goloka Sâroddhâr	*Shri Râdhâkrishna Mahâmantra Chandrikâ*
Adabhuta Chandrikâ	*Neelâdri Chandrikâ*
Puranmata Chandrikâ	*Rasa Kalpa Chandrikâ*
Shrimad Bhâgawat.	

Sant Jagannâth Dâs left his mortal body at the age of sixty but he was often seen at his different favourite places and postures for many more years after his departure. Shri Chaitanya Deva called him 'ativâdi', an extremist and his disciples are still called extremists.

45. Shri Shrichandraji Mahârâja

Shri Shrichandraji Mahârâja was born to Sikh Guru Shri Nânakdevaji and Sulakshanâ Devi in Tâlawandi, the present day Nânkânâ Sâhib, on *Bhâdrapada Shukla* Nawami in Samvat 1551. He had a different philosophy and established '*Udâsina Sampradâya*'. Although, he did not become a Sikh Guru but he was a great Sant that helped the people at different places and in different ways and with his magical words and miraculous deeds forced the Muslim Rulers to sanction concessions to Hindus in worshipping their Gods in their ways.

He was the incarnation of some illuminated soul. People could not come to a conclusion whose spirit he had but it was clear from his birth, as he is said to have born with, *jatâ*, (matted hair or plaits of hair) and *bhasma* (sacred soot). His sacred thread ceremony was held in time and he was sent to Kashmir for study. Within a short period he completed his study; and he became the disciple of Sadguru Awinâshrâmji; and stayed there for some time. Then he started traveling the country. From extreme north he went to extreme south and visited all the places of pilgrimages there. During that journey he showed right path to many and cleaned many sinners. They came on the right track and started leading a righteous life.

After a few years, he returned back to Kashmir and wrote commentaries on Vedas. He got the news that Hindus were suppressed and killed in Peshâwar. He traveled towards Kabul to save them. His memorials there tell the story of his success. Wajira Khân of Kabul became his Bhakt and started singing "*Hey Krishna Vishno Madhu kait bhâre*".

Shri Chandra established a sect called '*Udâsin Sampradâya*'. Many books were written on his life and works: *Shri Chandra Prakâsh; Udâsina Dharma Ratnâkar; Udâsina Manjari* etc. He is mostly associated with Thatatthâ; Vârhata; Shrinagar; Kândhâr; and Peshâwar that remained his abode from time to time.

Shri Chandra had such a control over Yoga that he lived for 150 years and remained young. He never grew old. It's sere wonder in itself! Living in the world for one hundred and fifty years he went towards the caves of Chambâ and was not seen again.

46. The Sants of Ashtachhâp: Devotees of Krishna

(a) Vitthal Nâth and Ashtachhâp

The way that Shri Vallabhâchârya showed gets divided into two. The philosophical branching is known as *'Shuddhâdvait'* and the devotional branching is called *'Pushtimârga'*. The *Pushtimârga* is a declaration of the fact that only because of the endorsement, assistance and wish a living being gets one's cosmic self, the *Brahman Swaroop*. The wish of God was called 'Pushti', endorsement. In the *Pushtimârg* only Lord Krishna, of Gokula is worshipped, particularly in his sweet form of a lover-child surrounded by the Passionate Gopikâs. Lord Krishna possesses infinite beauty and enchantment full of the oceanic currents of pleasing activities. The human soul dives in endless love, plays with the Lord and enjoys the blissful state of the lovely love-land.

There were many Sants and Poets and Sant-poets in the *Pushtimârga*. When after Shri Vallabhâchârya his son Shri Vitthal Nâth ascended his throne, he selected the best eight Sant-poets. They are called the Sant-poets of *Ashtachhâp*. In this way *Ashtachhâp* came into being.

Vitthalnâth organized both the philosophical ideas and the organization that had grown very large and covered most of the important regions of the country.

Vitthalnâth was also a poet but he is mostly known for his other works. Some fifty works are said to be completed by him. The following are the important ones:

1.	Vidwanmandan	9.	Bhakti Hetu
2.	Anubhâsh kâ Derh Adhyâya	10.	Shodash Granth Tikâyen
3.	Bhakti Hans	11.	Shringâr Rasa Mandan
4.	Bhakti Nirnaya	12.	Samskrit Âbhâ
5.	Vishapti	13.	Pada
6.	Nirnaya Granth	14.	Sphoot Strotra
7.	Nibandh Prakâsh Tikâ	15.	Granth aur Tikâ
8.	Subodhini Tippani		

He taught spirituality to Tânsen; Raskhân and Mohan.

There is a story about his end. It is known as *Leelâ-prawesh.* In Samvat 1642, when Vitthal Nâth thought that his work in the world was over he gave seven pilgrimages to his seven sons: Quotâ to Sureshji; Nâthhârâ to Vitthalnâthji; Rankroli to Dwârkâdhish; Gokul to Gokulnâthji; Kâmvan to Gokulchandramâji; Surat to Bâlkrisnaji and another Kâmvan to Madan Mohanji. Then he worshipped Krishna and offered the râjabhoga; and during the noon hours he reached a cave in Girirâj. He placed his rosary on the neck of Gokulanâth and entered the cave. One of his son tried to stop him by pulling his outer garment. He left that and saying to place it on his pyre he entered the cave.

There was a tradition to sing the songs composed by these Sants while worshipping Lord Krishna.

Ashtachhâp

The names of the Sant-poets of Ashtachhâp is expressed in a couplet:

Krishnaji kumbhandâs hain, sur hi permânand;
Nand arjundâs ju, ksheet swâmi govind.

1.	Sant Surdâs	5.	Sant Kumbhandâs
2.	Sant Nandadâs	6.	Sant Chaturbhuja Dâs
3.	Sant Krishna Dâs	7.	Sant Ksheet Swâmi
4.	Sant Permânand Dâs	8.	Sant Govind Swâmi

(b) Sant Surdâs

Sant Surdâs is a very respectable name in the whole of the country in the fields of Religion, Literature and Music. It is a proof of his universal recognition, of his importance and popularity that all blind singers are nicknamed as Surdâs. He is one of the greatest wealth of the Middle Ages. Surdâs is revered particularly for his *'Sursâgar'* that has oceanic width, depth and dynamism in poetic display on the enchanting life of Lord Krishna. He is the leading poet of *Ashtachhâp* and in the *Pushtimârga* his words are taken as its theory. He has become a living and dynamic symbol of deep unconditional love and devotion to the Lord.

From all the available sources the date of the birth of Surdâs was fixed as *Vaishâkh Shukla Panchami*, Samvat 1535. He was born in a poor Sâraswat Brahmin family near Delhi at Sihi. He was blind from the very birth. He was an expert singer and versed in calculating auspicious day and time. He became popular as Swâmi and at a very tender age he went out of the village and started living near a pond. At the age of eighteen he started living at Gaughât between. Âgrâ and Mathurâ. At that place he met Vallabhâchârya and became his disciple, although he had many disciples of his own. After knowing the life and activities of Krishna described in Shrimad Bhâgwat and narrated to him by his guru, he started singing that life of the God. He composed verses on all the 12 Chapters. They are thousand in number and are collected in *Sursâgar*. His Guru appointed him to sing hymn and chant the Name as Kirtan in the temple of Shrinâth at Gokul where Surdâs spent the rest of his life.

He had similar devotion for his guru and God, *bharoso dridh in charanan keo*, I have unshakable faith in these feet. When asked about the deeds of eyes and mind, he recited his two verses to declare his unconditional devotion towards Shri Krishna as if he was himself Râdhikâ. The verses are: *bali bali hon kumâri râdhikâ nand suwan jâso mati mâno* and *khanjan nayan rupa rasa mâte*. After reciting them Surdâs left his body.

The verses of Surdâs show his deep thinking and the power to see through the words of others and exact descriptions of the unseen happening. He had intense feeling and easy perception. His senses were fully alert that made him to describe the beauty of Vrindâvan, Krishna, grazing Cows, the playful Goipkâs and of course, Râdhâ. Since he was blind by birth so he displays childlike innocence, purity, virtuous, simple, emotional, loving and sweet. The beauty lies in the creation of emotional scenes and their exact and fitting descriptions. There are numerous such scenes from the outer world that only a man with clear sight and sharp vision, deep perception and emotional attachment could describe. Surdâs did all these with his blind eyes. He saw them in his heart, through the inner eyes. He must have found the most talked about pair of Krishna and Râdhâ in his heart and felt them playing there. So, he succeeded in describing the actions in minute details.

The wonder grows when he describes the worried mother and the playful child who is totally restless and keeps on doing different things all the times; in the popular verses like *maiyâ mohi dau bahut khijhâo; maiyâ mori main nahi mâkhan khâyo* etc. The spontaneity and correct detail, and creation of ethereal pleasure made the people doubt his blindness by birth and some people claimed that he must have become blind at a later age. Some say that the verses of Surdâs present both the worldly and heavenly truth simultaneously together. The reason may be that he was both a devotee and poet and he excelled in both the fields. The early critics gave Surdâs the honour of being the Sun of the world of literature by declaring '*sur sur tulasi shashi*.'

Another critic declared that there are three great 'Dâs' Sant Poets and Singers in India, Kabirdâs, Tulasidâs and Surdâs; and they represent *Satyam, Shivam* and *Sunderam*; Kabirdâs presented *Satyam*, the Truth; Tulasidâs presented *Shivam*, the Moral; and Surdâs presented *Sunderam*, the Beauty. A verse from Surdâs will show the beauty:

Chakai ri, chali charan sarovar, jahân na prem viyoga;
Jaha bhram-nisâ hoti nahi kabahun, soi sâyer such joga;
Jahân sanak-siva hans, meen, muni, nakh ravi prabhâ prakâs;
Prafullita kamal, nimish nahi sasi dar, gunjat nigam suwâs;
Jihin sar-subhag mukti-muktâphal, sukrit amrit rasa pijai;
So sar chhâri kubuddhi vihangam, ihân kahân rahi kijai;
Lachhami sahit hoti nit krirâ, sovit surajdâs;
Aba na suhât vishaya-rasa chheelar, wâ samudra ki âsa.

(c) Sant Nandadâs

The Sant Poet of *Ashtachhâp*, Nandadâs belonged to Râmpur and was a brother of Tulasidâs; according to '*do sau bâwan vaishnava ki vârtâ*' but '*dohâratnâwali*' claims that he was a cousin. He is famous as a devotional poet. He was devoted to Lord Krishna.

A story runs, that he was infatuated by the beauty of a *Khatarâni* but once he turned towards Krishna he forgot her beauty and remembered only the beauty, personality, love and *keli* of Krishna. It may be a possibility that under the influence of Vallabhâchârya and Krishna, Guru and Govind, his ways and attitude were changed and he got revelation and became a devotee of Lord Krishna that he fostered with spiritual care.

Nandadâs had studied Scriptures and classical books. He knew the classical rules and patterns of composing poetry and he followed them well. His poetical creation is based on the principles of poetry and *pushtimârga*.

His two books: *Râsa Panchadhyâyi* and *Bhawar Geet* are very popular. The first presents the *Râsa-leeela* with Krishna and Râdhâ at the central stage surrounded by the Gopes and Gopikas in and around the beautiful gardens, ponds, village streets and different sites of the bank of the river.

In the *Bhawar Geet* he has presented the victory of Devotion, Bhakti over the *Gyân-yoga-mârg* through the dialogues and discussions between Uddho on the one side and the Gopikâs on the other. It is full of dramatic element and witty comments. The Gopies emotionally answer reasoning of the learned scholar Uddho with clarity, vision and devotional logic. Their dialogues are not the products of books but the expressions of inner and powerful feelings that prove heavier to Krishna's messenger and he returns defeated:

Jau unake guna nâhin, aur guna bhaye kahân te;
Beeja bin taru jamai, mohi tum kahau, kahân te;
Wâ guna ki perchhâh ri, mâyâ darpan beecha;
Guna te guna nyâre bhaye; amal bâri jal keecha.

He gave two more important books *Rasamanjari*, that paints the playful love of Râdhâ and Krishna and *Anekârtha Manjari*, a dictionary. His all other books have the word manjari as for example: *Virah Manjari; Gyân Manjari, Mâna Manjari* and *Rupa Manjari*.

Nandadâs' works present variety and are rich both in quality and quantity. After getting the guru he devoted himself towards it and was successful in producing a lot for the people to follow a literary and religious path.

(d) Sant Krishna Dâs

Sant Krishnadâs was a disciple of Shri Vallabhâchârya and one of the Sant-poets of *Ashtachhâp*. Although, he was a Shudra but he was appointed as the head of the temple. Once, he was angry with him over something and stopped visiting his Guru. Mahâraj Birbala got him arrested and put him into the jail. The Guru freed him and re-established him on his previously held position, the head of the temple.

Krishnadâs has also composed many songs related to the love and playfulness of Krishna and Râdhâ that has been collected in "*Jugalmâna Charit*'. He wrote two other books *Bhramar Geet* and *Prema-Tatwa-Nirupana* but they are not available. He left this world in Samvat 1665 while singing the following verse:

Mo man giridhar chhabi pe atakyo;

Lalit tribhanga chhâl pe chali kai, chibuka chậri gari thatakyo;

Sajal shyâm ghan baran leen hwain, phiri chit anat na bhatakyo;

Krishnadâs kiye prâna nichhâwar, yeh tan jag sir patakyo.

(e) Sant Permânand Dâs

A Kannaujiâ Brâhmin Sant Permânand Dâs lived in Kannauj. He was very dedicated to his poetic creation and showed greater devotion towards Lord Krishna. His poetical creations lulled the listeners to lasting inner silence. It is said that after listening to one of his verses, his guru Shri Vallabhâchârya, remained engrossed in the inner self for many days.

It is said that when he sang in trance, the sweet, mellifluous and lilting song, bâla Krishna would come, sit in his lap and listen to the songs. He saw Lord Krishna in his sublime form and in person. The emotional devotees preferred to sit before him for hours to listen to the songs like the following:

Bahuri hari âbahugo kihi kâm;

Ritu basant aru makar bitite, aru bâdar bhaye shyâm;

Târe gagan ganat ri mâi, vitye châro yâm;

Aur kâja sabahu bisari gaye, hari leta tumhâri nâm;

Chhinu ângan, chhinu dwâre thâdi, ham sukhat hain ghâm;

Permânand prabhu rupa vichârat, rahe asthi aru châm.

(f) Sant Kumbhandâs

Shri Kumbhandâsji lived in Yamunâvat village near Govardhan Mountain. River Yamunâ flowed by the village. He was a farmer and remained busy either in agricultural work or in worshipping Krishna. He was a contemporary of Shri Permânand Dâs. He was completely detached from wealth, fame and respect. It pinched him throughout his life that once he had to go to Fatehpur Sikari, on the call of the Bâdashâh. He sang before him the following verse:

Bhagat ko kahân sikari so kâma;
Âwat jât panahiyâ tuti, bisari gayo hari nâm.
Jinako much dekhe dukh upajat, tinako kariyo paro salâm;
Kumbhandâs lâl girdhar binu, aur sabai bekâr.

He Bâdshâh ordered him to ask for something and he requested that he should not be called again.

Once, Mânsigh, the king of Jaipur came to him and offered bags full of gold and jewels and also a few villages. He refused to take. On the repeated request of the king to give him some order; he ordered him not to come again to him and try to cultivate lust in him. Although he was the Kirtankâr of Shrinâth Temple but he supported his large family with the meager agricultural produce.

Once, he had to go out of Govardhan for some time with the guru. They were on their way to Dwârkâ. He wept because of the separation, as he was unable to see his Shrinâth with whom he used to play. He sang his feelings:

Kite din hwai gaye binu dekhe;
Tarun kishore asika nand nandan kachhuka uthat mukha rekhe.
Wah saubhâgya wah kânti badan ki, kotika chand bishekhe;
Wah chitawani wah hâsya manohar, wah natawar bapu bhekhe;
Kumbhandâs lâl girdhar binu jivan janam alekhe.

The guru ordered him to return back. Before he left the world he composed 500 sweet verses.

(g) Sant Chaturbhuja Dâs

Once the guru said to Kumbhandâs that he had seven sants as his sons. Kumbhandâs said, "I have only one and half." The half was eaten away by a lion when he was looking after the cows of the temple. The remaining one is Shri Chaturbhuja Dâs. The day, a son was born to Kumbhandâs he was playing with Shri Nâth who was with his four arms. So, he named his son as Chaturbhuja Dâs. It may be the grace of the Lord that he became a Sant. Of and on, he would take his son to his God. On the 41st day after his birth when he took him to Shrinâth, He blessed him that he would talk spirituality whenever he wished. The boy started speaking.

Shri Chaturbhuja Dâs was rigid in one thing. He never sang in the absence of Shrinâth. Once the guru ordered him to sing far way from the temple. He said that my one audience Shrinâthji has not come, how could I sing? Gokunâthji said, "He is coming?" The Lord came there to save His devotee from ignominy; and Shri Chaturbhuja Dâs sang: *adabhut natabhes dharen jamunâ tat syâmsunder; guna nidhân giriwardhar râsa rang râche*. It is said that Shrinâth was also eager to listen to his songs.

(h) Sant Chheeta Swâmi

Chheet Swâmi was a rich and indisciplined Pandâ of Mathurâ. Under the influence of Vitthalnâthji he changed and became a calm, cool and tranquil Sant, and from then on he sang only in praise of Shri Krishna. Although, he had gone to deceive him but his look played a miracle and he prostrated before the guru and requested him to take him in his shelter.

His verses are found but there is no collection of his verses. He showed his love and devotion towards Shrikrishna and through him towards the place: (O God! Bless me to live in this Brajabhumi in every life.)

Hey vidhnâ! To son ancharâ pasâri mângaun
Janam janam dije yâhi braja basibo.

Chheeta Swâmi was the only Sant among the *Ashtachhâp* that spent the whole life as a Grihasta. But his songs were so lilting and he performed in such a way that even Akbar used to come in disguise to listen to him. He was the purohit of Birbal.

(i) Sant Govind Swâmi

Sant Govind Swâmi was born in Antari in Bharatpur state. He left his family and started living in Mahâvan. He became a disciple of Vitthalnâth who was so pleased with his art of singing and the poetic quality of his verses that he took him into *Ashtachhâp*. Govind Swâmi sang so well that Tânsena used to come to listen to his songs.

Later on he started living on Govardhan Mountain and planted numerous trees. The garden is still there and famous as '*Govind Swâmi ki Kadamkhandi*'. In his devotional songs he had shown friendship with Shrinâth as he sang for him as Kirtankâr.

His devotion to his Lord was as perfect as to his guru. So, when his guru entered the cave for Samâdhi, Govinddâs followed him and left the world with his guru. It is the only example of its kind

In the following verse he has described the childhood of Lord Krishna:

Prâ samaya uthi jasumati janani giridharsuta ko ubati nahwâvati;

Kari singâr basan bhushan saji, phoolan rachi-rachi pâga banâwati;

Chute band, bâge ati sibhati, bicha-bicha chova argajâ lâwati;

Soothan lâl phoodanâ sobhit, âjiki chhabi kachhu kahati na âwati;

Vividh kusum kimâlv ura dhari, shikar murali benta gahâwati;

Lai darpan dekhe shrimukha ko, govind prabhucharanani sir nâwati.

47. Sant Tyâgarâja

The people forgot the original name of Sant Tyâgarâja. His benevolent deeds and sacrificial attitude earned him a nick name 'Tyâgarâja'. It became his original and only name.

Tyâgarâja is equal to Surdâs, Tulasi Dâs and Meerâbâi in dedication, devotion, teaching, verses, and the ability to sing. Like their poetic creations the verses of Tyâgarâja are musical: lilting, mellifluous, sonorous and captivating. One of his biography-writer has claimed that his aim was to give a height to music. Of course, he gave music a height and depth but only as a means to an end. Complete surrender and total devotion to Lord Râma was his ultimate end. He showed it by clinging to the golden idol of Lord Râma throughout his life and by accepting Samyâs as the right age of 77. He lived eleven years more and departed from the world singing spiritual and devotional song before his Râma at the age of 88.

Tyâgarâja got that golden idol of Shri Râma during the partition in the family. But his elder brother threw it into the flooded Cauveri River. Tyâgarâja jumped into it in search of the idol. He did not think of his life. The idol was the aim. His earnestness gave him success. He found the idol and never parted from it again.

Tyâgarâja had no lust. He had least needs. He never thought of luxury. That is one reason that he refused the King of Tanjore to sing songs in his praise. He declared that he needs no wealth otherwise the golden idol of Râma could fetch enough wealth to live in luxury. Luxury takes away all the strength. It gives no energy. It is a synonym to weakness.

He was completely detached from worldly pleasures and attractions. All his incomparable works and deeds are the expressions and creations of the inner purity that Tyâgarâja possessed and exhibited. His works have the permanent beauty of spiritual life; it has nothing to do with worldly gain and loss. This very sense of the inner spiritual world enriched his work with refined, sensitive, sensible and celestial music and elements. It amply distinguishes him from others.

Tyâgarâja is Tyâgarâja, the king of sacrifices, in the true sense of the term.

48. Shri Dâmâji Pant

Shri Dâmâji Pant was a Subedâr in Mangalverha in the early Vikram Samvat 1600 in Mahârâshtra. It was under Muslim rule and was famous as the 'Bâdashâhi of Bedar'. Although, Shri Dâmâji Pant was an employee of the Bâdashâh but he was a religious, benevolent and a true devotee of Vitthal. It was the time of great famine which continued for seven long years. He had already given everything that he had to save the life of the people. But during the 7th year neither he had anything to offer them nor there was any other source left accept the granary of the Bâdshâh. He thought over it, and ordered the grain to be given to the starving and dying people. He knew, the result was sure death for him, as the Bâdashâh would never tolerate it.

But Dâmâji Pant could not see the people dying, so, he accepted the death penalty. The people were saved with it. The news came to the Bâdashâh. He ordered that Dâmâji Pant be arrested and brought before him. The order was obeyed. The soldiers came and arrested him. He was being brought to Bâdashâh. The night fell. They stayed at a village. The next morning, another order came from Bâdashâh that the price of grain has been deposited in the treasure by his servant 'Vithu Mehar', and that Dâmâji Pant be escorted to his abode with all honour.

When the order came Dâmâji Pant was performing poojâ. When he opened the Gitâ for chanting the Mantras, he found a receipt with the stamp of the Bâdashâh that the price of grain is being deposited. He wondered at it. In the meantime, he got the message.

Dâmâji Pant knew that, it must have been done by Vitthal Bhagawân. He bowed to him and performed the poojâ in full confidence that nothing could happen to a devotee of the Lord.

49. Shri Bhânu Dâs

Shri Bhânu Dâs, a Rigvedi Brâhmin, was a contemporary of Shri Dâmâji Pant. They were the devotees of Vitthal Bhagawân as a tradition of the family. At the age of only ten he went into penance and worshipped Lord Surya for seven days in the basement of a temple. The God appeared and blessed him. From there on he became Bhânu Dâs, and hence his original name is not known.

Shri Bhânu Dâs was forced to enter the cloth-market by the people who financed him. He was so sincere to his work, so honest to his customers and so dedicated to the Lord that within a few years he became very rich. Yet, he was regular with his worshipping and the self-study of the Scriptures, and never failed to worship Bhagawân Vitthal on Ekâdasi of Kârtika.

There is a miraculous story told about Shri Bhânu Dâs. Once, Krishna Roy, the king of Vijayanagaram came to Pandharpur to worship Bhagawân Vitthal. He liked the idol so much that he took it with him and placed in a temple in Vijayanagar. The people sat on hunger strike at the temple but none dared to request the king to return the idol.

Shri Bhânu Dâs announced that either he would bring the idol or give his life. He went to Vijayanagar and reached the temple at around midnight. It was locked but the locks opened. He entered the temple and requested the God to accompany him to Pandharpur. The God placed his nine-jewel-necklace on to the neck of Shri Bhânu Dâs. But he was arrested and in the morning was ordered to be hanged. He sat at the hanging place and called his Bhagawân Vitthal. He went into a trance. In the meantime, the gibbet (the wooden-cross prepared for hanging) changed into a green tree.

The king heard it. He came to the place. He prostrated before Shri Bhânu Dâs thinking him to be a Sant. He enquired into the matter. When he came to know of the real intentions of the man, he arranged a palanquin laden with jewels and sent the idol on it to Pandharpur with Shri Bhânu Dâs. The Ekâdasi of Kârtika was celebrated ceremoniously and is still celebrated with a lot of pomp and show.

It must be mentioned here that the famous Sant Eknâthji is the great grand son of Shri Bhânudâs.

50. Janârdan Swâmi

Janârdan Swâmi, a Rigvedi Brâhmin was born on *Chaitra Krishna Shashti* in Vikram Samvat 1561. He became the Subedâr of Châlisgaon and then of Devagarha that was later on changed to Daulatâbad. The Sultan had a lot of faith in him. He was a politician and a dedicated devotee of Dattâtreya. Because of his influence the markets etc remained closed on Thursday, the day of Bhagawân Dattâtreya.

Janârdan Swâmi was the guru of Shri Eknâth. He declared that there was no difference in Janârdan Swâmi and Bhagawân Dattâtreya. They were one and the same. He got the mystery of Brahman revealed to him by Dattâtreya and he gave it to Eknâth, perhaps his only disciple.

The greatness of Janârdan Swâmi lies in the fact that he achieved everything while leading a life of a householder. He remained a grihastha throughout his life. While in grihastha life he showed such '*ekanista bhakti*', great devotion to one Lord that Dattâtreya was pleased with him and appeared before Janârdan Swâmi to show him the path of salvation.

51. Sant Eknâth

Sant Eknâth was born in around Samvat 1590 as the son of Suryanârâyan who was the son of Chakrapâni and the grand son of Sant Bhânudâs. His parents died when he was only a child and so he was fostered by his grand father Chakrapâni. Eknâth was inclined towards spirituality and chanting the Name and singing songs to God from before the age of six when his sacred thread ceremony was performed. He was given proper education and finished the Râmâyana, the Mahâbhârat and the Purânas. He started searching an accomplished preceptor to know the Brahman only at the age of 12.

It is said that once Sant Eknâth was singing hymns during the fourth quarter of the night in a temple when an airy voice directed him to Sant Janârdan Swâmi. He went to him and served him in many ways. Janârdan Swâmi gave him the responsibility of looking after the account. Once, he remained awake till morning in correcting a minor mistake. Janârdan Swâmi was pleased with him and asked him to show that dedication to Bhagawân Dattâtreya. He taught him and with the grace of Janârdan Swâmi Eknath visualized the God; and later declared that his Guru Janârdan Swâmi and the Lord Dattâtreya are one and the same.

His guru suggested him to worship Lord Krishna and ordered him to go for penance on Shula Bhanjan Mountain. He returned after many years. Then the guru asked him to visit the places of pilgrimage and accompanied him up to Nâsika-Trayambakeshwar. In this long journey Eknâth completed his first book in *Obi-vritta* on *Chatusloki Bhâgawat*. He recited it to his guru in Panchavatti.

He returned back but stayed at the temple of Pippalewshwar Mahâdeva. His grand father came up with a written order of his guru to enter the life of a grihastha after getting married. He obeyed the order and proved to be a very successful grihastha. The most important part of his household life was the fact that everyday many people visited his place and they were welcomed and given food. He had acquired and showed all the qualities of a Sant. There are many stories related to his magical impact on others and of strange acts; and many people changed their way of living after listening to his lectures on Bhâgawat. It includes a prostitute that left her trade, and became his disciple. It is said that once he caught the thieves stealing his articles. He helped them carry those things but it changed their living-style.

Sant Eknâth lived a complete and satisfactory life and left his body at the bank of Godâvari in Samvat 1656. He had announced his day of departure earlier, so there was a great crowd and most of the people were singing hymns and performing religious rituals when he left the worldly abode.

Sant Eknâth wrote many books but the important among them are: *Bhâgawat Ekâdasha Skand*; *Rukminiswyamber* and *Bhâwârtha Râmâyana*.

52. Shankar Deva

Shankar Deva was born to Kusumbar Bhuyân and Satyavati at the midnight of the moonless night of Kârtika on Thursday in Vikram Samvat 1371 in the village Batadravâ in the Naugâon District of Âssâm. He had the body and appearance like Lord Shiva and was called His incarnation. Anyway, he had godly personality and divine attitude. He has been described by Mâdhavadeva, his diciple, in the following words:

Shrimant shankar gaur kalevar, chander yena âbhâs;
Brihaspati sam pandit uttam, yena sur parkâsh;
Padma pushpa sam vadan prakâshe, sunder ishat hânsi;
Gambhir vachan madhu yena srave, nayan pankaj pâsi.

Shankar Deva was such a Siddha Yogi that he would raise his body in air and remain still in sky without any support. He thought and declared that God can't be realized with logic and knowledge we can realize God with devotion in solitude and complete surrender:

Bhâi mukhe bolâ râma, hridaya dharâ rupa;
Yete ke mukti pâibâ kahi lo swaroop;
Pâpa samhârak harinâm mahâbali;
Yâra dhwani suni kampi palâya pâpa kali.

Shankar Deva observed and repeated that the Name of Lord had wonderful and magical effect: incomparable and all-giving:

Param nirmal dharma harinâma kirtan
Te samasta prânir adhikâr;
Yete ke harinâm samasta dharmer râjâ,
yehi sâr shâshtrârth vichâr.

With his knowledge and contribution he is called the father of Assamese literature. At the age of 120 at a green tree he left this physical body. That place, Vatadrawâ, the birthplace of Shankar Deva has turned into a teertha.

53. Bhaktrâja Bheekhajana

The *'Bheekhabâwani'* of Bhaktrâja Bheekhajana is very popoular in Râjasthân:

Manjâi kula bheda rakta kesar prasangâ;
Nâgar beli prasang sahat mâkhi mili angâ.
Kasturi mriga nâbhi, keeta pâtahin kula sohai;
Mani vishdhar upajant, pheema jutani jaga mohair.
Pâras vansh pakhân hai, sankha hâra sab kou kahai;
Hariguna hitawe bheekhajana, jâhin kula kâran chahai.

When Bhaktrâja Bheekhajan was stopped from going in and praying to Laxmi Nârâyan in his temple in Jaipur, he went behind the temple, sat down with the announcement that God will come to show himself he won't leave the place. He went on complete hunger strike. He sat still in single posture without taking food or water for three days. On the forth day, there was a miracle, the back wall of the temple tumbled down and the idol had moved towards bhakt Bheekhjana. The miracle brought lakhs of people to him.

Later on, after the death of Bhaktrâja Bheekhajanan, this incident was inscribed in the front of the temple. It is still there. The last line declares: *apano jana prabhu jâni ke daras diyo muha phera.*

Bhaktrâja Bheekhajana was born at Fatehpur, in Jaipur around Samvat 1600. It is said that he got the grace of God becaue of his deeds of the previous life.

54. Sant Beerbhâna

Sant Beerbhâna is the pioneer Sant of '*Sâdha*' sect. His time is said to be the mid-sixteenth century. His teachings are collected in a book called '*Âdi Upadesh*', which is kept secret by the followers of the *Sâdha* sect for the reasons best known to them but they say that they won't allow the teachings to be known to the followers of other sects. There are his twelve important teachings that they mention: Worshipping of One God; Kindness; Contentment; Frugality; Vegetarian food; one marriage; Non-violence; plain white clothing; etc. They are famous in India and outside for dying clothes.

Because Sant Beerbhâna said so, they treat Sant Kabir as an incarnation of God.

55. Sant Vyâsa Dâsji

Sant Vyâsa Dâsji was a great scholar of Samskrit but most of his works are in *Vrajabhâshâ* as he had turned to a Râdhâ-Vallabhiya devotee from Gaur sect. In this way he became Vyâsa Dâs from Harirâm. Earlier on he was proud of his knowledge and used to challenge the Sants and scholars. Once, he challenged Sant Shri Hita Haribashaji who gave a very polite reply:

Yeh ju yeka mana bahuta thaur kari kahi kaune sachu pâyo;
Jahna tahna vipati jâr-juvati jyon pragata pingalâ gâyo;
Dwai turang par jore chadhata hathi parat kaun pai dhâyo;
Kahidhaun kaun anka para râkhai jo ganikâ suta jâyo;
Jai shri hita haribansha prapanch banch sab kâla-vyâla ko khâyo;
Yeh jiya jâni shyâma-shyâmâ pada kamal sangi dir nâyo.

The words of the Sant shook Sant Vyâsa Dâsji so much from inside that he prostrated before him, requested for forgiveness and accepted him as preceptor. After taking lesson from the guru he came to Vrindâvana, got a temple constructed there and settled for the whole life. He returned the minister of and the Orchhâ king and refused to leave Vrindâvana, announcing that he is a ghost who wishes to get happiness after leaving Vrindâvana:

Vrindâvana taji je sukha châhat te hain râkshas preta;
Vyâsa Dâs ke ura mein vaithyo mohan kahi kahi deta.

Sant Vyâsa Dâsji was born at Orchhâ in Bundelakhand in Samvat 1567. He got proper education and was married but felt the urge and left everything behind. His wife joined him as yogini. He forced her to sell all her ornaments and feed the Sants. She obeyed and remained with him.

Once, Sant Vyâsa Dâsji, broke his sacred thread to tie up the musical bells of the idol of Râdhikâji while a *râsa lilâ* was going on in the temple complex. He declared it to be the best use of the sacred thread as Râdhikâji had participated in that *Râsa-lilâ.*

On another occasion, Sant Vyâsa Dâsji, tried to push into the hands of Shri Krishna an ornamental flute of gold presented by Orchhâ king. It cut the finger of Shri Krishna. Blood oozed out from the idol. He bandaged the bruise with a wet cloth.

He has written a lot, but an authentic list of his books is not available. Among his books '*Râsa Pancha Adhyâyi*' is very popular.

56. Sant Singâji

Sant Singâji was a devotee of Nirguna Brahman, the God without Qualities. He composed about 800 hymns and songs worshipping Him. They are called '*Anahadi Nâda*'. Like Kabir he too preferred pure and sincere love for spiritual realization:

Jala bicha kamal, kamal bich kaliyân, jahna vasudeva abinâsi;

Ghat mein gangâ, ghata mein yamunâ, wahin dwârkâ kâsi;
Ghar vastu bâhar kyon dhundho, vana-vana phirâ udâsi;
Kahai jan singâ, suno bhâi sâdho, amarpurâ ke bâsi.

Sant Singâji was born in the family of milkmen on *Vaishâkha Sudi Ekâdasi* in Vikram Samvat 1576 in Barwâni in Central India. His father shifted to Harasooda with his cattle and other belongings. When Singâji grew young he got the job of a messenger of the Râo Sâheb of Bhâmagarh.

Once, on his way he heard the nirguna bhajan of Manrangiji and became his disciple. He resigned from the job and accepted the new job as the servant of the Absolute Brahman. There is enough of excitement in complete surrender to God.

Sant Singâji knew the meaning of and benefit from sacrifice; and the need of control over the senses for sacrifice. Without control over the body, the physical self, one can't sacrifice the worldly riches for knowing the inner self. There are many tales related to his sacrifices.

Sant Singâji decided to take Samâdhi-alive when his guru was angry with him as he did not awoke him at midnight to worship Shrikrishna and celebrate his birth on the night of *Janmâstami*. He dug out a deep ditch, and descended into it with camphor light in one hand and a rosary in the other.

Now only the songs and hymns of Sant Singâji are left for the people to sing and remember him. They also remember him whenever their cattle are lost. They have the faith and they find their lost cattle. Sant Singâji sang his experiences in his songs:

Rupa nâhi, rekhâ nâhi, nâhi hai kula gota re;
Bina dehi ko sâhab mero, jhila-mila dekhu jota re.

57. Moreyâ Gosâwi

Moreyâ Gosâwi had accomplished all the *Riddhies* and *Siddhies* by worshipping Shri Ganesh. He would live for three weeks at a stretch on only the juice of '*durbâ*', a sacred grass, used in almost all the rituals in India. There are tales that he would sit in one postures for six weeks without moving. He enjoyed great power of penance. As a result, though he meditated in a forest at the bank of Pâwanâ River yet no wild animal or dangerous insect would come near him. People tell the stories that he gave eyes to the blinds and sons to childless parents. In the great tradition of Shri Ganesh he blessed people with prosperity and safety.

Moreyâ Gosâwi was a rare son of rare parents. His father, Wâman Bhatta and the mother Umâbai lived on the left over or fallen grains in fields. They would collect them and prepare food with only that. They got a son very late in their life and named him Moreyâ. They lived for a long time. The father died at the age of 125 and the mother at 105 within a very short period.

Moreyâ Gosâwi went for penance and performed it at three places: Moregâon (his birth place); Thedur and Chinchawad. The last one became his permanent abode as it was very close to an uninhibited forest at the bank of Pâwanâ River.

A poor Brâhmin gave his daughter to Moreyâ and they got a son. They named him Chintâmani.

The only son of Moreyâ Gosâwi is known for the *Brahman Vidyâ* he got from his father Moreyâ Gosâwi. It is stated at many places that Shri Chaitanya Mahâprabhu started calling him Chint Moreyâ Gosâwimani Deva and 'Deva' became the title of the Sants in that tradition.

In the western part of India at many places Moreyâ Gosâwi is remembered whenever the people worship Shri Ganesh.

Seven Sants in the family of Moreyâ Gosâwi known as 'Deva"

1.	Moreyâ Gosâwi	5.	Dharanidhar Mahârâja
2.	Chintâmani Deva	6.	Nârâyana Mahârâja (Junior)
3.	Nârâyana Mahârâja (Senior)	7.	Bâbâ Mahâraja
4.	Chintâmani Mahârâja (Junior)		

58. Bhakt Parameshti Darji

The God has His own system, working, thinking and doing. What we see is called an illusion created by His Mâyâ. That is one great reason that the wisest too have failed in unveiling the whole of the mystery that surrounds one's life. It is difficult to think and talk of the infinite numbers of mysteries in the infinite universe. What a rare co-incidence. A black, hunch-backed tailor was a great devotee of Bhagawân Jagannâth. His physical deformity shaped his inner being in a soothing and sublime way. That tailor had art of embroidery in his fingers and devotion for God at heart. He was not rich but benevolent; he was not strong but kind; he was not spendthrift but charitable. He had imbibed all the virtues. He saw god in all and hence gave utmost respect to one and all. He is remembered as Bhakt Parameshti Darji

Some four hundred years ago Bhakt Parameshti Darji lived in Delhi east. His wife Vimalâ was also pure like her name. She obeyed her param bhakt husband. He was lucky to have an obedient son and two beloved daughters. It was the grace of God that he was happy and satisfied.

Bhakt Parameshti Darji was famous for both his work and his devotion. The rich men, and the members of royal family and occasionally Bâdashâh would take his services and rewarded him amply.

Once, the Bâdashâh called Bhakt Parameshti Darji to his court and gave him a cloth which was specially prepared with thread of gold and embroidered with the pieces of pearl, ruby and diamond. He had ample faith in Bhakt Parameshti Darji. He gave him the cloth and asked him to stitch two pillows for him.

Bhakt Parameshti Darji prepared the pillows. They were amazing and a light was coming out of it. He thought of his God Bhagawân Jagannâth and in that state of trance offered one pillow to his Lord. When he regained his senses he was amazed to see only one pillow. He gave one pillow to Bâdashâh and narrated the story. The king was angry and put him into prison with the comment that only Jagannâth will give him food and release him from the jail.

It is said that Bâdashâh got a dream in the early hours of the next morning. He went to see Bhakt Parameshti Darji in the jail. All the gates of the prison were open and all the guards of the jail were sleeping. When he reached the cell of the Bhakt he was sleeping with ease and was completely free.

They all realized the power of devotion, purity and dedication. He was brought to the court and given suitable reward.

After his release and reward he left Delhi, and was not heard again.

59. Bhakt Kubâ Kumbhâr

It may be a record of some sort for the modern scientist and may be registered into some record book that Bhakt Kubâ Kumbhâr remained alive for one year inside fallen soil and sand wall of a well while it was being dug.

It is all the more important that unlike many learned-saints Bhakt Kubâ Kumbhâr belonged to the group of a few illiterate Sants who are known for their purity, simplicity, honesty, sincerity, devotion and virtues.

Bhakt Kubâ Kumbhâr and his wife, Puri, were very pious and contented souls. They prepared only thirty pitchers in a month and lived on the meager income that they generated with it. They shared a part of it with the guests also but they never complained. Instead, they utilized the rest of time in chanting the Name of God and worshipping Him the way they knew. They had earned fame on that basis.

Once, about two hundred Sâdhus came to that village. They searched a grihastha who could feed them. Some one mentioned the name of Bhakt Kubâ Kumbhâr. They reached his place and called, '*Sitârâma*'. Bhakt Kubâ Kumbhâr came out, realized the need, went to a merchant for loan of adequate food articles for 200 men and promised to repay it by working for him. The merchant asked him to dig out a well in lieu there of. He accepted, took the articles, fed the Sâdhus, and the couple was happy.

Bhakt Kubâ Kumbhâr and his wife had to prepare only one pitcher a day. So, they had time. They started chanting *'Harinâm'* and digging the well. His wife, Puri would carry the soil away. They continuously worked for months. At last, they dug up to the source of water and the water started rising slowly in the well. But the wall had no brick. It was all soil and sand. The wall caved in and Bhakt Kubâ Kumbhâr was crushed inside. His wife, Puri, was at the top. She wept, the people came for help but they realized and announced that nothing could be done. They brought Puri home. She wept and called her God but of no avail. She had to lead a life of a widow.

One year passed. The well became a plain land. Once, some Sâdhus stayed there. They clearly heard the sound and music of bhajan, devotional songs, coming from inside the earth. Throughout the night they sang in accompaniment with the sound coming from the earth. In the morning they told it to the villagers. They could not believe it. They came and heard the songs. They declared it to be the sound of the dead or crushed Bhakt Kubâ Kumbhâr. The news spread fast. People from other places came. The king also came to be a first hand witness to the magical music coming from inside the earth. Puri came and declared the sound to be of her husband. The king ordered to dig the place. Cautiously the work started. The sound grew louder. More men joined and within hours they took off the outer soil.

Then they witness an amazing sight. Bhagawân Hari was sitting and listening to the song that his Bhakt "Kubâ Kumbhâr" was singing. After a few minutes, Hari changed into an idol but there was no change to Kubâ Kumbhâr. He was brought out and Puri again became a married lady. From then on they started their normal work and worshipping.

From that day, the news kept on spreading and people kept on pouring in to see the man.

60. Bhakt Raghu Kewat

Bhakt Raghu Kewat was initially only a fisherman in all respect barring the fact that he did not like to kill and sell the fish. He lived with his wife and mother in Pipalichatti, some 25 kilometers away from famous Jagannâthpuri. Fishing was his traditional profession and that was the only thing he knew. On the other hand his heart was filled up with pity and sympathy for the fish whenever he saw them trying hard to come out of the net or jumping towards water. Their struggle for survival turned his heart sour. He disliked his profession. He would call the Lord, ask for forgiveness and bow to Him. He became a bhakt of Bhagawân Jagannâth, chanted his Name and sang songs in his praise. He wanted to leave the profession but he had no other way.

One day, after a gap of a few days, Bhakt Raghu Kewat went for fishing. He caught a large red fish. When he was taking it out of the net he heard in clear human voice, 'Raghu, rakshâ kar!' 'Ragu rakshâ kar!' (Save me Raghu! Save me Raghu!)

Bhakt Raghu Kewat was amazed at the strange request of the fish and at the human voice. Moreover, how the fish knew his name. At heart he was sure that it was a strange doing of the God. With the fish in hand, the request coming and vibrating in the ears, food for family in the mind and exuberant pity at heart Bhakt Raghu Kewat stood in trance for a moment: still and in trance, thinking nothing, feeling nothing and doing nothing. His senses returned back, he moved a few steps towards the river and put the fish back into water. He felt peace and exuberant pleasure when he saw the fish swimming away from him.

Bhakt Raghu Kewât sat at the bank. He could not decide what to do? He did not know whether he was completely empty or filled up to the brim. He felt satisfied. The night fell and passed. The morning came. He remembered his surroundings, the events of the last day and started chanting the Name of his Lord. He did not move away. He did not think of returning back. He sat and chanted the name. Another night came and passed. Raghu was there at the bank of the river chanting the name. The next morning made it clear that he won't leave the place. He was determined to spend the rest of his life there at the bank of the river. He had forgotten his family, his self, remembered only the God.

Before the next evening, an old Brâhmin came to Bhakt Raghu Kewat and asked who he was? What was he doing? Why was he sitting there? What was his problem?

At first Bhakt Raghu Kewat said nothing but on the insistence of the Brâhmin he declared his resolution that he wanted his God, Jagannâth and nothing less than that would make him move away from the place.

The Brâhmin changed into Chaturbhuja Bhagawân. He bowed to Him. The God asked him to spell out his wishes. Bhakt Raghu Kewat asked for unshakable devotion and got it. He repeatedly saluted the God, prayed to Him and praised Him. The God disappeared. He sat there for a long time. Then slowly he returned home. His life changed from that day. At home he was amazed to know that the Jamindâr had sent many things for their living. Only he knew it was the grace of the Lord. From that day, he did nothing but to chant the name of Jagannâth and moved here and there. The people realized and gave enough to his family for their livelihood. They asked for nothing more. The children declared him mad and made fun of him. He never retorted back. He heard all the taunts but kept on repeating the name. One day, a boy beat him hard with a thorny thick branch of wood. He tolerated the pain and returned home without saying a word. After an hour the boy died. It was surely a punishment. The people came to Bhakt Raghu Kewat. He prayed to Lord and the boy got his life back. It was a miracle that gave him popularity.

Once in a while, when he would get something good he would call Bhagawân Jagannâth and give Him the Bhoga. The Lord would gladly accept what Bhakt Raghu Kewat had to offer.

Once, Bhagawân Jagannâth was in Pipalichatti with Bhakt Raghu Kewat and it was the time of Bhoga at Jagannâthpuri. It was the tradition that the Bhoga was offered to the shadow of the Lord falling in a mirror at Bhoga Mandap. That day, the shadow was missing. The priests wondered. The information reached the king. He was worried. At night he got a dream that showed Lord Jagannâth taking Bhoga from Bhakt Raghu Kewat.

In the morning the king went to Bhakt Raghu Kewat and brought him to Jagannâthpuri along with his family. They were given a place in the temple complex to live. They spent the rest of their life chanting the Name of Prabhu and worshipping Him.

61. Sant Mahâkavi Vidyâpati

One of the great devotees of Shiva and Shakti Mahâkavi Vidyâpati has been kept confined to Maithili Literature although his great contribution lies in Samskrit Literature. Ironically enough, his other creations are not given preference only because of Maithili and a lot is forgotten about him. He has been called a mystic as allegation. Mysticism should be used to praise such great souls. In his writings, Vidyâpati combines *Shringâr* and *Bhakti*; sensuousness and devotion; reality and devotion; rituals and devotion. For these, and various political and social reasons Vidyâpati is often excluded from the list of Sants as he was a *grihastha, râjâshrayi* (dependent on a king), and has praised the kings also. The other reason may be the fact that he was very much attached to worldly life and worldly possessions. Yet he was a great devotee and did everything with the grace of Shiva and Shakti.

Except '*Vidyâpati Padâwali*' all other works of Vidyâpati are in either *Awahatta* or Samskrit. A glance at his works will make many things clear:

1. **Kirtilatâ**: The Praise of Mahârâjâ Kirti Singh in Awahatta.
2. **Kirtipatâkâ**: The Praise of Mahârâjâ Shiva Singh in Awahatta
3. **Goraksha Vijay**: Dialogues in Samskrit and Prâkrit but songs are in Maithili.
4. **Bhu-parikramâ**: The description of pilgrim places that he visited. It's a good book on Geography of India.
5. **Purush-parikshâ**: The Biographies of Historical figures like Harishchandra, Shibi, Pârtha.
6. **Likhanâwali:** A book on letter writing that includes different styles.
7. **Shaiva-sarva-swasâr**: A book on the rites and rituals of Shiva-Poojan.
8. **Shaiva-sarva-swasâr**: A collection of Purâns related to Shiva; and a collection of proofs of the worshipping of Lord Shiva, his God.
9. **Gangâ-vâkyâwali**: Devotional songs in praise of the river Ganges: with the main principles that the Ganges offered salvation to those whom none was able to make free; and the salvations that the Ganges has already offered outnumbers the stars in the sky: *kâhu ne na târe tinhe gangâ tuma târe; jete tuma târe tete nabha mein na târe hain.*
10. **Vibhâgasâr:** A discussion of the parts of 'dâya'.
11. **Dâna Wâkyâwali:** A discussion on Charity.
12. **Durgâ-Bhakti-Tarangini:** The book is related to the worshipping of Mâ Shakti, his Goddess.
13. **Gayâ-Pattalaka:** The rituals and offerings to the ancestors at Gayâ are discussed in this book.
14. **Varsha-kirtya:** It deals with the rites and rituals of all the year long.

15. Mani-Manjari: A short play.

16. Padâwali: Collection of Vidyâpati's verses in Maithili.

It is very popular about Mahâkavi Vidyâpati that Lord Shiva served him as his domestic servant Uganâ. It became clear when he was returning back home with Uganâ from Janakapur. He was tired and thirsty, and so was his horse. He stopped in a forest and asked Uganâ to bring water. Uganâ went away and returned soon with fresh and cool water. Vidyâpati drank it and asked Uganâ: 'Where did you get this water? It is the pious water of the sacred Ganges.' Uganâ laughed and changed into his Lord Shiva. He fell on His feet. The Lord blessed him.

It is also said that since he was Shâkt also so he was non-vegetarian. His king was vegetarian. Once the king visited his abode on the instigation of the competitors of Vidyâpati. The allegation was that he has non-vegetarian dish in his room covered by a red cloth. The king came there, saw the covered dish and asked Vidyâpati 'What is inside that cloth?'

Instantly and confidently Vidyâpati replied, 'Those are the flowers of *Odhawool* for worshipping Mâ Shakti.' The king had definite information. He pulled off the cloth, and Lo! There were only the flowers of *Odhawool* inside. Vidyâpati was saved. He immediately prostrated before the idol of the Goddess to pay his thanks and to offer prayers to her for saving him from sure disgrace. There are many such supernatural events that are narrated about his relation with Shiva and Shakti. He declared: How much can I praise thee? Who can be comparable to you? I feel shy when I try to compare you. *tohe sarisa eka tohi Mâdhava.* You are only like you.

Mâdhava kat tore karab barâi;
Upamâ tohar kahab kakarâ ham
Kahitahu adhika lajai;

Mahâkavi Vidyâpati was born in Samvat 1407 in Vispi Village in the District of Bihar; and departed from the world in Samvat

1507 after leading a life of ups and ups for one hundred years. Some calculate the time of his birth with reference to King Shiva Singh who ascended the throne and declare 1350 to be the date of birth. According to that calculation Vidyâpati lived for 157 years; and died at the bank of the Ganges in 1507. He belonged to a family of learned scholars who were attached to the court of the king because of their knowledge, character, and integrity.

Because of his learning and learned creations he was given the title of 'Mahâmahopâdhyâya Mahâkavi Vidyâpati' He belonged to the great tradition of the Scholars in the region. Happily enough, his descendents are still found. They were living on the mound in Vispi but about hundred years ago they shifted to Saurâtha, famous for Maithil-Marriage-Fair.

Mahâkavi Vidyâpati has also described the râsa-lilâ of Shri Krihna. Incidentally, his description of râsa is closer to that of Jaideva: beautiful, lilting, sensual and mellifluous:

Nava vrindâvana nava nava tarugana nava nava vikasita phool;

Nawal basant nawal malayânil mâtala nava ali kula.
Biharai nawal kishore, sakhi ri, biharai nawal kishore;
Kâlindi pulin kunja vana sobhan nava nava prema-bibhore.
Navala rasâla mukula madhu mâtala nava kokila kula gâya;
Nava juvati gana chitta umatâ yai nava rasa kânana dhâya.
Nava yuvarâja nawal nava nâgari milaye nava nava bhânti;
Niti niti yaisan nava nava khelana vidyâpati mati mâti.

In fact, Mahâkavi Vidyâpati is not a controversial figure; he was a genius that maintained a balance among heterogeneous elements and ideas. Those things are almost opposite in nature and character. He was in the care of a king but he is a poet of the mass; he composed sensuous poetry but is great devotee; he was Shaiva, Shâkt, Vaishanava simultaneously together and yet he was free from religious extremism; he was born and brought up in a cultured, refined, and ethical Brâhmin family yet he was not bound to morality or traditions or traditional rites and ritual; he was a great worshipper and spiritualist yet he enjoyed freedom of speech and attitude; and above all, he was able to move with equal ease and balance on the hard, logical, ethical mârga; and soft, dewy, green path of love and marriage songs of the young boys and girls.

62. Appayya Dikshit

Sant Mahâkavi Vidyâpati was a rasika Sant like Vyâsa Dâsji (Harirâma), the Appayya Dikshit was a Scholar Sant like Vitthal Nâthji. The fact is that Appayya Dikshit was a great Shiva-Bhakt and scholar.

Appayya Dikshit was simultaneously a Grammarian, Philosopher and Poetic genius. He had great command over *Alankârs*, the Figures of Speech.

Appayya Dikshit was born in 1550 AD during the time of Akbar and died in 1622 during the period of Shahjahân at a mature age of 72. Because of his parental heritage and the literary time that he developed into a composite whole. He became a literary class in himself.

The grand father of Appayya Dikshit was a famous Âchârya and was called Âchârya Dikshit. His father was Rangarâjâdhwari. He too was a learned scholar. He got his education from them. It was perhaps easier for him to grow into a devotee and a scholar because of the environment in the family. His family believed in Advait Philosophy that he was taught but he achieved a rare distinction in Shaivite Philosophy and became a staunch Shiva Bhakt. Yet he could not break his relation with Advait Philosophy because of the family pressure and the order of Shri Nrisinghâshram Swâmi that lived at the bank of River Narmadâ.

Appayya Dikshit worked hard for establishing Shaiva Philosophy and gave his first book *'Shiva Tatwa Vivek'*. Then came his three other great books that assimilate the best of Advait Philosophy. They are: *Parimal; Nyâya Rakshâ Mani* and

Siddhânta Lesh. He felt that Lord Shiva and Lord Vishnu are the same entity; and hence was able to maintain a balance between the devotion of the two.

The family of Appayya Dikshit suffered some financial crisis as they were dependent on Krishnadeva, the Mahârâjâ of Vijayanagaram, and he was defeated in Tâlikot battle and replaced by the IIIrd Dynasty. But it improved when Appayya Dikshit grew young and became the court Pandit of the new king Tirumallai and continued to enjoy that status even during the kingship of Chinnatigma and Venkatpati.

Appayya Dikshit has mentioned these and other kings in his books. It is apparent that he was respected by the kings otherwise he would have been replaced by the next king ascending the throne.

It is said that Appayya Dikshit, remained in Kâshi for a long time then returned back to south and when he thought that his end is coming closer he went to Chidambaram and left this world under the feet of his God, Devâdhideva Mahâdeva.

63. Shri Shribhatta Deva

Shri Shribhatta Deva was a gift of a Sant to Târâ Devi and was born in Pingalâ, popularly known as Pâta Bâusi, in the district of Kâmarupa in Âssâm in Shaka Samvat 1480. He showed devotion and other saintly qualities from childhood and due to him Vaishanava Dharma was rejuvenated and spread over the whole of the region. He wrote his books in Âssâmese. They are only four in number: *Bhaktisâr*; *Bhakti Viveka; Sharan Sangrah* and *Dâmodar Vyâkhyân*. His books are the proof of his deep devotion and wide knowledge. His hermitage is still there in Pâta Bâusi but in a dilapidated condition.

The following Teachings of Shri Shribhatta Deva is very popular and has universal acceptance. It is very close and similar to the questions and answers of Shri Shankarâchârya that he has given in '*Prashnottarmâlâ*'.

1.	With what boat we can cross over the worldly ocean?	The couple of feet of the Almighty.
2.	Who is imprisoned?	The person indulged in physical pleasure.
3.	What is hell?	Our body.
4.	What is heaven?	Lack of worldly longings.
5.	What is source of Salvation?	The memory of the Self.
6.	Who throws into the hell?	Attractive woman.
7.	What is the way to heaven?	Practice of non-violence.
8.	Who sleeps happily?	*Samādhinishta*; one that meditates.
9.	What are foes?	Our sense organs.
10.	Who are friends?	Our sense organs under control.
11.	Who is pauper?	That has exuberant lust.
12.	Who is a gentleman?	He who is contented.
13.	What is the resource of happiness?	Detachment from desires.
14.	What is the worldly net?	Affection and pride.
15.	What is enchanting like wine?	A seductive lady.
16.	Who is blind?	One that has passion for sex.
17.	What is death?	Notoriety.
18.	Who is a guru?	That teaches for one's real benefit.
19.	Who is a disciple?	A devotee to guru.
20.	What is the longest lasting ailment?	This mortal world.
21.	What is the panacea?	Ethical thinking.

22.	What is the ornament of man?	Pure and wider attitude.
23.	What should be always taken?	The teachings of guru.
24.	What is the best pilgrimage?	The knowledge of pure elements.
25.	What are the worst things?	Gold, woman and wine.
26.	What are the resources of the revelation of Brahman?	Company of Sants; Contentment, Control over senses, and ethical thinking.
27.	How can we be detached?	Through *Vairāgya*; by relinquishing all.
28.	What is the fever?	The anxieties at heart.
29.	Who is a fool?	That lacks conscience.
30.	What is the main religion?	Devotion to Lord Vishnu.
31.	What is learning?	Accumulating resources for knowing the Brahman.
32.	Who is patient?	That is not attracted by a woman's activities.
33.	What is essence?	The knowledge of Shiva.
34.	Who is the best?	A man with moral character.
35.	Who is handsome?	That possesses knowledge and wisdom.
36.	What is rare in the world?	*Satsang, Sadguru, Sarvatyāg, Ātmabodha* and ideas about Brahman.
37.	Who is an animal?	Displaced from one's religion.
38.	What is sweet poison?	Woman.
39	What is the topic of perennial thinking?	Truth; Self; World and Brahman

64. Sant Dâdu Dayâlji

Sant Dâdu Dayâlji was the devotee of the God without Attributes. His Nirguna Brahman was everything to him. He did not pioneer any Pantha but his teachings to his disciples created a pantha known as *'Brahman Sampradâya'*. But it did not last long and within a few years after the departure of Sant Dâdu Dayâlji, in Nârâyanâ village in Vikram Samvat 1660, it became known as *Dâdu Pantha*, and its followers are found everywhere in the country but they are limited in number.

Once, a Nâgar Brâhmin Lodirâma got a box drowning in the river Sâbarmati. It was *Chaitra Shukla Ashatami* of Vikram Samvat 1601. He opened it and found a smiling kid in it. He brought the boy home. He gave it to his wife who had no child. She was happy and brought up the child with care. The child became famous as Sant Dâdu Dayâlji. He tried to run away from home in order to take Samyâsa but was taken back by the parents and later on was married in Baranagar. He got two sons and two daughters.

It is said that at the age of 11 Lord Shri Krishna had appeared before him as an old man and given spiritual teachings. From then on he longed for the congregations of the Sants.

Finally at the age of 19 he got an opportunity, left his home, came to Râjasthân and started working as a carder in a village named Sâmbhar. The Kâji did excesses towards him and died. After that many other supernatural events gave him the reputation of a Sant and he became Sant Dâdu Dayâlji.

Sant Dâdu Dayâlji went for penance, and meditated over the world and the Brahman for the real knowledge for 12 years and got many Siddhis, supernatural powers but he rarely used them. He was against the use and misuse of the powers that the Lord endowed.

The teachings of Sant Dâdu Dayâlji are very close and similar to that of Sant Kabir. He claimed the showy nature of the ritual and the ways of idol worshipping to be useless.

Sant Dâdu Dayâlji had thousands of followers but only 152 are treated as original and important. Out of that 152 one hundred disciples did not go for hermitage and perhaps they did not make disciples. The rest 52 started hermitage and so were called *'Thambâdhâri Mahants'*. Their main place of pilgrimage is Nârâyanâ village. There is a Dâdu Dwârâ here constructed with white stones. There are Dâdu Dwârâs at other 52 places of the Mahantas also. In the Dâdu Pantha there are Nâgâs also that wear white dress. Others wear saffron (*bhagawâ*) cloths.

Among the 52 disciples of Sant Dâdu Dayâlji the following are very famous:

1.	Mahâtmâ Garibdâsji	8.	Vashanâji
2.	Sunderdâsji (Senior)	9.	Jaimalji Kachhawâhâ
3.	Rajjabji	10.	Jaimalji Chauhân
4.	Jagajivan Dâsji	11.	Jaggâji
5.	Bâbâ Banawâri Dâsji	12.	Jagannâthji Kâyastha
6.	Chaturbhujaji	13.	Sunderdâsji Busar
7.	Mohan Dâs Mewârâ	14.	Jana Gopâlji

65. Sant Rajjab

Sant Rajjab is a famous disciple of Sant Dâdu Dayâlji; and there is a very popular story, how he became the disciple of Dâdu. Once, Sant Dâdu Dayâl was sitting under a tree. A grand bârât, marriage party, flanked by musicians, was passing through that way. Rajjab was the groom and was on his way to get married. When it came near the Sant he recited a couplet. It is a very famous couplet and is often quoted in meetings and congregations whenever the name of Dâdu or Rajjab comes in discussion:

Rajjab tain gajab kiyâ, sira para bândhâ maur;
Âyâ thâ haribhajan koon, karai narak ko thaur.

(O Rajjab! You have done a strange thing. You are ready for marriage, though you had come for chanting the Name of the Lord; and you are making your abode in hell.)

Rajjab came down of the mare, went to Dâdu, touched his feet, sat down by him and decided to become a Samyâsi. Offering his *maur*, (the head gear for marriage) he ordered his younger brother to get married in his place. When the relatives accompanying the marriage party raised hue and cry, Dâdu asked him to follow their advice and get married otherwise he may start courting other woman. Rajjab silenced them, including Dâdu, by reciting a couplet:

Rajjab ghar-gharani tajai, para gharani na suhâya;
Ahi taja apani kanchuki, kâki pahire jâi.

It was clear that Rajjab was not interested in becoming a householder after getting married or in some other woman. He threw out all the responsibilities and became a disciple of Sant Dâdu Dayâlji. Later on he became popular as Sant Rajjab after getting revelation.

Sant Rajjab proved to be a true and sincere disciple. Once, the guru was to cross a muddy river or drain. He asked the disciples to place some bricks to avoid mud. Rajjab slept over the mud head down and requested the guru to pass over his body without getting the feet muddy.

After the departure of Sant Dâdu Dayâl, Sant Rajjab came to Jaipur and started living in Sângânera, which is very close to Jaipur. He was joined by Sant Sunderdâs. Later on, they departed from this world one after another.

One day, Sant Rajjab was going with his disciples to a householder on dinner. He met a hungry Brahmin on the way. He asked him to join them. In order to save the Brahmin from disgrace, Sant Rajjab gave him a seat by his own side. The disciples raised objections. He felt that the disciples have ego. So, he declared that Brahmin to be his heir.

Sant Rajjab sang numerous songs and chanted many couplets teaching his disciples and the people, and praising the Lord. They show his command over the subject, music and poetic diction:

Rajjab bhâgain bhajan suni, agha indri guna chore;
Jyon bhujang chandan tajain, taru sira bole more. (i)
Jana Rajjab Râmahin bhajai, pâpa rahai nahi sang;
Jyon topak ki trâsh suna, taruvar tajai bihang. (ii)
Pâle se paravat galahin, dekhi sura ki tâpa;
Aisi vidhi agha utarahin, jana Rajjab Hari Jâpa. (iii)
Guna târe, mâyâ timir, sheeta bhram, mana chand;
Rajjab sumiran sura son; sahaja pare sab mand.

The only book of Sant Rajjab is called '*Rajjab Vâni*', and is a collection of all his works; and has a lot to offer. The following chart will make it clear:

S.N.	Vidhâ, Kinds of Poetry	Number
1.	Number of books	13
2.	Total chapters	39
3.	Total number of all *Vânis*	10,013
4.	*Sâkhis* (Chapters 239)	5,425
5.	*Padas, Bhajans*	218
6.	*Aril*	083
7.	*Kavitta and Sawayân*	150
8.	*Chhappaya*	089

66. Sant Sunderdâsji

The author and poet of *Sunder Vilâs*, *Gyân Samudra*, *Sarvânga Yoga Pradipikâ* and *Sukha Samâdhi* etc forty-two books Sant Sunderdâsji represents *Sant Sâhitya* and *Sâdhanâ of Ritikâla*. His language follows the rules of Grammar and his poetical works are rich in figures of speech. He has presented pictures in poetry. His works are treated as the classical form of Sant Literature. He was philosophical and has powered *shânta-rasa* (calming effect) in them. He has used a mixed language and has written something in different languages i.e. Hindi, Awahatta, Panjâbi, Gujarâti, Purvi and Persian. The general mysticism is present in abundance in his works.

The following are the books of Sant Sunderdâsji:

1.	Gyân Samudra	22.	Panjâbi Bhâshâ
2.	Sarvânga Yoga	23.	Brahma Strotra
3.	Panch Indriya Charitra	24.	Peera Murida
4.	Sukha Samâdhi	25.	Ajab Khyâla
5.	Swapna Bodha	26.	Gyân Jhulanâ
6.	Vida Vichâr	27.	Sahajânand
7.	Adabhuta Upadesha	28.	Griha-Vairâga-Bodha
8.	Pancha Prabhâva	29.	Hari Bole Chitâwani
9.	Guru Sampradâya	30.	Tarka Chitâwani
10.	Guna Utapatti Nisâni	31.	Pawangam
11.	Sad Guru Mahimâ Nisâni	32.	Adillâ
12.	Bâwani	33.	Madillâ
13.	Guru Dayâ Shat Padi	34.	Viveka Chitâwani
14.	Bhrama Vidhwansak Ashtak	35.	Bârah Mâcâ
15.	Guru Kripâ	36.	Âyurbala Bheda

16.	Guru Upadesha	37.	Trividha Antahkaran
17.	Guru Deva Mahimâ	38.	Purvi Bhâshâ Barawai
18.	Ukta Anoopa	39.	Sunder Vilas (Sawaiyâ)
19.	Râmaji	40.	Sâkhi
20.	Nâma	41.	Pada-Bhajan
21.	Âtmâ Achal	42.	Phutakar Kâvya

Sant Sunderdâsji was well formed, tall and had a heavy body. His whitish colour was very bright and attractive. He had a big head and wide forehead. He had a sweet tongue and heavy speech. There was a smile on his face though he used to remain always serious.

Sant Sunderdâsji was so handsome, and Dâdu Dayâlji was so impressed by his personalitry that he named him Sunder Dâs.

Sant Sunderdâsji was born in Dyosâ, which was once the capital city in place of Jaipur. He was born to a Khandelwâla Vaishya Parmanand alias Sâha Chokhâ and Sati. There is a tale about his birth. He is claimed to be the incarnation of Jaggiji, a disciple of Dâdu Dayâlji and a Mahâtmâ, poet and writer. By mistake he blessed the couple with a son. So, he had to die and take rebirth as the son of the couple. Sunderdâs inherited all.

When Sunderdâs was only five years old Dâdu Dayâl visited that village and his father gave him to the Guru. He became a disciple at that tender age. He came to Kâshi at the age of eleven and studied Vedas, Vedânta and other Scriptures for 18 years (some say for 20 years). He returned back to Fatahpur, to his Guru and practiced Yoga for 12 years.

Sant Sunderdâsji traveled far and wide. In that process he saw a lot, learnt a lot and taught a lot. It was the accumulating effect of all this that he was able to write so many books. As mentioned earlier in the article on Sant Rajjab, Sant Sunderdâsji departed from the world at Sângâner 1689 AD.

There are many memoirs of Sant Sunderdâsji at Dyosâ, Sânganer, Fatahpur, and Jaipur. Nârâyan Dâsji; Gangârâmaji; Mahant Fatahpuria; Sevânand Dâsji and Thandrâmji were his prominent disciples.

Sant Sunderdâsji was very friendly, co-operative and compassionate. He had many friends outside the circle of the disciples of Dâdu Dayâlji.

67. Samartha Guru Râmadâs

An incarnation of Shri Hanumân, Samartha Guru Râmadâs was a great Sant, very able and completely detached. It was he whom Mahârâjâ Shivâji, his disciple, gave his kingdom through a Dân-patra and took a bag for begging but the great guru returned the kingdom and ordered him to rule. As a result Shivaji ruled under the direct guidance of Samartha Guru Râmadâs.

Samartha Guru Râmadâs was the younger brother of Gangâdhar who at the age of nine recited in a temple '*Mâruti-Kawach*' for eleven days in a row and forced Shri Hanumân to appear before him and bless him. He got the '*Darshan*' of Shri Râma with the grace of Shri Hanumân and became famous as

Râmi Râmadâs. With a bit of difference the same thing happened to Samartha Guru Râmadâs who used to offer 2000 Surya Namaskârs everyday. He too got the blessings of Shri Hanumân at the age of only 8 and through him got the '*Darshan*' of Shri Râma.

It is said that Samartha Guru Râmadâs was gifted by Bhagawân Surya Nârâyan to Suryâji Pant and Renukâ Bai, and was born on *Chaitra Shukla Nawami* in the Vikram Samvat 1665, exactly on the birthday of Lord Shri Râma. He was called Nârâyan.

There is a nice incident about his self-exile and Samyâs or how Samartha Guru Râmadâs escaped from the worldly ties, and freed himself to be a Sant. At the age of only 12 his marriage was being solemnized. There was a cloth between the bride and the bridegroom. When the Pandits started chanting the shlokas of Manglâcharan, Samartha Guru Râmadâs, suddenly, rose and ran away. He ran up for about 8 kilometers and came up to the bank of River Godâvari, swam it over and reached Panchawati in Nâsika. He met Shri Râma again in the Panchavati. He prostrated to his God and recited a hymn showing his pitiable condition and was blessed by Him.

Samartha Guru Râmadâs settled in a cave at Tâphali, the meeting point of the Rivers Godâ and Nandani. There he chanted the '*Trayodasha akshar Mantra*, (Thirteen Lettered Mantra); of Shri Râma and studied Râmâyana, the Vedas, Upanishads, Gitâ and Bhâgawat. He did it for three years and got all the '*Riddhis* and *Siddhis*'.

One day, Samartha Guru Râmadâs was performing '*Brahma Yagya*' at the meeting point of the river. A lady came there and saluted him. He blessed her with eight sons saying '*Ashtaputrâ Saubhâgyawati Bhava*'. She laughed and said, 'O Sant, in which birth will it be possible? I have to salute you as a part of the ritual. I am about to get burnt with my dead husband on his pyre. How can I get eight sons?'

Samartha Guru Râmadâs ordered her to bring the husband to him. She returned. People brought her husband there. He sprinkled sacred and *abhimantrit* (sanctified with Mantras) water on the dead body and the man came alive chanting Shri Râma.

Samartha Guru Râmadâs announced, "I blessed you with eight sons, with the grace of Shri Râma I add two more. You will be the mother of ten sons. Of course, she got ten sons. She offered her eldest son to the Guru. The son himself became popular as 'Uddhava Gosâwi'.

Samartha Guru Râmadâs completed his penance of 12 years and for the next twelve years he traveled to all the pilgrim places of the country. During that journey he met 'Shri Sewta Mâruti' at the mountain peak. He gave him Topa, Mekhalâ, Valkala, Saffron cloths, Rosary, wooden slippers and Kubari. In the course of the same visit a co-villager recognized him and informed about the pitiable condition of his mother who had lost her eyes only because of weeping for her beloved son. It moved him and he returned back home where he begged forgiveness from the mother and gave her eyes back by touching them.

During that long journey of 12 years five Sants came closer: Samartha Guru Râmadâs; Jairâma Swâmi of Baragâon; Ranga Nâth Swâmi of Nigadi; Ânand Swâmi of Brahman Nâla; and Shri Keshava Swâmi of Bhâgâ Nagar. They are famous as '*Dâs Panchâyatan*'.

Samartha Guru Râmadâs settled at Shâhpur about 12 kilometers away from the meeting point of the Rivers Krishnâ and Kopanâ, known as '*Preeti-Sangam*'. He got 'Pratâp Mâruti Temple' constructed at Shahpur. Many people became his disciples. The prominent among them are: Subedâr of Châphala; Subedâr Pârâji Pant Barbe of Kolhâpur; his sister Rakhumâbâi and her two sons Ambâji and Dattâtreya; and Shivâji Mahârâja.

During the travels Samartha Guru Râmadâs established eleven Mâruties, the temples of Shri Hanumân at the following places:

Shâhpur;	Masur;	2 at Châphala
Dambraja	Shirasapta	Mana Pâdalen
Vâragâon	Mâjagâon	Shinganwâdi

and Bâhen.

During his lifetime he established the Hermitages at the following places:

Jâmba	Châphala	Ujjan Garh
Tâphali	Tanjâvar	Domagâon
Mana Pâdalen	Maraja	Râshiwade
Pandharpur	Prayâg	Kâshi
Ayodhyâ	Mathurâ	Dwârakâ
Badri-kedâr	Râmeshwaram	and Gangâ Sâgar.

During his life time Samartha Guru Râmadâs wrote the following books:

Dâsabodha	*Manobodha*	*Karunâshtak*
Purânâ Dâsabodha	*Âtmârâma*	*Râmâyana*
Obi Chaudah Shatak	*Sphuta Obiyân*	*Shad Ripu*
Panchikaran Yoga	*Chaturtha Mâna*	*Mâna Panchak*
Panchamâna	*Sphuta Prakaran*	and *Sphuta Shloka*

Samartha Guru Râmadâs needed tall and beautiful idols of Shri Râma, Sitâ and Shri Hanumân. He came to know about a person who was a great sculpture but had lost his eyes. He went to Tanjâvar to meet him. He gave him his eyes back and asked him to make the idols which he did and the idols were ceremoniously placed in the temple of Sajjanpur on *Phâlguna Krishna* Panchami in Vikram Samvat 1738.

In the same year on *Mâgha Krishna Nawami* Samartha Guru Râmadâs declared his departure. In the presence of the people and disciples he performed poojâ and ceremoniously sat before the idol of Shri Râma, and went into a trance. After a few hours, he started chanting '*Har Har Râma*'. The moment he pronounced it the 21st time a bright light came out of his mouth and entered the idol of Shri Râma.

68. Sant Tukâ Râma

Sant Tukâ Râma had the sense of detachment from the very beginning but he became a Sant very late in his life.

The life of Sant Tukâ Râma is a tale of pain, suffering, anxiety and agony that comes out of the household. Because his elder brother was not interested in household and left home after the death of his wife, his father gave him all the responsibilities of the family but Sant Tukâ Râma could not do justice to it. He was badly defeated in the worldly affairs; and when he was crushed under the debts and his first wife and the only son died he started spending his precious time near the river, on the mountains, reading books, chanting Name and creating *abhangs*. His popularity grew with his spiritual songs and people started treating him as a Sant. It was unbearable to a Brâhmin Nâganâth. He asked him to throw the abhangs into the river and leave the village.

Sant Tukâ Râmaji threw the *abhangs* but instead of leaving the village he sat on a stone before the temple of Bhagawân Vitthal Nâth, and remained seated for 13 days and that many nights without taking food or water. At last, the God appeared and blessed him and it is said that He entered the body of Sant Tukâ Râma after blessing him and announcing that his *abhangs* were safe in the River Indrâni.

When the fame of Sant Tukâ Râma touched the sky, the Brahmin Nâganâth was ordered in a dream to take shelter of Sant Tukâ Râma. He came to him but the Sant kept on saluting him as a Brâhmin.

Mahârâjâ Shivâji used to come to listen his teachings and the stories of Shri Hari. He tried to become his disciple but it was known to all that he was a disciple of Samartha Guru Râmadâs so Sant Tukâ Râma declined it. Shivâji continued to come to him.

He lived for another fifteen years, then he departed but his body was not found so it is claimed that he was carried away to heaven along with his body.

The *abhangs* of Sant Tukâ Râma are gifts and prized possessions of Sant literature. The following are some couplets (*Dohe*) in Hindi:

Lobhi ke chit dhan baithe, aru kâmini ke chit kâma;
Mâtâ ke chit puta baithe, tukâ ke mana râma. (i)
Kahe tukâ jaga bhulâ re, kahâ na mânat koi;
Hâth pare jab kâla ke, mârat phorat dhoi. (ii)
Tukâ milanâ to bhalâ, jab mansoon man mil jâya;
Upar-upar mâti dhasi, unaki kaun barâya. (iii)
Kahe tukâ bhalâ bhayâ, huâ santan kâ dâs;
Kyâ jânoon kaise maratâ, na mitati man ki yâs.(iv)

69. Sant Shri Vâman Pandit

Sant Shri Vâman Pandit was a contemporary of Sant Samartha Guru Râma Dâs. He was a Brâhmin that used to study and chant the Mantras of Rigveda. He was born in Beejâpur. He studied at Kâshi and duly completed his education within a short period. During his lifetime he wrote many books. The following books are important among them.

The Important Works of Sant Shri Vâman Pandit

Karma Tatva	*Nâma Sudhâ*	*Brahman Stuti*
Suma Shloki	*Gitâ Tikâ*	*Bhartrihari ke Teena Shatak*
Anubhutilesh	*Siddhânta Vijay*	*Shrutikalp Latâ*
Nigam Sâra	*Yathârtha Dipikâ*	

A poet named Goro Pant has claimed that 'Shri Krishna Dwaipâyan Veda Vyâsa was the **Secretary** of Gitâ; Shri Shankarâchârya and Madhusudan were the **Yogis** of Gitâ; Sant Gyâneshwar was the **Representative** of Gitâ; and Sant Shri Vâman Pandit was the **Prince** of Gitâ.'

Sant Shri Vâman Pandit departed from the world in Vikram Samvat 1752. His Samâdhi (Tomb) is still there in Bhogâon at the bank of Krishnâ River in Satârâ district.

The Samâdhi of Sant Shri Vâman Pandit was recently renovated by Shri Râmchandra Shankar Takki. His *punya tithi* is ceremoniously celerated here every year.

71. The Sants of Râm Sanehi Sampradâya

(a) Jaimal Dâsji

Jaimal Dâsji was the guru of Harrâm Dâsji who used to go to Dulachâsar in Bikâner every evening to meet him. He ordered him to come once in a month.

(b) Hari Râm Dâsji

Hari Râm Dâsji is the first âchârya of Râm Sanehi Sect, which is very popular in Mârwâr. He was born in Bikâner at Singhathal to a Brâhmin named Bhâgya Chand. He studied the Vedas and Scriptures and was baptized into Samyâs in Samvat 1700. His teachings have been collected in '*Vâni*' :*Sânchâ mukha mânava tanâ, jâ mukh nikase râm;Jana hariyâ mukh râm bin, soi mukh bekâm.* His disciples had planned a ceremony to celebrate his birthday but he died earlier. They were weeping bitterly at the time of his death, so, he took a month's time from the God and returned back. After the ceremony he announced his departure and at the designated time he died.

(c) Râm Dâsji

Râm Dâsji was a disciple of Harirâm Dâsji and is known for spreading the 'Sect' all around from the center that he created at Jodhpur. For this he was asked to leave the country but was called back again.

(d) Dayâlu Dâsji

Dayâlu Dâsji was one of the 52 disciples of Râmdâsji. When he was in penance, a beautiful dame came to bring disgrace to him but he did not open his eyes. She cursed and he lost his eyes after great pain. For relief he worshipped Râm and wrote '*Karunâ Sâgar*'. He got his eyesight back.

(e) Râmcharanji

Shri Râmkrishna became Râmcharanji when he was baptized into Râma Sanehi Sect. He was born in Vikram Samavt 1776 in Sodâ village. He had a long life of about 80 years. He had many disciples.

(f) Râmajanji

A disciple of Râmcharanji, Râmjanji was born in Vikram Samvat 1808 in Chittaur in a Vaishya family.

(g) Devâdâsji

A disciple of Râmcharanji, Devâdâsji was born in Vikram Samvat 1811 in Jaipur

(h) Bhagawân Dâsji

Bhagawân Dâsji was born in the village Pipâda in Mârwâr in a Vaishya family, and was a disciple of Râmcharanji. He said:*Swârath* swâd *moha taji bhâjo lâgo jan saranâi; Bhagawândâs bhavasâgar bhâri tab sahaje tar jâi.*

(i) Dariyâva Mahârâj

Dariyâva Mahârâj was Râm Sanehi Dharmâchârya. He was born on *Bhâdrapada Krishna Ashtami* in Vikram Samvat 1733; and departed on *Agahan Purnimâ* in Samvat 1815. He was the son of Manasarâmji and Gigâ Bâi; and the disciple of Premadâsji. He resided in Jaitâran village in Mârwâr.

71. Shri Râmkrishna Paramhans

Shri Râmkrishna Paramhans adopted different religions and ways to know the Self, the Brahman or God; realized the inner truth; came to the same conclusion that our Rishis showed myriads of years ago and preached their '*Sanâtan Mânav Dharma*'; Eternal Human Religion by declaring that He is One and has thousands of Names; one can call him by any name one wishes or prefers. He entered the realms of other faiths, dived deeper to know that way of worshipping and worshipping thus he reached at the apex of each religion; only then he was able to teach confidently that all religions are different ways to reach the God.

He is again the first modern Sant that called Mâ to Shakti, Eternal Energy, and placed woman on the highest pedestal again which once they enjoyed and which has gone into oblivion during the long period of slavery.

Shri Râmkrishna Paramhans got his name from his preceptor Totâpuri who baptized him into Samyâs, although he had followed the instructions of many other.

Shri Râmkrishna Paramhans was the first modern Sant of India who became popular in Europe as many articles and a book were published in English within years after his departure in 1886.

Shri Râmkrishna Paramhans was born on 17 February 1836 in a village called Kâmârpukur in the Hugli district of West Bengal to Khudirâm Chattopâdhyâya and Chandramani. They were poor but very religious. He was named Gadâdhar. He was a playful child, little interested in study and more interested in extra curricular activities including singing devotional songs that described Krishna. For his songs and other activities he was popular among the teachers and villagers. Before his sacred thread ceremony he promised to a Shudra to first accept his gifts as alms during the sacred thread ceremony. It created a problem at the right time but Gadâdhar was adamant, and his wishes were given preference. It was the first incident of breaking away from the tradition.

But the greatest break through for Shri Râmkrishna Paramhans was to treat his wife as and call her Mâ. It turned to be spiritual love and prostrating before her he said her that he would obey her, do whatever she says as a child obeys his mother. He had no children but they treated their disciples as their children. Particularly his most glorious disciple Swâmi Vivekânand was their most favourite child.

Once Shri Râmkrishna Paramhans had intense pain in his throat that continued for a long time. Swâmi Vivekânand asked him to request the mother when she appears before him to cure him and free him from the pain. He bade his disciple to do it for him as Mâ usually appeared in his meditation. He accepted but in meditation when Mâ actually appeared before him he was so full in her bliss that he could not ask to cure his guru. He accepted before his guru that it was almost impossible to ask for anything when that infinite energy is physically present in her enormity.

When his elder brother Râmkumâr became the poojâri and caretaker of a temple at Dakshneshwar in Kolkata Shri Râmkrishna Paramhans was also called there. After the premature death of his brother he took his position and the years of penance started that continued for 12 years. When he failed to get the revelation he turned into an extremist and started behaving in strange fashion. It was the time when he returned to his village and was married to Shârdâ Mani, the daughter of Shri Râmchandra Mukhopâdhyâya, who became Shârdâ Devi.

It marked another beginning in his life that led Shri Râmkrishna Paramhans to a Samyâsini, an expert of Tântrik Sâdhnâ, then to Gopâl Ray, a Sufi Sant, then to Christianity. He completed the circle when he took Samyâs from Totârâmji.

From there on his story is that of worshipping and teaching. He used simple and common Bengâli language to teach people who came from different places and distant land. Shri Râmkrishna Paramhans said that:

As a lamp can't burn without oil so a man can't live without a God.

As a fruit laden tree bows down so if you wish to make your life fruitful then be gentle and humble.

The anger of humble and saintly people is a line drawn on water. It never lasts for long.

The sunrays fall with equal intensity on all but is greatly reflected by water, glass and brighter surfaces. The light of God is also like that but is reflected back only by true and pious hearts.

God is also in a tiger but don't go to him. God is also in cunning and cruel fellows but don't keep their company.

The farmer irrigates his field but the water vanishes through the pores in the soil because he wishes to get rich crop. In the same way, he that worships God for fame, wealth and luxury loses the effect because of the spunge like desires.

The freedom from anxiety and pain is the proof of total dependence on God.

They have no fear who have surrendered to God.

Shri Râmkrishna Paramhans showed 'seven steps' to the stair that leads to the revelation of God. The following are those seven steps. These are somehow either based on or deeply related to the states of 'Kundalani'.

1.	The Company of Sants	Through the company of Sants, respect towards the God grows inside the heart.
2.	Respect	Respect gives rise to dedication.
3.	Dedication	Dedication ensures that the Self is interested in nothing other than the God. A dedicated soul can worship any God with or without attributes. Dedication develops devotion.

4.	Devotion	Devotion is the result of the maturity in devotion. When devotion matures, it takes the form of abstract ideas. In that state, the moment the God comes to mind one becomes silent.
5.	Silence	Most of the worldly people rise only up to the state of silence. They cease to grow more.
6.	Illumination	Illumination comes after revelation and is known as '*Mahâbhâva*'. It is the extreme form of the devotion to God. They never feel the body who achieve this rare state. They generally behave in strange fashion.
7.	Love	After revelation the Self remains engrossed in deep love. Revelation and love, in a way, are integrated whole. The feeling of the body is lost. It is called the state of '*Videha*', body-less-ness. Very few achieve this highest state.

72. Swâmi Vivekânand

Swâmi Vivekânand and his Preceptor Shri Râmkrishna Paramhans were the two figures that sought and achieved a balance between the western and eastern philosophy, spirituality and religiosity with their visions of completeness and the whole. He combines the best of both Shri Shankarâchârya and Mahâtmâ Buddha. He had fresh, clear and deeper ideas about everything social, political and religious.

Everywhere Swâmi Vivekânand is quoted for his enchanting and revealing speech at Chicago in the "Parliament of Religions"; that changed the thinking of the western world and in modern era for the first time the world looked towards India with respect. Indians regained their lost cofidence.

Swâmi Vivekânand, a great Sant of modern times, was born on 12th January, 1863 to a famous advocate and was named Narendra Nâth. His mother was deeply religious and the father represented the intellectual. He inherited both the qualities and became the greatest intellectual and religious figure; one that was capable of analyzing and discerning and also in assimilating, synthesizing and expressing with devotional force to magically enchant the audience.

His education started at home but he got his Bachelor Degree from Scottish Church College, Kolkata. First he came in contact with Girish Chandra Ghosh who shook him from inside and then with Râmkrishna Paramhans who enriched him from inside. He had immense spiritual wealth to pour out in torrent and yet he felt flooded with them.

The life of Swâmi Vivekânand is usually and safely divided into four phases: Childhood and Youthful Vigour; Five years of learning Spirituality under the preceptor from 1881 to 1886; Extensive and intensive journey to different parts of the country from 1886 to 1893; and the later phase of teachings. The phases give clear insight into the life and achievements, learning and teaching, revelation and revealing processes of the most powerful and enchanting figure of Modern India. He stands alone as an idiosyncratic and towering personality that has the supernatural power to observe and absorb all and to satiate each one with definite knowledge and confident expressions.

Swâmi Vivekânand denied to marry and accepted Samyâs despite the opposition; and became Swâmi Vivevekânand to combine the three *Sat, Chit* and *Ânand*. At that time, his family needed him most to take them out of the financial crisis. He preferred to solve the national and international crises and boldly ignored the personal needs and pleasure. He traveled from Kolkatâ to Dwârkâ and from Himalayas to Kanyâkumâri. He established Râmkrishna Mission on the 1st May, 1897. In 1899, he again went to America and traveled to other western countries like England, France, Austria, Balkan, Greece and Egypt.

Swâmi Vivekânand departed from this mortal world on 4th July, 1902 at 9 PM in Vellure Matha; at the age of 39 but had performed such great tasks that the combined effort of centuries and of many men won't accomplish.

The world in general and India in particular awoke after listening to Swâmi Vivekânand and to listen more from him. He became an ideal of the young and the old alike. Swâmi Vivekânand gave an aim and became an aim, the hero and the mask. Even now people wish to be like him. The reason behind that was the fact that like his preceptor he too taught 'Sanâtan Mânava Dharma', Eternal Human Religion and laid stress on the duties to be performed during the four phases of the four âshrams and to achieve the four pursuits.

Swâmi Vivekânand Said:

The Soul is a form and a part of the God. The soul is felt to be tied to the body, but if we get rid of the feeling the Soul will be seen in Free State. Vedas say that Salvation is to be free from life and death, pleasure and pain and imperfections. We can get Salvation only with the grace of the God; and the grace of God is showered only on a pious heart.

Hindu Dharma was born out of Vedas; and Vedas have no beginning and no end; Vedas are infinite and indefatigable. One should not wonder to hear that the Vedas have no beginning and no end because the Vedas are not books they are the collections of such theories that can't be refuted.

Those that gave those theories and definitions are called Rishis. There are many women among them, called Rishikâs. They were before we came to know of them and they will remain when we won't be here. They are beyond Time.

The Vedas tell us to worship God to be free from Death. Bhagawân Shri Krishna, the Perfect Incarnation, has also showed the same path. Follow it for Salvation.

73. The Sants of Modern Age

(a) Âchârya Mangaldâs

Âcgârya Mangaldâs belongs to the tradition of Âcgârya Râmânand. He was born in a Brahmin family in Dâkor and became a disciple of another Vaishnava Sant of Âgrâ Shri Sahaj Râmdâsji. Shri Hanumân appeared before him as he had completed the *anushthân* of *Sunderkând*. Later on, he got many temples of Shri Mâruti Râi constructed at different places. *Sur Druma Manjari; Dharma Mahodadhi; Veda Stuti Chandrikâ* and *Shri Divya Râma Stavarâja Bhâshya* are his books.

(b) Gosai Dâsji

Shri Gosai Dâsji was born in a Brahmin family in Vikram Samvat 1727 to Brahmânand and Sumitrâ Devi. He became a disciple of Jagajivan Swâmi. His three books: *Shabdâwali, Dohâwali* and *Kakaharânâmâ* are written in praise of Shri Râma.

(c) Shri Khema

Shri Khema Dâsji was a Brahmin and Dâsji lived in Bârâbanki district at Madhanâpur. He became a disciple of Jagajivan Swâmi.

After baptism, he went for penance for 12 years. He has written three voluminous treatises: *Kâshikând; Tatwasâr Dohâwali* and *Shabdâwali*.

(d) Newalâdâs

Newalâdâs lived at Dhaneshâ village of Sultânpur and completed '*Sukhsâgar*' there. Later on he added five more: *Gyân Sarovar; Bhagawat Dasham Skand; Ratnagyân; Shabdasâgar* and *Kakaharânâmâ.*

(e) Mauni Bâbâ

Mauni Bâbâ came to Gorakhpur and stayed under a tree in a kaupin (waist-cloth). He would sit silently on a deerskin. One day, his seat, the deerskin rose about two feet high with Mauni Bâbâ and he spent eleven days above the earth. People from different places, came to see this magical event and his supernatural power.

(f) Swâmi Abhayânand

Swâmi Abhayânand was born in Gorkhâ, Nepâl in a Thâpâ Kshatriya family. After practicing Yoga for 12 years, he entered life and as Colonel reached Lhasa and learnt many specialties of Tântrika Yoga from Tibbetan Lâmâs. He remained in penance for more than five years in one posture in a cave. He has written four books on Yoga: *Dhyâna Yoga*; *Mantra Yoga; Lakshya Yoga* and *Vâsanâ Yoga*. He departed to other world from Kâshi but only after showing his supernatural power by bringing food on empty leaf-plates of many invitees.

(g) Nârâyana Swâmi

Nârâyana Swâmi was born in Râwalpindi in Vikram Samvat 1885 in a Brâhmin family. At a mature age he came to Vrindâvan and worked in a temple to take part in the *Satsanga* and *râsa lilâ* at night. As Samyâsi he lived at Kusum Sarovar and composed devotional hymns and songs that are collected in '*Vraj-Vihâr*.'

(h) Prabhu Jagat Bandhu

Prabhu Jagat Bandhu was born in Murshidâbad in a Brâhmin family in 1871 AD. At an immature age he developed the qualities of Sants like detachment, kindness, and devotion that people started coming to him to listen to his bhajans. Later on, he started moving from place to place. He glowed with divine brightness.

(i) Sant Vijaya

Sant Vijay Krishna is said to be a master Krishna of both the *Tântrika Sâdhanâ* and *Sahaja Sâdhna*. It is said that he was able to change his body into smoke. He taught both '*aham Brahman* and *aham buddhi*.

(j) Chainrâm Bâbâ

Chainrâm Bâbâ was born in a Brahmin family at Badhâva in Balia district. He was given divinity by a sâdhu. There is his samâdhi in Sahatwâr.

(k) Tulasi Sâheb

Tulasi Saheb was born in a Brâhmin family in 1760 AD. He settled at Hâtharasa. *Ghatarâmâyana* and *Ratnasâgar* are his important books.

(l) Râmânand Swâmi

The guru of Swâmi Nârayan Shri Râmânand was born in Ayodhyâ in a Brâhmin family to Ajay Sharmâ and Sumati. It is said that Krishna had appeared before him. He went for penance on Girnâr Mountain.

(m) Gunâtitânand Swâmi

Moolaji became Gunâtitânand after taking Deekshâ and spent rest of his days in Junâgarh. For the last *Samâdhi* he went to Gondal where Trishikhari temple was constructed in his memory.

(n) Paramahans Pânapdâsji

Paramahans Pânapdâsji belonged to the family of Birbala. When he was left alone under a tree he was taken away by a Tirshân who fostered him. Later on he became a disciple of a Kabirpanthi, Magani Râm. He preferred to live in secrecy. He worked as a labour. The jealous workers de-shaped a wall and blamed him. In their presence he only touched the wall and it became straight. The master of the house was so impressed that he donated the house. It is still there and famous as Mahal. He has composed his teachings in *Vânis*.

(o) Shyâmâcharan Lâhiri

Shyâmâcharan Lâhiri was such a Sant that helped the people with his supernatural power and without trying and getting name and fame departed from the world. He spoke little and spent most of his time in either meditation or in self-study. He came to Kâshi in 1880 and spent rest of his time there writing commentaries on different branches of Indian philosophy.

□□□

6

The Sants Said

(One)

Physical hunger is never satiated with food. Even the whole of the food of the world, if and when eaten, bring the hunger back after some time when it is digested.

See, Feel, and Absorb God; and forget him. It is the greatest of remembrance of God.

When you go deep down inside your self, shun the self from the outer world and when there is no outer feeling; you are Enlightened.

The brightness of God is enough to intoxicate one to feel Him, to see only Him and praise only Him.

(Two)

The best form of kindness is charity. One should give charity without getting in doubt or dilemma; without thinking of sin. One should offer one's all as charity. One should give charity even if that charity leads to sin because it is better to endure the pain of hell than to break the expectations of others. The expectations of others should never be broken at any cost.

(Three)

The sins that begin with fear of God and ends with begging forgiveness from Him may bring one closer to God; but the penance that begins with ego and ends in pride will take the person far away from God.

(Four)

The God resides in us invisible like the black ant sitting on black stone in a black night.

He knows all that got the revelation of God, which is possible only after complete surrender and shaking of the ego and pride.

(Five)

God is far away from you till you are confined to your physical self, working for it, feeding it and providing it pleasure; but the moment you turn to your inner self, start working for it, feeding it and thinking for its comfort God will be before and with you.

(Six)

He is immensely enriched who saves the eyes from looking at dirty and sinful; who saves the sense organs from indulgence in luxury; who purifies his self with meditation and good deeds and who fosters the self and family with ethical and lawful earning.

(Seven)

Detachment is the way to salvation. Be detached without exposing it. Exposition incites others and hardens the pressure.

(Eight)

Remember God with humility and love; follow dharma with reverence and dedication; be with and serve the pious souls with respect and eagerness; be pleased and happy with family, friends and relatives; be kind and sweet to ignorant people; behave in gentle and civilized way with workers, servants and needy; you will become sublime and divine.

(Nine)

He has great tolerance that remains engrossed in God without the worries of tomorrows.

(Ten)

To be afraid of God is a characteristic of prosperity. It is complete destruction to commit sins and expect the grace of God.

(Eleven)

He is a companion of God who fears none but God; and has expectations with none but God.

(Twelve)

Lust of wealth; expectation of respect and wish to be famous are three most dangerous enemies. Be cautious.

(Thirteen)

There is no fall in the way of God; it is incessant and continuous ascending towards prosperity, peace and salvation.

(Fourteen)

Be content with what you have and where you are; and travel inside for greater things and better places.

(Fifteen)

There are four types of the state of mind: dead; unhealthy; lazy and healthy. Irreligious has a dead mind; a sinner has an unhealthy mind; selfish and lustful has a lazy mind; but only a pious, religious and spiritual person possesses a healthy mind.

(Sixteen)

While consuming and enjoying keep it in mind that the God is looking at you; while speaking be conscious that truth is not destroyed and while looking be sure to save morality.

(Seventeen)

Whatever the science sells the price is always religious spirit. In return it takes the great wealth of religion.

(Eighteen)

He is wise who has no worldly attachment. He is wise who neither thinks of nor waits for death. He is wise who knows that his God is pleased with him.

(Nineteen)

Talk least to men and a lot to God; take least from men, a lot from God but give all to men and nothing to God.

(Twenty)

The people are afraid of him who is afraid of God. The people have no fear of the man who has no fear of God.

(Twenty-one)

It is very easy to get indulged in worldly affairs it is very difficult to come out of it.

(Twenty-two)

Your thoughts are your mirror. Keep them clean to see your brightened self.

(Twenty-three)

While enchanting the world gives a lot but when lured it takes all.

(Twenty-four)

Let music go down deep and touch the inner self; don't miss the eternal music that flows all around and always.

(Twenty-five)

Least in security is better than plenty in fear.

(Twenty-six)

Lust spoils, contentment satisfies.

(Twenty-seven)

Be a gourmet not a gourmand.

(Twenty-eight)

Collect stalks of good deeds and pods of spiritual accomplishment.

(Twenty-nine)

Outer eyes see the outer world while inner eyes look at unknown Infinite with adoration.

(Thirty-one)

Success is impossible without Truth and Tolerance.

(Thirty-two)

There are three characteristics of Faith: To look towards God; to dedicate each deed to God; to spread hands for begging only to God.

(Thirty-three)

Scriptures and Sants generate Faith; Faith intensifies Curiosity; Curiosity gives rise to Detachment; Detachment teaches Ethics; Ethics leads to Revelation and Revelation gives Final Salvation that is our ultimate end.

(Thirty-four)

It is enough to have only God as friend if not then develop friendship with only those that have God as friend.

(Thirty-five)

Whose heart is not pure his deeds can't be pure.

(Thirty-six)

That man is blind that does not see God in other living beings. That man is a beast that does not have compassion for other living beings. That body is dead that does not serve other living beings.

(Thirty-seven)

There are three steps to atonement: Self-lassitude; Committing no more crime or sin; and Self-purification.

(Thirty-eight)

Carry and keep your God wherever you go and whatever you do.

(Thirty-nine)

He who knows God is charitable like a river; bounteous like the sun and tolerant like the earth.

(Forty)

Debates, Oratory, Egotism are outer presentations inside there is complete silence, immobility and tranquility.

(Forty-one)

Do whatever you can do in coming closer to God; but always take that as God's grace.

(Forty-two)

Don't be proud if you get immense riches; don't get aggrieved if you get nothing; think of God and do your duties.

(Forty-three)

If you know God, you don't need to say that you know God, the light of God will inform all.

(Forty-four)

Always be alert as the Creator is in you, and in all others, and He sees and knows all.

(Forty-five)

Only they have revelation that either have been in the company of Sants or have truly followed saints.

(Forty-six)

Don't search the world it is big, uneven, hard or flooded. Keep aloof from it then you are free.

(Forty-seven)

Don't try to possess God, surrender to Him and be possessed by God.

(Forty-eight)

How can he love God, the Infinite Creator of all, who does not love small beings?

(Forty-nine)

Be of God, God will be yours.

(Fifty)

You are bound to leave this world when you die; then leave it now when you are living and are not dead.

(Fifty-one)

The moment you completely surrender to Him, the moment he takes all your responsibilities.

Do you need money?

To remember God everyday early in the morning.

To behave in a gentle and humble way.

To speak to others without showing anger.

To show patience in adverse situations.

To give due respect to all whom you know.

To respond to others with a 'ji'.

To show obedience to parents and grand parents.

To grow from inside and work with zeal and skill.

To try to be better in thinking and expression.

To be determined to finish a work within the time limit.

To acquire higher qualities from the life of the great.

To show sympathy, kindness and compassion.

To take fresh air everyday as far as practicable.

To try to remain always fresh and happy.

To feel content with what you have and what you get.

❑❑❑

7

Rare Sacrifices by Sants

Dharma Veera Gaja Sukumâl

Dharma Veera Gaja Sukumâl was a grihastha. He had his wife and children. One day, he heard the teachings of Shri Nema Nâtha Prabhu and decided to take Samyâs. He sought permission from his mother who tried to persuade him to reconsider and change the decision but he was determined for it. At last the mother gave him the permission. He took Samyâs under the guidance of Shri Nema Nâth Prabhu. When the Samskâr was over he asked his Guru, "What is the easiest way to get salvation?"

The Guru said, "First purify your heart, speech and body then meditate upon God, you would get salvation."

After completing the preliminaries he started sitting in *dhyân* (meditation) at a burning ghât outside the village. He used to concentrate hard and was successful in it.

One day, his father in law, Somil Brâhman was passing through that way. He saw his son in law in the garb of a Samyâsi. He was angry. He started chiding and abusing him but Gaja Sukumâl heard nothing. He did not allow any ill will to enter his heart. The anger of the man grew to such an extent that he took a mound of mud put fire in it and placed it on the head of Gaja

Sukumâl. He felt the heat but did not move. The heat kept on growing he endured all. He did not even think of taking the fire off from the head. At last, his head burst out. What a rare event!

Dharma Veera Shri Dharma Ruchi

There was a lady that was expert in cooking. One day, she prepared sweets and cooked vegetables for some celebration. The smell was not healthy. She got suspicious. She tasted a bit. It was very bitter in taste. She collected them in a big pot and went out to throw them into a ditch.

It was just a chance that at that moment Dharma Veera Shri Dharma Ruchi reached there for begging food. Without thinking anything the lady gave the sweets and vegetables to the Sant. The Sant brought them to his Guru and opened it to eat. The guru smelled it and inspected it closely and announced that the food had poison in it. He admonished his disciple not to eat that. He asked him to throw that food to a distant place.

Shri Dharma Ruchi recollected it, tied it and went out to throw the poisoned food. He stopped at a place and tried to untie it. In the meantime one drop of sweet juice dropped there. The ants collected, tasted the drop and died. The Sant looked at it. He thought over it. If one drop of it can kill so many ants then the total food will kill many animals and birds. He decided, "No, it is not correct. He won't throw it for other beings to die."

He untied the food and ate out the whole food resulting into his instantaneous death. What a rare sacrifice!

Dharma Veera Khandhak Muni and Sunandâ

Once, King Kanak Ket ruled over Shrâvasti. Malay Sundari was his queen. They had a son Khandhak and a daughter Sunandâ. When she grew young Sunandâ was married to a prince. Time passed by.

One day, the king went with his son Khandhak to meet a Sant. The Sant was preaching the people. They sat there and listened to him. The speech and teaching of the Sant impressed Khandhak so much that he decided to become a Samyâsi. He expressed his desire. The parents were not ready but the young prince was determined and at last the parents were forced to give their consent. Khandhak went to the same Sant and became a Samnyâsi. Time passed by.

It was just a chance that Khandhak once came to the city of his sister. He started searching out her house. When he reached at her house she was sitting in the balcony on the upper roof with her husband. She saw her brother in the garb of a Samyâsi. Her heart felt the pain and her eyes deceived her. Two drops of tears rolled down. The husband saw the tears and thought that his wife has immoral relation with the Samyâsi. He did not ask anything. He called his servants and loudly ordered to peel out the skin of the Samyâsi. The sister heard it. She wanted to say something but she looked at the face of the man and thought that it's useless to say anything. He won't believe. The brother heard it and looked at the man and his sister and checked himself. He knew the man was mad in rage. He won't listen to reason. Anger is the greatest enemy.

The servants came to the Samyâsi; saw his face and stepped back. There was great peace and innocence on the face. The Samyâsi said, "Obey the orders of your master!" They obeyed. The skin of the Samyâsi was peeled out but the pain did not come to surface. It was not on his face. He was in deep trance. The vultures started coming and taking away the red flesh of Khandhak. His sister Sunandâ saw it. She was disillusioned. She came out, bowed to his dead brother and became a Samyâsini.

What a rare tolerance!

Maharishi Metârya

The day, the one month long complete fasting of Maharshi Metârya was over he went to beg for food. He reached the place of a famous gold smith. He was making some ornaments and had prepared many gold balls to fit in it. He saw the Sant and immediately went inside to bring some alms for the Sant.

In the meantime a bird sitting nearby was attracted by the gold balls and gulped many balls. The Sant saw it and tried to distract the bird. The bird flew away, and sat at its place. The goldsmith returned and found so many balls missing. His suspicion went directly towards the Sant. He thought that the man is not a Sant. He has stolen the gold-balls. He asked him. The Sant was in a fix. He knew what had happened but the moment he would divulge the information the bird would be caught and killed. It would mount to violence. He was against violence. How can he sacrifice a bird? He decided to sacrifice his own reputation to save the bird. He kept mum. He did say nothing.

The gold smith was angry. He tied the Sant in the scorching heat with a pillar, and tied a wet piece of leather tightly around his head. The Sant sat in Samâdhi. It was the only answer to the torture. The leather dried up and hardened and pressed the head hard and with it the nerves. The scorching heat was burning his body that had not taken meal for the last thirty days. The pain of the Sant can be only imagined it can't be expressed.

But there was peace on the face of the Sant. He felt nothing. He sat there in trance. The goldsmith wondered at the ease on the face of the Sant. In the meantime the bird started excreting the gold balls, as it was not digestible. The goldsmith saw it and realized his mistake. He untied the Sant and begged for forgiveness. The Sant knew that the goldsmith was right in his own way. He forgave him. But could he have forgotten the torture! What a torture and what tolerance! Man can be divine only with non-violence, tolerance and compassion.

Vidyuchchar

Vidyuchchar was the eldest son of the king of Hastinâpur but he turned to be a robber. He could not keep the great tradition of his parents. The king was aggrieved and angry and declared him dethroned. It made no difference to Vidyuchchar. He raised his great band of 500 robbers.

The Prince of Râjgriha changed his life. He became a Sant along with the complete band. They all knowingly died in a natural calamity, although they were in a position to avoid it. It happened in the following sequence.

In the course of robbery once he came to Râjagriha, famous capital city of the time and of the country. At that time Bimbisâr was the ruler.

Vidyuchchar entered the city to search a house of a rich man for robbing him. He found the town neat and clean and decorated well. It was ready to welcome someone. He was informed that the Victorious Prince Jambu Kumâr is returning back. He waited for him and was attracted by the ornaments and jewels that the Prince wore. He decided to rob him at proper time and in proper way.

Prince Jambu Kumâr had his own problems. He had decided to take Samyâs but it was deferred by his deft and experienced father. He had decided to marry the Prince to bind him to the life of a household. He had selected eight beautiful girls from the nagar for the Prince. The Prince got the news and sent words to the father of each of the girl to refuse to marry him as he would become a Samyâsi the next morning after the marriage but it did not work. He was married with all the eight girls.

It was the night that Vidyuchchar selected to rob the king. He led his band and went up to the window of the Prince. The Prince was preaching all his newly wed wives after declaring that the next morning he was to take Samyâs. The robber heard him patiently and was impressed particularly by the fact that the man was a Prince, and had all the luxuries of life along with eight newly wed beautiful brides. He returned back.

The next morning, the Prince took Pravrajyâ and left the palace. Vidychchar followed him and became his disciple along with the band. They all wished to get atonement for their wrong deeds.

One evening, Vidyuchchar decided to spend the night at a place. People came and informed him that the place was not safe for staying at night. A natural calamity is bound to come. But as the night had fallen and as a Sant he was not allowed to make journey or change place during the night so he decided to stay there which proved deadly for them but like great Sants they peacefully faced their death for the much needed expiation.

What a grand Prâyashchit, expiation!

Sant Parents and Sant Children

Sant Vitthal Pant was the only son of Govind Pant who was born as the elder son to Sant Trayambak Pant. The younger one was killed in a battle. Only after that the grand father became a Sant. He duly completed his education in Vedas and Scriptures. A learned Brahmin Sidhopant was pleased with his brilliance and married his daughter Rukmini with Vitthal Pant. After traveling to different pilgrimages they returned back to their parental village Âpegaon.

Vitthal Pant wanted to be a sant but it was not possible without the permission of his wife. One day, he deceived his wife in giving him permission. He asked, "If you permit me then I would go to the Ganges for the bath for salvation."

She did not understand the real intention of her husband and said, "You should go. Mukti Snân is real bath." He was pleased. He went to Gaini Nâth and took Samyâs. It was a painful life for the woman that had neither the husband nor children. The pain grew manifold when she came to know about her husband.

Once, Gaini Nâth visited her village. With other women she also went to hear him. She saluted the Sant when they were returning back. The Sant blessed her: 'May God grant you children.' She laughed hilariously and other women smiled. The Sant asked and was narrated the story. The Sant was aggrieved.

So, when he met Vitthal Pant again he ordered him to return back to grihastha âshram to his wife. At first he denied but he had to obey his guru. He returned back and re-entered the grihastha âshram. In a few years he got four children. But he was not accepted by the society. It was the worst crime to re-enter the grihastha-âshram. He and his family were ousted from the society.

It was not a big problem for the couple but when the question of the Samskârs and education of their children came, the society was adamant and refused Samskârs and education to the children, as they were not acceptable to the society because of their parents. The crisis grew. They wanted their children to prosper but they were unwanted citizen. The parents decided for atonement. They asked what could be the expiation for their crime. They were told that only their death could bring back the children to the social set-up. They decided to sacrifice their life for their children who were still neither grown mature nor wise.

When they were ready to go for the sacrifice, Sant Nâmadeva came there and consoled them. They gave their children to the Sant and started their last journey.

They came to Prayâga and offered their body to the Ganges at the meeting point of Gangâ, Yamunâ and Saraswati called Triveni.

What a sacrifice!

Despite the death of their parents the children did not deviate from the path of salvation. All the four became famous Sants: Nibriti Nâth; Gyâneshwar; Sopân Deva and Muktâbai. It is that famous Sant Gyâneshwar who made a buffalo chant the Veda Mantras at the age of only 11.

Âchârya Kumârila Bhatta

Âchârya Kumârila Bhatta completed his education and vowed to make the Vedas: the Shrutis and Smritis popular again. But it was the time of the rise of Buddhism. It was at its peak. For the popularity of the Vedas it was essential to show that Buddhism had come out of the Vedas and that the Vedas were the original books of Religion and Knowledge and that they possess all and are indefatigable. For achieving his goal it was essential for him to know Buddhism well. He met the Boddha Scholars and learnt Buddhism from them.

Then, Âchârya Bhatta started *shâshtrârths* against Buddhist scholars and defeated many of them one by one and re-established the popularity and supremacy of the Vedas.

One day, Âchârya Kumârila Bhatta realized that the act of debating against and defeating the Buddhist scholar was not a moral or ethical deed as he was the disciple of Buddhist Scholars. It mounted to revolt against the guru. It was a sin. He had committed a sin. Regret or remorse is not enough to be freed from the sinful act. He decided for expiation. The only atonement possible of such a grievous crime was death. He decided to die by burning the body slowly in the husk of paddy called *Tushâgni*. It burns very slowly and steadily. It was the extreme type of expiation that he opted.

His pyre was ready at Triveni in Prayâg. He sat on the burning fire and his body started burning. It was the time that Shri Shankarâchârya reached him for shâshtrârth. He directed him to his disciple Mandan Mishra and confirmed that his defeat will be taken as the defeat of Âchârya Kumârila Bhatta. Later on, Shri Shankarâchârya defeated Mandan Mishra who became his disciple but he always adored Âchârya Kumârila Bhatta as his guru and has mentioned him in his book as '*Bhagawatpâd*'.

People tried to dissuade him but it did not work on the determined Âchârya Kumârila Bhatta. His living body burnt to ashes: slowly, steadily, increasing intense pain every moment.

What a grand remorse! What a great atonement!

□□□

8

THE ONLY AIM: TO BE A SANT

The hearts of the Sants are like fresh 'butter': smooth, melting, satisfying, and giving sweetness, energy and changing the bitter taste of mouth into agreeable freshness. The greatest quality of butter is seen in the Sants; but with a difference. Butter melts on its own heat but the Sants easily melt if others' heat comes to their contact. The Sants will not be aggrieved at their own pain but they will weep at the pain and suffering of other persons. Only he is a Sant that feels the pain and suffering of others:

Sant hridaya navaneert samânâ;
Kahâ kavin pai kahai na jânâ.
Nija paritâp dravai naneetâ;
Par dukh dravai so sant punitâ.

If one lives for oneself, feels only his personal pain, works for personal gain and leads a self-centred life, then is not more than an insect or an animal. His living and life is meaningful that carries the burdens of others along with his own. He is strong that takes the responsibilities of and for many; feeds many and fosters many. People have changed the meaning of *lakhapati*, a millionaire; they say that he is a millionaire that has that much money with him. No, it was not the meaning and it is not correct.

A millionaire is he who has million living beings under his control and gets their unconditional respect.

To be a Sant or Saintly must be the immediate goal of each human being only then one can be said to be 'Human'; and can show that human beings are different to other animals as they have a very developed mind and the backing of the millions of years of human knowledge: collected, saved and transferred to the next generation. If one can lead a life like that of a Sant he would have 'all'. It is not a difficult thing. It needs only purity, determination, dedication and devotion. There are three ways declared by the wise ancestors: *Prabritti Mârga*, *Nibritti Mârga* and *Bhakti Mârg*. One can follow any of the three.

But the big question is will some one like to be melting butter to be readily taken away by others when each one is vying for and trying hard to overpower the other?

What the Sants immediately get is 'instant respect'. The modern life is devoid of respect. All men are looking towards others with expectations that whether he/ she shows respect or not. It is there from the highest office and authority in each department and each country to the lowest rank of the labourers. One punishes another (including the parents and grand parents; teachers and employers;) and the most heinous thing is that in order to show respect most of the people are showering rewards, giving ads, hanging hoardings, arranging meetings, writing articles to show respect to those who never deserve it but only to those who have the power to give some financial benefit to others. The criminals have been awarded again and again out of lust or out of fear. Where has man fallen to? Can man regain the height? Can individuals be civilized, sublime and saintly enough to get instant and genuine respect from others? When it will happen the earth will turn into a heaven. At present the earth is boiling like hell.

The Sants are like the Swan that drinks the milk from a mixture of water and milk; and leaves the water intact like something unhealthy and not required, as *vikâr*:

Sant hans guna gahahin paya, parihari vâri vikâr.

Will the man discard and abolish all such things that are helping the diseases to grow, that are injurious to health, that are destroying life and life element in any way, including the weapons and weapons for mass destruction. Will man ever think of detaching the self from everything wrong, unethical and harmful; *vikâr*?

When man will vanish the *vikârs* from his life then man will feel Oneness, Equality and Equanimity. Man will be man as envisaged by the Creator. A mother will never think of her children destroying each other. The Creator has created the ways, means and reasons of destruction. Creation and destruction is his responsibility. Living, enjoying and procreating is our responsibility. We must think of that and follow all the four pursuits: *Dharma, Artha, Kâma* and *Moksha* and never only the two, half of it: *Artha* and *Kâma*. Only then we can live a complete and happy and satisfactory life.

Tulasidâs went many steps ahead to declare that if God is the ocean, then the Sants are the clouds that keep the ocean filled up to its brim; and if the God is the Sandal wood then the Sants are like air that blows its fragrance to other people and places:

Râma sindhu ghana sajjan dheerâ;
Chandan taru hari sant samirâ.

The Sants have the qualities of Honey. It must be the aim of all and declared purpose in life to adopt the qualities of the Sants and to be Sweet; Lighted; Fragrant; Delighted; after absorbing the sweetness, light, fragrance, delight from ever changing, ever active, ever creating Nature. Will man distribute sweetness, spread light, spray fragrance and give delight? If man can do it then, (to repeat the earlier given statement) the earth will become a heaven. It is the only place that has life and it will become the only place to preserve life, give health, and give happiness to all. But then we need to be a Sant.

There are easier ways and means to become a Sant and lead a saintly life: healthy, happy, full of prosperity. Incidentally, prosperity includes everything: wealth, health, children, relatives, friends, good company, and inner growth, worldly-respect and so on. It is not confined only to wealth. The following are the easier ways:

1. To live on and by pious and ethical income; follow frugality; regularity in work and food too. One must be free from anxiety for the regular and right expenses but must stop all sorts of wrong, fruitless, wasteful and illegal expenses. He must be afraid of them: *vyaya ki nahi rahati chintâ mujhe, upavyaya se daratâ hun.*
2. Sweet and Truthful speech.
3. To serve all, as far as practicable without **affection** or **ego**.
4. To avoid making disciple as far as possible.
5. To avoid being swept away by respect and fame.
6. Not to indulge in discussion, debate, levying or refuting charges, conflict and clashes.
7. To feel to be own God and own ways to be the best but not to look down upon others'.
8. To control and keep the senses pure.
9. To be free from declared six enemies.
10. To collect and keep least articles.

The world knows Gitâ, reads Gitâ, analyses Gitâ; will the world follow Gitâ? What is summed up in 'mahâjano yena gatah sa panthâ'; that is the way that the gentlemen follow; Krishna declared in the Gitâ 3:21: what behaviour of a 'shreshtha' (better/great) man shows; others follow the same; what such men prove the others accept and follow it:

Yadyad âcharati shreshtah tat devetaro janah;
Sa yat pramânam kurute lokah tad anuvartate.

Will man follow these very common and general teachings and follow the pious ways of the Sants and not of the Scientists; Terrorists and Selfish persons? Will man achieve control and balance; and regain lost hope and faith? If man can do it then, (to repeat the earlier given statement) the earth will become a heaven, at least a far better and safe place to live on. But again we need to be a Sant.

□□□

More shades of Hinduism...

H.B. 399

H.B. 150

H.B. 96

80

60

150

80

80

H.B. 399

80

80